INVISIBILITY IN AFRICAN
AMERICAN AND ASIAN
AMERICAN LITERATURE

INVISIBILITY IN AFRICAN AMERICAN AND ASIAN AMERICAN LITERATURE
A Comparative Study

Klara Szmańko

McFarland & Company, Inc., Publishers
Jefferson, North Carolina, and London

LIBRARY OF CONGRESS CATALOGUING-IN-PUBLICATION DATA

Szmańko, Klara.
 Invisibility in African American and Asian American literature : a comparative study / Klara Szmańko.
  p. cm.
 Includes bibliographical references and index.

 ISBN 978-0-7864-3952-2
 softcover : 50# alkaline paper ∞

 1. American literature — African American authors — History and criticism. 2. American literature — Asian American authors — History and criticism. 3. Self-consciousness (Awareness) in literature. 4. Identity (Philosophical concept) in literature. 5. Ethnicity in literature. 6. Group identity in literature. I. Title.
 PS153.N5S99 2008
 810.9'896073 — dc22
                                                                2008029320

British Library cataloguing data are available

©2008 Klara Szmańko. All rights reserved

No part of this book may be reproduced or transmitted in any form or by any means, electronic or mechanical, including photocopying or recording, or by any information storage and retrieval system, without permission in writing from the publisher.

Cover photograph ©2008 Corbis Images. Front cover design by TG Design

Manufactured in the United States of America

McFarland & Company, Inc., Publishers
 Box 611, Jefferson, North Carolina 28640
  www.mcfarlandpub.com

Acknowledgments

I thank Professor Jadwiga Maszewska for her careful reading of the book, for all her comments, suggestions and for her staunch support.

I am grateful to Professor Dominika Ferens, who initiated me into the arcane of American literature and has guided me all the way through. I definitely need to mention the books which I have borrowed from Professor Ferens over the years.

I express my deep appreciation for Professor Werner Sollors for his reading of the book, for all his kindness and advice.

My warm thanks go to Professor Traise Yamamoto for her forthcomingness with help and advice.

My debt of gratitude goes to my Mother (Bożena Szmańko), Father (Tadeusz Szmańko), and Grandmother (Helena Golec) for all their love, help and support.

I thank the DAAD Commission and John F. Kennedy Institute for North American Studies in Berlin for scholarships which enabled me to compile most of the literature indispensable to complete this study.

I am indebted to Professor Mirosława Ziaja-Buchholtz and Professor Agata Preis-Smith for their comments and suggestions.

I thank the Director of the English Department at the University of Wrocław, Professor Leszek Berezowski, for his generous support of young scholars and his commitment to the international exchange of ideas.

I also thank Doctor Chitra Divakaruni for the permission to cite her poem "Yuba City School" (copyright © 1990 by Chitra Divakaruni; first appeared in *Black Candle* published by Milkweed Editions; reprinted by permission of the author and the Sandra Dijkstra Literary Agency). I am equally grateful to Kelly Sonnack for helping to secure the permission.

TABLE OF CONTENTS

Acknowledgments v
Preface 1
Introduction 3

**ONE. Different Faces of Invisibility:
Ralph Ellison's *Invisible Man*** 25
    Invisible Both to Whites and Blacks 28
    Invisibility — a Double-Edged Sword 34
    Invisibility, Tricksterism and Performativity
        of Human Identities 43

**TWO. Through Invisibility Towards Visibility:
Sam Greenlee's *The Spook Who Sat by the Door*** 55
    Invisible Freedom Fighters and Black Nationalism
        of the 1960s 56
    Invisibility of the Black Ghetto 69
    Dan Freeman's Literal Invisibility and Mimicry
        as a Linchpin of Literal Invisibility 79

**THREE. Performing Towards Visibility:
Maxine Hong Kingston's *Tripmaster Monkey*** 90
    Asian American Invisibility versus
        African American Invisibility 92
    Staging Chinese American Identity/Invisibility 104
    The Pitfalls of Recentering 111

Table of Contents

**FOUR. Multicultural Invisibilities:
Chang-rae Lee's *Native Speaker***   123
    "Uneasy Coalition of Our Colors" and the
        Black-Korean American Conflict   127
    Beyond Conventional Identity Politics Towards
        a Politics of Translation   141
    Mimicking for the Mainstream   152

Conclusion   157
Chapter Notes   173
Bibliography   195
Index   213

Preface

I hope that this comparative interdisciplinary study of the invisibility trope in African American and Asian American literature will help all scholars who are interested in interracial connections in American literature and American studies. While the focus of my investigation falls on four novels: Ralph Ellison's *Invisible Man*, Sam Greenlee's *The Spook Who Sat by the Door,* Maxine Hong Kingston's *Tripmaster Monkey* and Chang-rae Lee's *Native Speaker,* I place these works in a wider context of sociohistorical and literary references. I develop such critical concepts as (in)visibility, performativity, mimicry, and identity politics, laying special emphasis on the need for transformational identity politics consisting in cooperation between various racial groups. Of interest to me is not only the invisibility of marginalized racial groups to the mainstream society but also their invisibility to their own communities and to each other. I conduct my research in the spirit of critical multiculturalism, scrutinizing power dynamics inside and between distinct racial groups. I put into perspective mechanisms of oppression, stereotyping and resistance. Since this is a New Historicist study, I stress throughout the project that history unfolds here and now, before the eyes of people living at a given time.

I specifically address the book to scholars specializing in African American and Asian American literature as well as Asian American studies, African American studies and whiteness studies. The book should be particularly helpful to the scholars for whom invisibility is a research theme, even if they do not pursue their research in ethnic studies but in gender studies or queer studies. The manuscript offers the genealogy of the term and a theoretical dissection of the trope, distinguishing between various kinds of invisibility. I also envision as my audience anyone interested in the politics of location.

Preface

I owe my debt to all scholars who have paved the way for me in the discipline of interracial studies, among them Gary Okihiro, Manning Marable, King-Kok Cheung, James Kyung-Jin Lee, Reginald Kearney, Heike Raphael Hernandez. Having said that, I would like to stress that the book is the first comparative study of the invisibility trope in African American and Asian American literature.

Why do I find it important to analyze authors from different racial backgrounds together? For one thing, this makes it possible to look at racial relations in the United States from a broader perspective. It is true that black versus white and white versus other binaries no longer hold as much currency as they did, especially with the recent focus on Hispanic voters. However, the binaries still refuse to go away. No one feels it more profoundly than the Asian American population. Hence all studies that subvert racial dualism help to promote a more all-inclusive model of American democracy. Subjectivities emerge in multi-dimensional space. Binaries confine subjectivities to flat space. Multiracial projects also dislodge whiteness from its self-proclaimed position of centrality. Whiteness is no longer the only point of reference, but one of many points of reference. Such a study can never be fully exhaustive. While I bring African Americans and Asian Americans together, I omit Native Americans, Latinos and ethnic groups which are phenotypically white, but still feel marginalized in the United States. I want to emphasize that it is by no means my intention to detract from the value of projects that concentrate on only one minority literature. There is no doubt that the authors of such projects are more knowledgeable about the field than I am. They can also analyze the experience of a particular racial or ethnic group in greater detail than I do. I hope to compensate for all possible shortcomings by putting things into broader context and shedding light on commonalities as well as differences between respective African American and Asian American authors.

Introduction

This is a comparative study of invisibility in African American and Asian American literature. While I explore invisibility in a myriad of African American and Asian American literary texts, the main focus is on four novels: Ralph Ellison's *Invisible Man*, Sam Greenlee's *The Spook Who Sat by the Door*, Maxine Hong Kingston's *Tripmaster Monkey* and Chang-rae Lee's *Native Speaker*. Bringing African American and Asian American authors together, I hope to undermine the black and white dyad and complicate the picture of interracial relations in the United States. In my analysis of interracial interactions I stress the multidirectional nature of power. Rather than focus only on the invisibility of African Americans and Asian Americans to white people, I also look at various patterns of invisibility inside and between both communities. It is essential to emphasize the interdisciplinary nature of this project. I do not limit myself strictly to textual analysis, but draw on racial studies, the realm of sociology and the discourse embedded in politics of location. While African Americans and Asian Americans are invisible in a different way, it is difficult to overlook the similarities in their experience of invisibility. Ellison, Greenlee, Kingston and Lee point to white blindness as the chief cause of African American and Asian American invisibility. They throw just as much light on the white apparatus of power as they do on their own people. In all four novels invisibility is not only a burden, but also a springboard for creative action. The protagonists of the texts examined in this study make the most of their invisibility. Yet none of them settles for invisibility, but sees visibility as the final goal. Striving for visibility is an interweaving thread of my research.

Stating at the very outset that my research is embedded in the discourse devoted to politics of location, I need to acknowledge such authors

Introduction

as Susan Stanford Friedman, Analouise Keating, Neil Smith, Cindi Katz, Kathleen Kirby, Liz Bondi and Stuart Hall, to name just a few. Positionality and relationality[1] are crucial terms for me. All of us, notwithstanding our race or ethnicity, speak from a particular place and are positioned in relation to each other in a particular way. Our positions are never set in stone. They may change together with the changing background. Depending on whom we speak to and with whom we interact, certain traits of our identity can become more or less vivid. Therefore it is all too important to emphasize the relationality of our identities. Relationality is no less significant when we deal with racial categories. Once again I believe that in order to get the full measure of the relationality of human identities, we need to go beyond binaries which juxtapose the experience of a marginalized group with that of the dominant group. We also need to draw a clear line between the contextualization of human identities and othering practices. All identities are contextual and referential. However, they should not be oppositional. If we define ourselves by stressing who we are not, rather than say who we are, we will sooner or later end up excluding certain groups and people. Instead of seeking connections and common points with other human beings, we will erect walls between ourselves and those supposedly unlike us. That is why it is crucial to avoid self-definition based upon "othering."

Apart from being multiracial, this study is also diachronic. It is not accidental that the works which I have chosen to analyze come from different historical periods and deal with African American and Asian American invisibility at different points of American history. Invisibility has never been stable. The changing socio-historical context inevitably impinged on how successive generations of African Americans and Asian Americans experienced their invisibility. The action of Ralph Ellison's *Invisible Man* (published in 1952) unfolds in the 1930s, the time of the Great Depression, a harsh period for all Americans and even more so for African Americans. I have decided to include Ralph Ellison's canonized text here because it is the first such extensive study of racial invisibility. All three other authors discussed in this project allude to Ellison's novel. There is no denying that racial invisibility was a literary trope long before the publication of *Invisible Man*. However, *Invisible Man* is the first such explicit and extensive study of racial invisibility. If there is any single text which may serve as a matrix of racial invisibility then we may risk a claim

Introduction

that *Invisible Man* is the one. It definitely is a matrix text for three other authors discussed here. Sam Greenlee's *The Spook Who Sat by the Door* (published in 1969) takes place in an altogether different climate than *Invisible Man*. Set in the 1960s, the novel provides a fertile ground for the discussion of black nationalism. The protagonist of the novel — Dan Freeman — rejects the Invisible Man's peaceful integrationism, espousing separatism and opting for military struggle.

The Spook Who Sat by the Door dovetails nicely with Maxine Hong Kingston's *Tripmaster Monkey*, published in 1989 and also unfolding in the 1960s. Like Dan Freeman, the protagonist of *Tripmaster Monkey*— Wittman Ah Sing embraces nationalism. However, his is not militant nationalism, but cultural nationalism. Asian American activists of the 1960s and especially cultural nationalists modeled themselves after their African American counterparts, admiring them for their racial pride, cultural distinctness and activism. Similar as they are, both nationalisms differ in significant ways. African American nationalists often saw themselves as separate from the nation which refused to acknowledge them. Asian American cultural nationalists emphasized their cultural distinctness but at the same time they put a strong accent on their Americanness, underlining that they were no less American than other racial and ethnic groups living in the United States. Kingston overtly reflects on the differences and similarities in African American and Asian American experience of invisibility. Unlike Sam Greenlee, who is sympathetic towards the nationalist cause, Kingston (also an activist of the 1960s) approaches the nationalist philosophy with an air of distance. Wittman Ah Sing modeled after Kingston's arch critic — Frank Chin, may be a cultural nationalist, but Kingston herself draws our attention to the blind spots of the discourse.

Finally, Chang-rae Lee's *Native Speaker*, published in 1995 and set at the beginning of the 1990s is closest to our present day reality. The novel presents the most complex and all-inclusive view of interracial relations in the United States. Although Lee devotes the most space in his novel to Asian American invisibility, he does not limit himself to discussing just the invisibility of Asian American people. Instead, he examines interracial and interethnic relations between various minorities — both long-time citizens of the United States and fresh immigrants. The interaction between Korean Americans and African Americans comes to the foreground in the patchwork of these interactions. The events depicted in *Native Speaker*

Introduction

take place during the time of interracial conflict between Korean Americans and African Americans — following the Latasha Harlins incidents and before the Rodney King rebellion in 1992. Lee shows us how invisibility functions in an ostensibly multicultural state. At a conference I was asked why I insist on speaking about the invisibility of American minorities if they are so visible today: African Americans — omnipresent in popular culture, Asian Americans — an embodiment of the American success. *Native Speaker* illustrates how one can be seemingly visible and at the same time hyper-invisible in the modern multicultural American state.

The very term — invisibility — is very popular nowadays in literary studies, racial studies, gender studies, queer studies and other disciplines. While a number of scholars are quick to use the term in reference to stigmatized people, most of them treat it homogenously, without noticing the plurality and heterogeneity within the phenomenon of invisibility. I distinguish between different kinds of invisibility. Rather than speak about invisibility in the singular, I would like to explore multiple invisibilities. Apart from analyzing the invisibility of African Americans and Asian Americans to the white world, I trace various patterns of *internal invisibility*: invisibility between various strata of Afro-American and Asian American community as well as invisibility of Afro-Americans and Asian Americans to each other. I also distinguish between *figurative* and *literal invisibility*. Minorities are figuratively invisible when the rest of society looks at them through the prism of stereotypes about people of color. They are *figuratively* invisible through no agency of their own, simply "because of a particular disposition of the eyes of people with whom [they] come in contact. A matter of the construction of their *inner eyes*" (Ellison 7). People of color are *literally* invisible when the outside world literally cannot see them. They become literally invisible after assuming alter identities and after making a conscious decision to be taken for someone else than they are. Most often they achieve literal invisibility through the manipulation of stereotypes attributed to them. In all cases discussed here literal invisibility is a direct result of figurative invisibility. Realizing that the outside world is unwilling to see them as they are, some oppressed decide to capitalize on their invisibility. Rather than be simply passively invisible, they begin to utilize the misconceptions of the outside world to their own advantage. Their underlying reasoning is: if you do not want to see me as I am, I will let you see even less than you would otherwise see

Introduction

in order to put your watchfulness to sleep and pursue my own agenda. Instead of submitting to your hallucinations about me, I will control them and use them to my own benefit. Literal invisibility usually serves as a protective device. It is a source of protection for trickster figures in *Invisible Man*. Dan Freeman from *The Spook Who Sat by the Door* takes literal invisibility one step further and uses it to liberate his people rather than only ensure their survival. Henry Park from *Native Speaker* abuses literal invisibility, employing it against his own people. Unlike Freeman who spies on whites, Park spies for them, initially working against the oppressed. The expiation comes only when he embarks upon his narrative. Ellison and Kingston focus first of all on figurative invisibility, whereas Greenlee and Lee devote more space to literal invisibility.

Throughout this study I emphasize that power never flows in just one direction. Exploitation is not a sole prerogative of the white apparatus of power. Although minorities find themselves in a subordinate position to the white mainstream, they do not speak from the vantage point of complete powerlessness. Frequently they mimic structures of oppression in relations with their own people. Therefore I argue that the oppressed can be invisible to each other as well. Internal invisibility is a major theme in all four novels discussed here. Sam Greenlee highlights the tension between the black middle class and people from the ghetto. Chang-rae Lee sheds light on the antagonism between people of diverse racial and ethnic origin. Exploitation within an immigrant community gains a central place in his novel. Maxine Hong Kingston delineates the internal stratification of the Chinese American community at various levels: invisibility of fresh immigrants to long-time Chinese Americans, invisibility of completely assimilated Chinese Americans to those who cherish the Chinese American heritage, invisibility of lower class Chinese Americans to elite members of the Chinese American community. In *Tripmaster Monkey* Kingston not only makes her people visible, but also levels an indictment at Asian American nationalists. All authors analyzed in this study emphasize that white society is partly responsible for the invisibility of minorities to each other. Ellison's observation "Use a nigger to catch a nigger" (421) reverberates in three other texts. Ellison, Greenlee, Kingston and Lee underscore the role of whiteness in aggravating the tensions inside marginalized communities.

We can speak not only about the invisibility of racial minorities but also about white invisibility. Still, the invisibility of white people is markedly different than that of marginalized racial groups. It is not thrust upon them by anyone but self-constructed. Just as we can distinguish between different kinds of invisibility pertaining to people of color, we can also distinguish different kinds of white invisibility. Many whites render themselves invisible by unmarking themselves and marking non-white racial groups. A lot of white people opt for a negative, oppositional definition of identity — that is, to be white is not to be a number of things (Frankenberg, "Whiteness and Americanness" 70). Whiteness, as seen by many whites, is an empty signifier, free of any internal heterogeneity. The white self constitutes itself by constructing a range of "others." The invisibility of racial others helps white people to define themselves. Hence the invisibility of racial and ethnic minorities hinges on white invisibility. Secondly, whiteness renders itself invisible by concealing its own power and privilege. The white apparatus of power conspires to make structures of oppression invisible. Additionally, it obscures its own role in instigating the hostilities inside and between marginalized racial and ethnic groups. Whenever tensions flare — as was the case during the Rodney King rebellion — the white apparatus of power removes itself from the picture, creating an impression that the conflict is solely between minorities. Only the articulation of all oppressive forces of whiteness can render marginalized racial and ethnic groups more visible.

Lee, Kingston, Ellison and Greenlee not only make their own people visible but also make whiteness visible, exposing white oppression and emphasizing internal heterogeneity within whiteness. Examining an intricate process of stereotyping, Kingston delves into the white mentality. Ellison draws a diversified picture of the white world, depicting different social groups and accounting for their attitudes towards African Americans. Both Ellison and Greenlee devote a lot of space to unmasking the hypocrisy of liberal whites, who claim to rise above racial divisions. Lee also accentuates internal stratification within whiteness, distinguishing between more and less privileged white ethnic groups.

The underlying premise of this study is that invisibility is not only a burden but also carries a hidden potential. All characters analyzed here use their invisibility constructively. For the Invisible Man invisibility is a wellspring of creativity. His narrative is woven out of his invisibility. Without invisibility there would be no story to tell. Invisibility is no less a

Introduction

source of inspiration for Wittman Ah Sing and Henry Park. Wittman constructs his whole play around the invisibility of his people. His earlier works: poetry and attempts at fiction writing are also informed by Chinese American invisibility. It is invisibility that prods Wittman to action. Invisibility fills him with anger and that anger in turn tells him to channel his invisibility and "make something of it" (277). The first-person narrator of *Native Speaker*—Henry Park—says openly: "only you [broader American society] could grant me these lyrical modes" (320). Invisibility fuels his creativity. Society made him invisible and now he shares with society his experience of invisibility. Invisibility also prevents him from speaking out for most of his life. Henry's silence is the direct result of his invisibility. The narrative releases him from silence, providing him with an outlet for everything he has so far kept hidden from the eyes of the outside world. For Greenlee's Dan Freeman invisibility is not a source of creativity, but he still uses it no less creatively than three other characters. Playing upon white stereotypes of blackness, he tricks whites into believing that that he is their ally, while at the same time preparing an African American ghetto rebellion.

For many oppressed people invisibility is also a source of "second-sight" (Du Bois 5). They may be unseen by the outside world, but many of them enjoy remarkable powers of perception. Usually they can see more than people around them. Their prescience often contrasts sharply with white blindness. Invisibility sensitizes them to the intricacies that escape the attention of other people. Their illumination is two-fold. Themselves exposed to exploitation, they have a much better understanding of power relations in the United States. Invisibility also allows them to "see around the corners" (Ellison 10). Unlike most people, they do not trust appearances, but search for the meaning under the surface. All their experiences have an enlightening power. The Invisible Man says: "I have been boomeranged across my head so much that I now can see the darkness of lightness" (5). Most of the invisible have been "boomeranged" from their original plans and expectations. Invisibility sharpens their vigilance, making them more cautious to the swindles of the outside world.

In 1897[2] W.E.B. Du Bois used the term second-sight in reference to African Americans in his double-consciousness formula: "The Negro is ... born with a veil, and gifted with second-sight" (Du Bois 5). Second-sight gains a semblance of a visionary quality, counterbalancing the alienating power of the "veil,"³ which stands for the invisibility of African Americans, their alienation from the world of privilege. African Americans are by no means the only minority gifted with second sight. The invisibility of other non-white racial and ethnic groups makes them equally predisposed to the gift of second sight. Maxine Hong Kingston's Woman Warrior "can see behind [her] like a bat" (36). "Seeing behind" symbolizes the completeness of vision. It protects the Woman Warrior from any mischief on the part of her enemies. The protagonist of *Native Speaker*— Henry Park claims: "You can keep nothing safe from our eyes and ears" (320). The lack of security and certainty enhances the watchfulness of American immigrants who occupy central place in the novel.

All of the authors analyzed here see invisibility first of all as an illuminating force, but they also acknowledge that it can be blinding. The blinding power of invisibility becomes especially conspicuous in the mutual relations between people of color. Their own invisibility can blind them to other people's oppression. Maxine Hong Kingston claims that Wittman's second sight is not yet fully fledged: "Foolish ape wants more vision" (126). The blinding power of invisibility is also visible in the attitude of nationalists to the white world. Some of them, for example Ras from *Invisible Man*, treat whites as a homogenous group, as oppressors who need to be annihilated. Overall, however, it is second sight of the marginalized, not their blindness, that comes to the foreground in all texts.

As I stated at the very beginning, the interweaving thread of this research is striving for visibility. The protagonists of all four novels tap the dormant potential of invisibility, but none of them settles for it. Visibility is their ultimate objective. They choose diverse paths towards visibility. Wittman hopes to achieve visibility for himself and for his people through theatre. Aiming at cultural and social visibility, he wants to popularize Chinese American culture, hoping that it will win the acclaim of the mainstream, just as jazz and blues did. Unlike Wittman, Henry and the Invisible Man, Dan Freeman believes that his people can become visible only through military struggle—underground guerrilla warfare. He does not strike out for visibility in a direct, open fashion. He does not try to set whites straight on their misconceptions. Instead, he lulls them to sleep. Launching a ghetto rebellion, he literally explodes all these misconceptions in the faces of white people.

The Invisible Man and Henry Park strive for visibility through auto-

Introduction

biographical writing. Constructing their autobiographies, they undermine their invisibility and achieve a higher degree of perception. They strive not only for their own visibility, but also for the visibility of all others who are unheard and unseen. The construction of the narrative is an act of self-definition and individualization. They reach for autobiography to move closer to visibility, but autobiography as a genre is not entirely unproblematic. When one takes upon oneself the task of speaking for others, there is always a danger of misrepresentation. Asian American nationalists were quick to identify autobiography as a "white" form of writing that went against racial "authenticity." I address these points of contention while discussing *Invisible Man* and *Native Speaker*.

My aim is not only to dismantle invisibility, but also to problematize the notion of visibility. Various factions of the African American and Asian American community envision their visibility in different ways. The Invisible Man sees African Americans and white people living together in an integrated country. Dan Freeman believes that African Americans can never be fully integrated and hence he wants African Americans to separate themselves from the white state. Wittman Ah Sing is a cultural nationalist, but he sees people of different races living together side by side. His most immediate concern, however, is the fate of his own community — Chinese Americans. Henry Park goes beyond representing the interests of his closest community — Korean Americans. Identifying with all American immigrants, irrespective of their racial or ethnic origin, he pictures a state that would truly embrace all of these people, not just in letter, but in reality. As a critical multiculturalist, he accentuates unequal power dynamics between all these diverse groups. He also exposes the sham nature of American multiculturalism that tries to conceal power differentials, to render them invisible.

Problematizing the term visibility, we need to address the question of identity politics. How do minority communities position themselves in relation to other groups? Do they preponderate their own experience over that of other oppressed people or do they seek similarities? It is vital to distinguish between conventional identity politics and transformational identity politics (Keating 39). Proponents of conventional identity politics set themselves apart from other groups, prioritizing their own interests over those with whom they might strike potential alliances. Supporters of transformational identity politics cherish their cultural distinctness, but at the same time they search for points of convergence with other distinct units, often pursuing broader coalitions. It is not unusual for oppressed groups that subscribe to conventional identity politics to attack other marginalized people. Transformational identity politics, on the other hand, underscores the very experience of oppression that unites all oppressed. It acknowledges the differences, but it sees those differences as strengths, not weaknesses. The differences help to save the world of heterogeneity. They do not necessarily need to block potential alliances.

The works analyzed here differ in their approach to identity politics. Focusing on African Americans and their experiences, the Invisible Man still strongly valorizes diversity: "Whence all this passion toward conformity anyway?—diversity is the word.... America is woven of many strands" (435). Yet he does not bring other racial or ethnic groups into the picture. While he asserts that America is "woven of many strands," his strands remain black and white. The brotherhood poster designed by the Invisible Man includes a Native American couple ("representing the dispossessed past"),[4] a blond man in "overalls," an Irishwoman "representing the dispossessed present," an African American man and a young white couple "surrounded by children of mixed races" (290). The man "in overalls" shows that Ellison is sensitive not only to racial difference, but also to class difference. The inclusion of Irish Americans in the poster also proves that he can differentiate between different shades of whiteness. The caption under the poster reads: "After the Struggle: The Rainbow of America's Future" (291). Overall, however, Ellison's novel has a limited spectrum of colors, because it dwells on the relations between African Americans and whites.[5]

As a militant nationalist who espouses separatism, Dan Freeman to a great extent personifies conventional identity politics. However, unlike many of his nationalist colleagues, he does not target other oppressed groups: Jews, homosexuals, immigrants, or women. He does not forge alliances with them, but does not attack them either. Wittman Ah Sing becomes trapped in some of the pitfalls of conventional identity politics. In theory, he wants people of diverse racial and ethnic origin to live side by side. Yet in practice he has problems with accepting people different than himself. Fresh immigrants and women, especially those who refuse to embrace cultural nationalism and marry within the race, attract his strong criticism. The third-person narrator of *Tripmaster Monkey* does not

Introduction

subscribe to conventional identity politics. As mentioned earlier, she highlights inconsistencies in Wittman's philosophy. Among the characters discussed here only Henry Park as an already self-conscious narrator supports transformational identity politics. In his vision of struggle against oppression, people from diverse backgrounds unite their forces, just the way they unite behind John Kwang, the man who tries to build up a large multi-ethnic and multiracial coalition. It is not without significance, however, that Henry Park speaks thirty years after Dan Freeman and Wittman Ah Sing. He confronts a different reality than any of his predecessors.

Conventional identity politics treats identity as a stable, an essence, whereas transformational identity politics recognizes the performativity and plurality of all identities. Identity performance is crucial in all texts discussed here. The performance of identities happens at various levels. I notice that both Asian American and African American nationalists perform their identities, although they are not always aware of it. The term performance gains special prominence in *Tripmaster Monkey*. The performance of Chinese American identity in Wittman's play goes side by side with Wittman's real life performance of his Chinese American nationalist identity. He performs his nationalist identity both through ideology which he promotes and through the lifestyle which he leads, including his dress, haircut and body language. His pacifism contradicts the pose of a Chinaman samurai that he adopts for the outside world. Similarly, his play includes a number of war scenes. The contradictions in Wittman's ideology and in his play stem from the contradictory demands placed on Chinese Americans by the mainstream and contradictions ingrained in the portrayal of Chinese Americans: an alien, Yellow peril, a "gook," a model minority citizen, an effeminate eunuch, an oversexed Asian American woman. These are some of the stereotypes clinging to Asian Americans. Fashioning himself as a warrior and staging his epic play, Wittman tries to subvert the stereotype of an Asian American as submissive, cowardly and passive.

The performance of identities is also central in the model minority discourse, which comes up as a theme in three novels discussed here: Greenlee's *The Spook Who Sat by the Door*, Kingston's *Tripmaster Monkey* and Lee's *Native Speaker*. Exploring invisibility in each of these novels, I examine how the model minority rhetoric plays a part in generating interracial invisibilities and what responses it invites from Asian Americans and

Introduction

African Americans. The model minority discourse receives the most attention in Lee's *Native Speaker*. Lee notices that in some cases Asian Americans feel compelled to perform the model minority myth, which like other stereotypes is thrust upon them.

Discussing the performativity of identities, I problematize the terms "mimicry" and "slippage," both popularized by Homi Bhabha. All the characters analyzed here are conscious of their mimicry, employing it as a deliberate strategy in their struggle against invisibility. Ironically, invisibility enables them to reach for mimicry and mimicry in turn becomes a weapon in the battle against invisibility. The exploitation of mimicry comes to the foreground particularly in *The Spook Who Sat by the Door* and in *Tripmaster Monkey*. In both texts mimicry relies on conscious manipulation of slippage. However, it is not exactly slippage defined in Homi Bhabha's essay "Of Mimicry and Man." Bhabha's slippage implies an unconscious lapse, a slip, something that evades the control of a mimic person. Both Wittman and Freeman use slippage consciously and strategically, turning it to their advantage. Yet both of them aim at diametrically different results. Wittman employs a tactical slippage in his play to render certain stereotypes hyper-visible. Exaggerating some of those stereotypes, he hopes to sensitize the audience to their constructedness. Spectators are to see the absurdity of their own inventions. By contrast, Dan Freeman does not try to jolt other people's consciousness, but to make them feel secure in their misconceptions. Their feeling of security allows him to pursue his hidden, subversive agenda. Freeman's slippage is much more subtle than that employed by Wittman. While Wittman exaggerates certain stereotypes to expose them, Freeman is careful not to overdo his performance. I also distinguish between Freeman's conscious mimicry and the imitation practiced by the black middle class. Some members of the black middle class have an illusion of full integration into white society, although more than once they are proved wrong on the issue.

We can trace a certain affinity between mimicry and tricksterism. Nowadays the term tricksterism seems to be used less and less frequently, having in some respects given way to mimicry. This is not to say, however, that both terms are equivalent. I emphasize that tricksterism is always conscious, while mimicry can sometimes be unconscious, even though that is not the case in the texts discussed here. Unlike tricksters who are always aware of their signifying,[6] mimic men may not always be conscious

Introduction

of their impersonation. It may seem to them that they are one with their embodied role. This happened especially when colonizers took to impersonating people from colonies. They were not always aware of the difference between their target personality and their embodiment of it. Richard Burton, the author of *Personal Narrative of a Pilgrimage to Al-Madinah and Meccah* and *The Book of the Thousand Nights and a Night* claims that he was a colonial official by day and a "native" by night (Roy 194), as if he could ever be both almost at the same time. Although the term "trickster" recurs in various minority literatures of the United States, it is most frequently used in the African American context. All trickster figures in Ralph Ellison's *Invisible Man* use mimicry in their impersonation, though they do so in different ways and with different ends in mind.

Mimicry and tricksterism are not always subversive and recalcitrant. A mimic person and a trickster usually strike out against a more powerful opponent. Still, they do not have to speak from the position of powerlessness.[7] Nor do they need to represent the interests of their community. Unlike Dan Freeman, who is referred to as a black Prometheus, Bledsoe and Rinehart from *Invisible Man* turn against their communities. Henry Park also becomes a mimic man in order to spy for white people and against other people of color. He is pushed onto the way of betrayal by his invisibility in American society. Unlike Rinehart, he does not cheat his people solely with an eye for profit. Psychological compensations are much more important for him.

Ellison, Greenlee, Kingston and Lee do not write in a vacuum but inscribe themselves in a long tradition of invisibility writing. William James reaches for a visibility and invisibility metaphor in his discussion of the social self in his 1890 book *Principles of the Self*.[8] According to James, visibility is the cornerstone of our social self. All of us crave recognition from other human beings. Without such recognition we are not fully fulfilled and we do not entirely belong to society. We want to be seen in a positive light:

> we have an innate propensity to get ourselves noticed, and noticed favorably, by our kind. No more fiendish punishment could be devised, were such a thing physically possible, than that one should be turned loose in society and remain absolutely unnoticed by all the members thereof. If no one turned round when we entered, answered when we spoke, or minded what we did, but if every person we met "cut us dead," and acted as if we were non-existing things, a kind of rage and impotent despair

Introduction

would ere long well up in us, from which the cruelest bodily tortures would be a relief; for these would make us feel that, however bad might be our plight, we had not sunk to such a depth as to be unworthy of attention at all [294].

Invisibility as described by James in many ways parallels that experienced by racial minorities in the United States, especially in the past. The rest of society refused to recognize them, acting as if they were non-entities rather than fellow-citizens or fellow-human beings. If they were recognized, then most often for exploitation purposes.

Invisibility goes together with inaudibility. People who are unseen are also usually unheard. James's student — W.E.B. Du Bois — reflects on the inaudibility of people exposed to "caste segregation:"

It is difficult to let others see the full psychological meaning of caste segregation. It is as though one, looking out from a dark cave in a side of an impending mountain, sees the world passing and speaks to it; speaks courteously and persuasively, showing them how these entombed souls are hindered in their natural movement, expression and development; and how their loosening from prison would be a matter not simply of courtesy, sympathy, and help to them, but aid to all the world. One talks on evenly and logically in this way but notices that the passing throng does not even turn its head, or if it does, glances curiously and walks on. It gradually penetrates the minds of prisoners that the people passing do not hear; that some thick sheet of invisible but horribly tangible plate glass is between them and the world. They get excited; they talk louder; they gesticulate. Some of the passing world stop in curiosity; these gesticulations seem so pointless; they laugh and pass on. They still either do not hear at all, or hear but dimly, and even what they hear, they do not understand. Then the people within may become hysterical. They may scream and hurl themselves against the barriers, hardly realizing in their bewilderment that they are screaming in a vacuum unheard and that their antics may actually seem funny to those outside looking in. They may even, here and there, break through in blood and disfigurement, and find themselves faced by a horrified, implacable, and quite overwhelming mob of people frightened for their own existence [*Dusk of Dawn* 649, 650].

Unlike James's invisible, Du Bois's inaudible and invisible do not mingle freely with the rest of society but are segregated from it. Du Bois devotes more place to the reactions of prisoners and the reactions of the outside world. This should come as no surprise, since as an African American Du Bois was to a great extent invisible himself, perhaps not as invisible as other more underprivileged black people, but invisible nonetheless.

Introduction

Initially, people behind plate glass are both invisible and inaudible. If they talk "evenly and logically," "the passing throng does not even turn its head." Only after showing signs of frustration, they manage to evoke some response from the passing crowd, inadequate as it is. They do not achieve any meaningful visibility or audibility. A significant communication gap occurs between the two worlds. The prisoners' despair merely arouses curiosity. Passers-by show no empathy. Dispassionate bemusement of the passing throng contrasts with extreme agitation of people behind "invisible but horribly tangible plate glass." In *The Souls* an equivalent of the glass is the already mentioned veil. Both stand for discrimination and prejudice that separate people of color from the world of privilege. It is not without significance that the glass is invisible. Invisible to whom? Those imprisoned behind the glass can see it all too well. They are fully aware of the barriers erected between themselves and the outside world. People who erected the barriers pretend not to see them. As I pointed out earlier, structures of oppression can be equally invisible as people exposed to them. At the time of Du Bois those structures of oppression were much more visible than now. Still, most of the society pretended not to see them. Therefore they looked in bewilderment at the excited gesticulations of the prisoners, as if wondering: "What's all the fuss about?"

In his 1945 Introduction to *Black Metropolis* Richard Wright overtly refers to James's passage on invisibility, concluding that "the American Negro has come as near being the victim of a complete rejection as our society has been able to work out" (xxxiii). Like Du Bois, Wright points to the effects of isolation on the minds of the oppressed. He predicts racial riots that will be the direct result of white policies. Desperate to make themselves seen and heard, African Americans will, in the end, try to break free from their "steel prison" (xxxiii). He denounces the three hundred year old policy of "knowing niggers and what's good for them" (xxxiv). Keeping African Americans at a distance, most white people still assumed an air of eloquence on the "Negro problem." Wright emphasizes the hypocrisy of white Americans who were quick to see the hardships of people in foreign lands but failed to acknowledge the adversities confronting people living around the corner. According to Wright, America had its consciousness split. In a sense he extends elements of Du Bois's double consciousness formula to white people. If in *The Souls* Du Bois speaks of "unreconciled strivings," "the double-aimed struggle," and "the waste of double aims" in reference to African Americans, Wright accentuates the division in white racial consciousness.

Invisibility has been no less an issue for Asian American authors than for African American ones. Several years after Du Bois published *The Souls* (1903), Sui Sin Far, a Chinese American author published *Leaves from the Mental Portfolio of an Eurasian* (1909), in which she reflects on her own invisibility and the invisibility of other Chinese Americans. Sin Far's experience of racial difference at many points bears striking resemblance to that of Du Bois. Both learned of their presumable difference in similar circumstances during the years of their childhood. For Du Bois the bitter revelation came when a white girl refused his visiting card, making him feel inferior, different and subhuman. The first germs of double-consciousness started to sprout in his mind just then: "Then it dawned upon me with a certain suddenness that I was different from the others; or like mayhap, in heart and life and longing" (4). Sui Sin Far learns of her difference when a child announces to another child that Sin Far has a Chinese mother and therefore they should not play with her. Sin Far mentally registers the incident. She clearly remembers the day "on which [she] first learned that [she] was something different and apart from other children" (886). The event leaves an indelible imprint on her brain.

Both Du Bois and Sin Far notice that they are not really seen by people around them. Whenever someone looks at them, it is most often not for the purpose of establishing contact, but simply to fix them with an ethnographic gaze. There is palpable tension and a communication gap between Du Bois and the white world:

> Between me and the other world there is ever an unasked question.... They approach me in a half-hesitant sort of way, eye me curiously or compassionately ... instead of saying directly, How does it feel to be a problem? [3].

Du Bois's experience of racial difference is not nearly so graphic as Sin Far's encounters with the white world.[9] Growing up in the predominantly white Great Barrington, Du Bois was to a great extent shielded from discrimination unleashed against other African Americans. Sin Far, on the other hand, recounts multiple examples of hostility towards herself and her siblings. She comes up with the whole gamut of expressions that render the attitudes of other people. They "scan [her] curiously from head to foot," "survey [her] critically," "call [her] from play for the purpose of

Introduction

inspection" (886). They "gaze" upon her, "very much in the same way that [she has seen] people gaze upon strange animals in a menagerie" (887).

Sin Far draws overt comparisons between her own invisibility and the invisibility of black people. She came into the most immediate contact with representatives of the black race while working as a journalist on the island of Jamaica. Unlike other inhabitants of the island, Sin Far refuses to look down on black Jamaicans. She refutes various pseudo scientific theories which many of her contemporaries trace back to the Bible:

> I am also surrounded by a race of people, the reputed descendants of Ham, the son of Noah, whose offspring, it was prophesied, should be the servants of the sons of Shem and Japheth. As I am a descendant, according to the Bible, of both Shem and Japheth, I have a perfect right to set my heel upon the Ham people; but though I see others around me following out the Bible suggestion, it is not in my nature to be arrogant to any but those who seek to impress me with their superiority [891].

Shuddering at prejudice towards black people, she declares: "I too am of the brown people of the earth" (891). The declaration is a clear rebuttal of an earlier cited hierarchy, the hierarchy which is anything but set in stone. While the Bible passage places the Chinese above blacks, in reality many whites thought otherwise. Sin Far cites such statements as: "A Chinaman is more repulsive than a nigger," "I would rather marry a pig than a girl with Chinese blood in her veins" (889). To illustrate the place that African Americans were assigned in the American world, Du Bois also employs a genealogical metaphor: "After the Egyptian and Indian, the Greek and Roman, the Teuton and Mongolian, the Negro is a sort of seventh son" (*Souls of the Black Folk* 5). Black people feature as last and first in the above cited hierarchy. They come last in the American world, but they come first in the Duboisian history of civilization. Having charted the African American present, Du Bois looks back to the glorious past of his ancestors: "The shadow of a mighty Negro past flits through the tale of Ethiopia the Shadowy and of Egypt the Sphinx" (*The Souls* 6). In a similar vein, young Sin Far is proud to find out that "China is the oldest civilized nation on the face of the earth" (889). Both authors insist that it is institutional injustice, not some inborn imperfection that keeps their people from the world of privilege.

Du Bois and Sin Far brace themselves from their youngest years to be a credit to the race, to prove the rest of society wrong in its indignation for their people. People of color constantly have to assert their

Introduction

equality: "That sky was bluest when I could beat my mates at examination-time, or beat them at a foot-race, or even beat their stringy heads" (*The Souls* 4). Like Du Bois, Sin Far exudes a sense of triumph when — as a little girl — she wins a skirmish with her oppressors: "We have won the battle," she proudly announces to her Chinese American mother (887). Little Sin Far goes as far as to prepare herself for the role of a martyr who will die at the stake for the cause of her people. Ultimately Du Bois and Sin Far have the same goal: to have their humanity acknowledged. According to Sin Far, people will be able to "see and hear distinctly" only when the brotherhood of mankind will take upper hand over other malevolent forces within "human family" (890).

In their disenchantment with the American democracy both Sin Far and Du Bois pose a similar question: "Why did God make us to be hooted and stared at?" (Sin Far 888), "Why did God make me an outcast and a stranger in my own house?" (*The Souls* 5). Estrangement from the American land is seen both in Asian American and African American writing. Several sentences after addressing his indirect question to God, Du Bois calls the United States a "prison-house" rather than a true home that African Americans are still searching for (5). I argue throughout this project that Asian Americans often experience even more profound alienation from the American reality than African Americans. Estranged as Du Bois is, he nonetheless calls the United States his house, imperfect as it may be. Many Asian Americans could not go so far as to call the United States their house or home. They had an aspiration to belong to the United States, but they were constantly banished outside its borders, either figuratively or literally. In "Chinese Workmen in America" Sin Far reflects on the absence of Chinese Americans from the American imagery: "In these days one reads and hears much about Chinese diplomats, Chinese persons of high rank, Chinese visitors of prominence, and others, who by reason of wealth and social standing are interesting to the American people. But of those Chinese who come to live in this land, to make their homes in America, if only for a while, we hear practically nothing at all. Yet these Chinese, Chinese-Americans I call them, are not unworthy of a little notice" (231). Respective Exclusion Acts of 1882, 1884, 1886, 1902, 1907, 1917, and 1924 barred Asian Americans from the United States (Lowe 180). Neil Gotanda very appropriately captures African American and Asian American alienation from the American land. According to Gotanda,

Introduction

African Americans are a "domestic" other, while Asian Americans are an "external Orientalized other" (133). Texts analyzed here show that this division and this perception of African Americans and Asian Americans still to a great extent hold. They are alienated from the United States in a different way.

Invisibility remains a recurrent motif in African American and Asian American writing. Civil rights gains of the 1960s did not prevent African Americans and Asian Americans from perceiving themselves as invisible in the American world. Some seventy years after Du Bois called the United States a "prison-house," Sam Greenlee referred to it in very similar terms in "Prison Poems," arguing that all black people write from behind bars (*Blues for an African Princess* 33). In "Blues for Ronda Davis" Greenlee says that black existence verges on virtual non-existence (ibid. 21), which strikes a chord of Ellison's "black is and black ain't" (*Invisible Man* 8). African Americans are still often suspended between being and not being.

The editors of the first Asian American anthology *Aiiieeeee* (published in 1974) claim that "for seven generations" Asian Americans had been "no show" (xvi). Trying to undermine their invisibility, Asian American writers look to the past and to the future, in the hope of exposing past omissions and preventing future erasures. Being "no show" is nowhere more visible than at the beginning of Asian American presence in the United States, during the inauguration ceremony at Promontory Summit, Utah, following the completion of the transcontinental railway on May 10, 1969. Chinese Americans are left out of the picture commemorating the solemn occasion. Maxine Hong Kingston recreates the event in her 1980 book *China Men*.[10] The narrator's mythic great grandfather — Gwan Goong — portrays the United States as a place of crushing solitude for Chinese Americans, a place where they are barely noticed: "The Gold Mountain is lonely. You could get sick and almost die, and nobody come to visit. When you're well, you climb out of your basement again, and nobody has missed you" (38). Whenever Asian Americans are noticed, it is usually for the purpose of ostracism and propaganda. Asian American workers[11] were blamed for stealing the jobs from white workers and lowering their salaries. An example of such early anti–Asian American propaganda comes in a petition drafted by the Japanese and Korean Exclusion League in 1906. The authors of the petition alarm American citizens of the danger that "hordes"

Introduction

of Mongolians pose to the white race (in Ichigashi 274). They appeal for the extension of the Chinese Exclusion Act to the Japanese and Koreans. The petition ends with a call: "Stop the Mongolian invasion" (Ichigashi 274). Similar rhetoric surfaces again in a contemporary setting described in *Native Speaker*, when a group of steel workers stages a demonstration in front of the house belonging to a Korean American politician. Asian Americans and especially Asian American immigrants remain convenient scapegoats.

As I stress throughout this project, African Americans and Asian Americans battle a different set of stereotypes. While African Americans are portrayed as rebellious rabble rousers that scream for recognition (as they, in the end, do in Du Bois's metaphor), Asian Americans are frequently seen as submissive model minority citizens who quietly work away, pursuing an Anglo-Saxon version of the American dream. Asian American invisibility spans two extreme ends of the stereotyping spectrum: on the one hand, they are sees as permanent aliens that will never be fully American, and on the other, as perfectly assimilated citizens who merge with the rest of society. One of the lingering convictions is that Asian Americans corroborate their invisibility, because unlike African Americans, they stay quiet rather than clamor to be heard and seen. Some Asian American authors admit that in some cases this may indeed be true. A Japanese Canadian narrator of Joy Kogawa's *Obasan* says: "we seek the safety of our invisibility" (38).[12] Still, other Asian American writers categorically reject the stereotype of Asian American silence and meekness. In an interview with Virginia Lee Frank Chin avers: "I don't want to be measured against the stereotype anymore" (*Aiiieeeee* xxix). In a similar vein, Wittman Ah Sing is compared to Daruma the Shouter (Kingston 307).

Ultimately none of the characters in this project agrees to be measured against stereotypes. All of them aim at being seen in a sharp and clear light. They admit that invisibility can have its compensations. Yet these compensations can never take the place of visibility. Active as African Americans and Asian Americans are in their striving for visibility, they will succeed only if the white world changes the construction of its "inner eyes." It would be an oversimplification if we focused only on the invisibility of people of color to whites and overlooked their often contradictory and conflicting subject positionings in relation to each other.

Introduction

Therefore I emphasize that the invisibility of African Americans and Asian Americans to white people takes place within a larger network of mutual invisibilities. However, those mutual invisibilities do not happen in a vacuum, but under the shadow of the always present yet seemingly invisible white interference.

One

DIFFERENT FACES OF INVISIBILITY
Ralph Ellison's *Invisible Man*

Invisibility becomes the main source of contradictions in Ralph Ellison's *Invisible Man*. Contradictions underlie the very concept of invisibility. The Invisible Man lives in the solid material world, but he remains unseen by most Americans. Their gaze can hardly ever see beyond the surface of his black skin. His blackness produces a number of fixed, stereotypical images in the minds of white Americans. Society has a uniform vision of all African Americans, failing to embrace them as individuals. Ellison's valorization of contradictions may have exerted an impact on his treatment of invisibility. Originally, invisibility entails the discrimination of African Americans, their disbarment from full participation in the American democracy. The disfranchisement of black people gives rise to their suffering and the feeling of marginalization. The Invisible Man is all too aware of disadvantages stemming from invisibility. However, he also realizes that it does not entirely shut blacks away from the world of possibilities. Invisibility can be potentially illuminating. The Invisible Man derives inspiration and creativity from his invisibility. Through the very act of writing he transcends invisibility. The invisibility of African Americans accounts for their discrimination. Yet it may also serve as a tool to overcome the barriers standing in their way. The Invisible Man discovers that invisibility opens a hatch to tricksterism. Although Ellison notices positive sides of invisibility, he leaves no doubt that the ultimate objective of African Americans is to triumph over their invisibility, not acquiesce to it.

The recognition of invisibility is a precondition of the Invisible Man's self-discovery. The Invisible Man has numerous premonitions of his invisibility. Yet he does not grasp the magnitude of the problem. It takes him a while to realize that he is invisible practically to everyone. Only a real disguise gives him the full sense of his invisibility. Invisibility lies at the core of all his misfortunes. Everything revolves around his invisibility and every aspect of his life is somehow connected to it. Therefore the recognition of his invisibility is crucial for the achievement of self-understanding:

> I myself, after existing for some twenty years, did not become alive until I discovered my invisibility.... It took me a long time ... to achieve a realization everyone else appears to have been born with: That I am nobody but myself. But first I had to discover that I am an invisible man! ... I *was* and yet I was invisible, that was the fundamental contradiction [10, 19, 383].

Only after recognizing his invisibility to society does he become fully visible to himself. The Invisible Man frees himself from remnants of his illusions and gains a better grasp of interracial relations in the United States. The principle of invisibility does not pertain exclusively to him but to all Afro-Americans. However, not all people of color are willing to admit their invisibility. The Invisible Man knows that blacks will never overcome their invisibility unless they acknowledge it. The refusal of some African Americans to see their invisibility plays into the hands of whites. The Invisible Man's recognition of his invisibility is also essential for his acceptance of second-sight.[1] After discovering that he has fallen prey to the manipulations of white people, the Invisible Man can no longer blind himself to reality. Nor can he remain oblivious to the fact that invisibility is part of Afro-American reality in the United States.

At the time when the events described in *Invisible Man* unfold — the 1930s — African Americans were invisible because most whites made no effort to see them as they really were. Nursing false preconceptions about black people, they usually associated and many of them still associate blackness with different stereotypes, refusing to accept the humanity of African Americans. Deeply-ingrained prejudice prevented white people from perceiving African Americans as individuals endowed with complex personalities. The Invisible Man is aware that for most whites he has no personality and individuality. Projecting their fantasies about blackness upon Afro-Americans, whites attempt to make blacks live out stereotypes attributed to them. The invisibility of black Americans stems from the blindness of white people:

One: Different Faces of Invisibility

> I am invisible, understand, simply because people refuse to see me ... it is as though I have been surrounded by mirrors of hard distorting glass. When they approach me they see only my surroundings, themselves, or figments of their imagination — indeed, everything and anything except me.... That invisibility to which I refer occurs because of a peculiar disposition of the eyes of those with whom I come in contact. A matter of the construction of their *inner* eyes [7].

The "mirrors of hard distorting glass" bear reminiscence to Du Bois's "invisible yet horribly tangible plate glass," already cited in the Introduction (*Dusk of Dawn* 649, 650). Most researchers dealing with double-consciousness[2] have focused on the sight of African Americans, virtually gliding over the problem of white people's blindness. Their impaired vision is the main cause of racial problems in the United States. Suffering from distorted perception, white Americans saw not black people but their caricatures. Yet the Invisible Man realizes that it is not some inborn imperfection that prevents whites from seeing him. Being flawed by greed and blind pursuit of profit, most whites found it much more comfortable to nourish themselves on illusions about blacks. The bias against African Americans was, to a great extent, fuelled by financial factors. As George Lipsitz observes, whites have a "possessive investment" in privileges that accrue to their whiteness (1). Very much in line with Lipsitz's reasoning, Cheryl Harris sees whiteness as property cautiously guarded by its bearers. Protecting privileges attached to their whiteness, whites create an "exclusive club," afraid lest some intruders compromise its exclusivity (Harris 1736). In the 1930s whites feared that enfranchised African Americans would pose a challenge to their own superior material status. Segregation and discrimination helped whites to hedge a privileged position. Racist theories concocted by white people were supposed to further entrench blacks in their invisibility. Whites gave a scientific shape to their views in order to cover up their real motives. The biological concept of race underlay for example theories of polygenesis and monogenesis, Arthur de Gobineau's theses, social Darwinism, the eugenicist movement initiated by Darwin's cousin — Francis Galton.[3] Although Franz Boas, Horace Meyer Kallen and Robert E. Park undertook the first attempts to undermine the pseudoscientific notions of race already at the turn of the nineteenth and twentieth century,[4] those theories were still alive and well in the 1930s and they circulated in a variety of forms in the southern United States until the 1960s.

Invisible Both to Whites and Blacks

The Invisible Man is invisible to all social groups in the United States. Presenting a diversified picture of the black and white world, Ellison shows the Invisible Man interact with representatives of various social classes both within the black and white community. All these interactions are marked by his invisibility. Some African Americans remain unseen by the immature Invisible Man as well. African American invisibility to white people often impinges on their mutual interactions.

It becomes apparent that for most whites the Invisible Man has no personality during the hospital scene. Doctors do not approach him as a human being, but as a primitive, underdeveloped creature, which needs to be conditioned to the life in the civilized world. They would like to turn him into an automaton that would perform mechanically, without thinking. Doctors think that by applying the right kind of pressure, they can bring about a change of the Invisible Man's personality. Trying to manipulate his consciousness, they fail to recognize the Invisible Man as a subject, treating him as an object. Ellison's doctors resemble Foucault's doctors who represent a "system of centralized observation" ("The Eye of Power" 146). They are to ensure the "visibility of bodies" within this system (146). This is the only kind of visibility offered to the Invisible Man by the society in which he lives. Incarcerated in a lobotomy machine, the Invisible Man resembles Foucault's inmates, be it pupils, soldiers or patients who stayed in glassed-in cells which enabled observation from a "central observation-point" (Foucault 148). One of the hospital doctors is described as looking at the Invisible Man out of the "bright third eye that glowed from the centre of his forehead" (176). The hospital ordeal intensifies the Invisible Man's search for self-consciousness. He says: "When I discover who I am, I will be free," which suggests that he has understood that the key to freedom lies in self-discovery and his self must emerge from within, not from the outside (185).

Whites who purport to be benefactors of the black race cannot really see the Invisible Man either. Norton is the best example of superficial white philanthropy. He does not approach African Americans as individuals but as a black, shapeless mass that needs uplifting. The Invisible Man calls him a "teller of polite Negro stories," a "bearer of the white man's burden" (39). Perceiving himself as a pioneer of progress, Norton believes

One: Different Faces of Invisibility

that he is responsible for the enlightenment of black people. He assumes a patronizing attitude towards them. His philanthropy reaches only a very narrow spectrum of black population. Like a lot of other affluent whites, Norton sees only what he wants to see, banishing from his mind everything that might disturb his conscience. The cabins inhabited by tenant farmers teetering on the brink of survival shatter Norton's idyllic vision of African American life. His "polite Negro stories" do not match reality and are discredited by Trueblood's story. Norton is not selfless in the devotion to the racial cause. His charitable deeds help him soothe his conscience. He is convinced that his own fate and salvation hinge on what will happen to blacks. The old man's charity is spurious and it does not come free. Black students who attend the college sponsored by whites are imbued with white indoctrination. They are to subordinate themselves to white people's expectations. White benefactors overlook the fact that the value of education obtained by blacks is questionable, because color line divisions will probably make it impossible for them to get the job they deserve. The vet from the Golden Day can see through Norton's sham principles, observing that Norton needs the Invisible Man to include him in the catalogue of his achievements and convince himself of his own benevolence. The vet's claim that for Norton the Invisible Man is a "black amorphous thing" finds the confirmation years later when Norton cannot recognize the Invisible Man at the subway station (87). Not being able to distinguish between individuals, he can see African Americans only as a whole. Trueblood proves no less invisible to Norton than the Invisible Man. Norton projects his own desires onto Trueblood , who serves as a scapegoat for him.

The Invisible Man is invisible in a different way to representatives of the white working class. Unlike upper class whites, union members in the paint factory show open hostility towards him. Factory workers utter clearly racist theories. Considering the Invisible Man to be less developed, they claim that he was born a fink. The animosity of union members deeply hurts the Invisible Man. He is bewildered to find out that even people from the lower class look down on him. Listening to their offensive comments, he feels humiliated, scared and enraged. What infuriates him most is that they are trying to thrust their interpretation upon him without allowing him to voice his own opinion. Their hostility is propelled not only by deeply rooted prejudice but also by economic interests. Fearing that blacks will take their jobs, factory workers perceive African

Americans as competition, a threat to their status. Entrepreneurs exploit cheap black labor, paying black workers lower wages. A number of African Americans employed in the Liberty Paints factory are students working there to cover their tuition bills. The Invisible Man internally rebels against the fact that whites expect black people to work mechanically, without thinking and asking questions. Carl Degler maintains that one could encounter much more hostile attitudes towards African Americans among the lower class rather than among representatives of the upper class (135). Cheryl Harris makes similar observations, also noting that the white working class was much more likely to identify with the bourgeoisie than with fellow black workers (1741). In *Black Reconstruction* W. E. B. Du Bois argues that the discrimination against black people not only gave members of the working class comparatively higher wages, but also offered a significant boost to their ego. Du Bois calls it "compensatory wages of whiteness" (*Black Reconstruction* 700). Working class whites derived a considerable comfort from the fact that there was still someone lower in the hierarchy. Exposed to class oppression, they were free of racial oppression and apparently that was enough to keep them from identifying and targeting the real enemy. The result of such a reasoning on the part of the white working class was that "the wages of both classes could be kept low, the whites fearing to be supplanted by Negro labor, the Negroes always being threatened by the substitution of white labor" (*Black Reconstruction* 701). Ultimately people who set up the system drew the largest dividends. The Invisible Man gets lost in an intricate web of social relations. The paint factory is a miniature of the American society, the society which sends contradictory messages to black people. The unions label the Invisible Man a company fink, whereas Brockway believes him to be a union member. Brockway's antagonistic behavior shows how blacks can be invisible to one another.

The Invisible Man is also unseen by people who claim to rise above color line divisions. The Brotherhood welcomes everyone irrespective of their skin color. In the eyes of the organization all human beings are equal. However, under the veneer of lofty goals there is nothing but yearning for power. Giving black Americans a false sense of action and belonging, top brothers use blacks as a political instrument. In their ostensible color-blindness they see neither the different socio-historical background of African Americans, nor their humanity (384).

One: Different Faces of Invisibility

Brotherhood leaders are not interested in black people as individuals. Minor brothers do not represent any value. What counts is the number of votes and marchers they can provide. The Invisible Man compares brothers to the great white father. Like some slaveholders, they propagate the myth of paternalism, perceiving themselves as guardians of ignorant black masses, whom they need to guide and protect. Pretending to be friends of Afro-Americans, Jack and other leaders expect blind, unquestioning obedience. Whenever blacks get too vociferous in their demands, they do their best to silence them. Anyone who refuses to toe the party line is eliminated. Instead of granting African Americans their civil rights, whites palm them off with their friendship. White brotherhood leaders are not prepared to give up any of their privileges. The Brotherhood is sponsored by whites who want to hold blacks in check. When demonstrations reach a crescendo, inching towards accomplishing something, white leaders immediately bring them to a halt. Brothers concentrate on the virtual non-issue of black Sambo dolls, but are not concerned by the problem of police brutality. The movement would like its members to look at themselves from the perspective of the organization. Talking to Hambro, the Invisible Man comes to see that the powerful keep exploiting the underprivileged, maintaining that it is done for their own good. Jack, like Barbee, is figuratively blind. During the committee meeting Jack tells the Invisible Man to repeat the word "responsibility." Accidentally, it is the same word he was asked to repeat at the battle royal. Members of the Brotherhood can exercise no personal responsibility. Interrogating the Invisible Man, the Brotherhood leaders shed all appearances and show their true face. Like the battle royal whites, they make it clear to him that he should keep his place.

The Invisible Man is just as invisible in the South as in the North. In the South the discrimination against African Americans assumed much more drastic forms. Blacks were openly abused and denigrated. Facing open hostility from whites, black Southerners tried to remain as unpretentious as possible. Some blacks pretended to be chauffeurs while driving their own cars.[5] Forms of discrimination in the North were much more refined and subtle, but equally effective in disfranchising African Americans. Although most whites in New York are polite and seemingly unbiased, they hardly see the Invisible Man: "I felt that even when they were polite they hardly saw me, that they would have begged the pardon of the

Jack the Bear, never glancing his way if the bear happened to be walking along" (129). Their politeness is insincere. Northern whites are impersonal and impermeable. At the time when the events described in *Invisible Man* take place — the 1930s — Northern cities were already segregated into white and black districts. The level of segregation in New York was 5 percent in 1900 and 42 percent in 1930, in Chicago 10 percent in 1900 and 70 percent in 1930, in Cleveland 8 percent in 1900 and 51 percent in 1930 (Denton, Massey 31). The segregation of the Northern cities began in 1900 as a result of the increasing migration of African Americans from the South. The movement of African Americans to the Northern cities was speeded up by:

1. the changing situation in Southern agriculture: the shift from cotton production to food crops, which led to significant downsizing of the workforce;
2. the decreased demand for unskilled labor in the South accompanied by the increased demand for such labor in the North,
3. floods of 1915 and 1916 led to further aggravation of Southern agriculture; and
4. World War I, which stemmed immigration from Europe, producing a labor shortage to be filled by African Americans from the South (Denton, Massey 28).

The numbers of black migrants from the South ballooned from 174,000 in the 1890s to 525,000 between 1910 and 1920 and 877,000 in the 1920s (Denton, Massey 29). The influx of African Americans unleashed a wave of panic in the North. Especially hostile were the whites who shared the same neighborhoods with black people.

White animosity towards African Americans living in the North took manifold forms. The beginning of the 20th century saw an outbreak of communal riots against black people. During such riots African Americans were attacked at random, mostly by roaming bands of whites: New York in 1900, Springfield, Illinois in 1908, East St. Louis, Illinois in 1917, Chicago in 1919 (Denton, Massey 30). Communal riots gave way to targeted violence in the 1920s: threats against black individuals inhabiting white neighborhoods, ransacking and bombing of their houses. Real estate agents: both white and black waged the most successful battle against integrated settlements.[6] They successfully channeled the flow of Southern immigrants[7] to black districts, preventing them from settling in other parts

One: Different Faces of Invisibility

of the city. They also frustrated the attempts of the black middle class to move to better-off neighborhoods. Middle class African Americans living in white neighborhoods faced enormous pressure to move to other sections of the city (Massey, Denton 39). "Restrictive covenants" served as one of the most powerful weapons in the segregation crusade.[8] Property owners who signed the covenants agreed to exclude African Americans from a given area for a specified period of time. Any violation could be pursued in the courts. The Supreme Court did not outlaw the covenants until 1948 (Denton, Massey 36).

The Invisible Man encounters open belligerence in the North when he unsuccessfully tries to dispose of the "Negro bank." The antagonism of white Northerners manifests itself in its undiluted form. All their prejudice and hatred burst to the surface. A white man calls the Invisible Man a confidence man, voicing sentiments prevailing at that time in the American society. White Americans perceive blacks as cheats and parasites preying on their benevolence. Whites loathe African American presence to such an extent that they could not even stand the idea of having a piece of black garbage in their neighborhood. White segregation policies show themselves much more drastically during the eviction scene of an elderly couple that suddenly finds itself on the street with all its possessions. During his affiliation with the Brotherhood the Invisible Man initiates a campaign against evictions.[9]

The Invisible Man is aware that he is invisible not only to whites, but to his own people as well. Various sections of African American community do not see each other. It becomes fully clear to the Invisible Man during the Harlem riot: "I was invisible ... even to their eyes" (422). Just as the Invisible Man is invisible to virtually all classes of white people, he is also invisible to all tiers of the black community. He is not seen by the black middle class upstart Bledsoe. As already mentioned, he is invisible to Brockway—a working-class black man. His invisibility to Ras the Exhorter—a black nationalist—almost costs the Invisible Man his life. It is just when he is about to be hanged by Ras that he sees the full import of African Americans' invisibility to each other:

> It's simple, you've known it a long time. It goes, "Use a nigger to catch a nigger." Well, they used me to catch you [African Americans in Harlem] and now they're using Ras to do away with me and to prepare your sacrifice. ... look they've played a trick on us, the same old trick with new variations [423].

Manipulating African Americans to their own advantage, whites create as well as exploit the already existing rifts within African American community, sapping its strength. Rather than unite against people who want to keep them in their place, Ras, the Invisible Man and other African American factions fall prey to white manipulations and end up fighting one another.[10]

Other African Americans are not entirely visible to the immature Invisible Man either. He looks down on lower class blacks, believing that they bring ill fame on the whole black race. Trying to emulate whites and their standards, the young Invisible Man detests any contact with black belt African Americans. Together with other college students he is ashamed of black peasants' uncouth manners and their spiritual chanting, which he sees as "animal sounds" (47). Looking at his attitudes already from the perspective of maturity, the Invisible Man attributes his derision for black-belt people to "fear," fear of being "pulled down" (47), of going back where he came from. The Invisible Man himself comes from a poor sharecropper family. His youthful hostility towards people from the black belt parallels the animosity of the black middle class to people from the ghetto, of which I am going to talk in Chapter Two. The Invisible Man's grandfather — a former slave — is initially unseen by the Invisible Man too. He wonders "what an old slave could know about humanity" (268). At the beginning the Invisible Man is not sure whether the pursuit of individuality does not entail the negation of one's blackness. All these doubts visit the Invisible Man's mind because of white indoctrination, which often questioned the humanity of black people. Only after completely rejecting the outlook of the white world, does he become fully certain that individuality cannot be built on the eradication of one's racial consciousness.

Invisibility — a Double-Edged Sword

The mature Invisible Man realizes that invisibility is a part of his identity. Therefore he introduces himself to the reader as an invisible man. To society he is no one else but an invisible man and invisibility finds its way into his self-assumed proper name. The Invisible Man defines himself through his invisibility and he will not allow others to name or define him. As a self-conscious narrator, he is no longer prepared to accept labels coming from the outside world. Whites see in him everything but what he really is. Adopting his own name instead of accepting names invented for him by others, he assumes responsibility for shaping his own identity. Now his identity emerges from within, not from the outside. Naming himself, the Invisible Man rebels against the existing system of signification and looks inside for his identity:

> I always tried to go in everyone's way but my own. I have also been called one thing and then another while no one really wished to hear what I called myself. So after years of trying to adopt the opinions of others I finally rebelled. I am an *invisible* man [433].

In the end the Invisible Man is just himself. Anglo-Saxon rules of naming do not apply to the Invisible Man. His name is meaningful, because it is born out of his invisibility. Thomas Vogler observes that the Invisible Man's name would be compatible with the Native American system of naming. Among Native Americans "everyone had to wait until he had earned a name through some significant action, or until he had revealed enough of his basic personality for a name to be chosen that adequately reflected his individuality" (141). The Invisible Man earns his name through his experience of invisibility.

He admits that invisibility lies behind the ordeal African Americans go through. The effects of invisibility are not always tangible and feasible to the outside world. Invisibility results not only in physical deprivation, but also in psychological trauma. The anguish of black people can be much more devastating than any privations they suffer because of their invisibility. Ignorance and insensitivity of the white world angers the Invisible Man. Some blacks internalize antagonistic attitudes, feeling degraded and excluded. Although the Invisible Man emphasizes that he is a man of flesh and blood, he confesses that invisibility makes him wonder whether he really exists or is only a figment of other people's imagination. It annoys the Invisible Man that whites ignore him, treat him as a nonentity. Facing the indifference of the world, the Invisible Man must reassure himself that he really belongs to it, "striking out with [his fists]" to make himself seen (7–8). His metaphor of desperately banging on the door of the world to be recognized makes him similar to people from Du Bois's metaphor cited in the Introduction. Both the Invisible Man and people incarcerated in the glass cave reach the crescendo of desperation, but in both cases their desperation fails to produce the desired reaction from the outside world.

Invisibility in African American and Asian American Literature

Desperate for recognition, African Americans want to be perceived as an essential part of humanity. Blacks and whites work at cross purposes. Afro-Americans crave full integration into society, whereas whites refuse to accept them as their equals. The white man that offends the Invisible Man does not see him as a human being. To him he is just an object on his way, an object to be pushed aside or passed without notice. Being banished to the margins of society, many black people had an impression that everyone and everything conspired against them. Confronted with discriminatory and segregationist policies, African Americans often wrestled with piercing solitude. The Invisible Man says that "there is acoustical deadness in [his] hole," which might indicate that he has no one to talk to (11). The Invisible Man's alienation is compounded by the fact that his isolation is not only figurative, but also literal.

Invisibility blurs distinctions between good and evil, making everything relative. Hostility and indifference of the white world fills African Americans with rage and a desire to strike back. Invisibility may change their picture of external reality. Facing bias and victimization, some African Americans find it difficult to keep things in perspective, to draw a line between oppressors and the innocent. Everything loses its right proportions and becomes twisted out of shape. Invisibility robs the world of whatever love it has, turning it into the site of malice and hatred. The world looks at the Invisible Man through "mirrors of distorting glass," yet sometimes he also seems to look at the world through distorting glass:

> When one is invisible he finds such problems as good and evil, honesty and dishonesty, of such shifting shapes that he confuses one with the other, depending upon who happens to be looking through him at the time ... all life seen from the hole of invisibility is absurd [432, 437].

Invisibility can have a desensitizing effect on Afro-Americans. Having been severely wronged, black people need great determination and enormous strength of character not to turn hostile and indifferent. As the Invisible Man confesses, "you begin to bump people back" (7). And the Invisible Man bumps the insulting man back, but unlike Guitar in *The Song of Solomon,* he does not hit back at random. He can still distinguish between good and evil. Hard as it is, the Invisible Man manages to put everything in context, refusing to get lost in the absurd world of invisibility. However, some do get lost. Unlike the Invisible Man, Ras the Exhorter is blinded by his invisibility. Being consumed with hatred, he would like to

One: Different Faces of Invisibility

wipe all whites off the face of the earth. The Invisible Man maintains his objectivity and does not get carried away by emotions. For him invisibility is not so much a blinding, but rather an illuminating force.

The Invisible Man is familiar with all downsides of invisibility. Yet he by no means suggests that invisibility is all gloom and doom. Putting a positive spin on things, the Invisible Man emphasizes that even invisibility has certain compensations. Its deleterious effects can be counterbalanced. As I stressed at the very beginning, invisibility involves contradictions. It comprises both positive and negative sides. The Invisible Man is clearly aware of the contradictory nature of invisibility: "I'm an invisible man and it placed me in a hole — or showed me the hole I was in.... All sickness is not unto death, neither is invisibility" (432, 16). His invisibility is not only the source of his suffering and alienation, but also the source of his illumination. Invisibility is potentially enlightening. All his misfortunes and tribulations give him an ultimate insight, leading to his illumination. The Invisible Man can see where others are blind. Neither Norton nor Jack, nor Emerson is able to get under the surface of things, to see their real depth. Power and security makes influential whites overconfident, throwing them off guard and blunting their perception. The Invisible Man's invisibility forces him to ask the questions that would never cross Norton's or Jack's mind. His insight goes beyond racial awareness, reaching a much more universal dimension. Rising above the color line and uniting with all human beings, the Invisible Man poses existential questions. The statement "None of us seems to know who he is or where he is going" concerns the nature of human condition[11] (436). His invisibility sensitizes him to the fate of the whole mankind. Invisibility also taught the Invisible Man to "classify stenches of death" (438), making him much more alert to other people's fraudulent tricks.

Invisibility propels his creativity and it lends a spark to the creation of the narrative. Weaving the story out of invisibility, the Invisible Man turns his ordeal into a work of art. The Invisible Man's narrative is born out of his invisibility and alienation. Something essentially negative becomes transformed into something constructive: "I play the invisible music of my isolation ... you hear this music simply because music is heard and seldom seen, except by musicians. Could this compulsion to put invisibility down in black and white be thus an urge to make music of invisibility?" (16). The Invisible Man's narrative transcends the medium he employs to write it. Telling his story or rather "putting it down in black and white," he "makes music of invisibility." His prose is elevated to the level of music. At certain points the syntactic structures he uses seem to imitate sound, for example in the Prologue, during most of his speeches and in the Epilogue. Invisibility endows the Invisible Man with greater sensitivity, enabling him to hear and see music.

He traces an affinity between himself and Louis Armstrong. What primarily unites them is their invisibility. The Invisible Man makes music out of his invisibility, whereas Armstrong "made poetry out of being invisible" (11). Armstrong also reaches beyond the confines of his artistic medium. Thanks to his own invisibility the Invisible Man can fully understand and appreciate Armstrong's music. Both Armstrong and the Invisible Man use their invisibility constructively. Their creativity is inseparably interwoven with all the torment and anxiety accumulated inside:

> With Louis Armstrong one half of me says, "Open the window and let the foul air out," while the other says, "It was good green corn before the harvest." Of course Louie was kidding, *he* wouldn't have thrown old Bad Air out, because it would have broken up the music and the dance, when it was the good music that came from the bell of the old Bad Air's horn that counted [438].

"Old Bad Air" is an essential ingredient of their creativity. However, ultimately, it is "good music" that counts. What really matters is how someone utilizes their invisibility. The Invisible Man discovers a potential dormant in invisibility. That potential materializes in his narrative. The Invisible Man wants the reader to hear his music, just as Armstrong hopes that the listener will see his poetry.

Writing becomes a device helping the Invisible Man to undermine his invisibility. It makes him more visible to himself and to other people. Telling his tale, he has been trying to "look through himself" (432). The Invisible Man is no longer afraid to look back at his life, no longer shuddering from digging into the events of the past. He understands that he cannot erase the past, but he can at least learn from it. Therefore he "belatedly studies the lesson of his life" (432). Yet his writing, like his invisibility, involves contradictions. It is excruciating and cathartic at the same time. In order to put everything down, he has to relive the painful events of the past. Telling the truth and opening his mind before the reader is not easy. As the main participant of all events in his story, the Invisible

Man needs to struggle to remain objective. However, constructing the narrative, he also cleanses himself, "whips it all up" (433). The very act of telling the story and sharing his experience with the reader negates at least part of his anger and bitterness. Creating the narrative, the Invisible Man gets the maximum of insight: "I've illuminated the blackness of my invisibility—and vice versa" (16). The self-analytic undertaking of writing an autobiography has illuminated him, just as invisibility has illuminated him. By narrating his story, he "illuminated the blackness of his invisibility." Charles Taylor points out that our life becomes fully meaningful only if we see it as a narrative, as a story (47). Thomas Vogler comes to similar conclusions, arguing that the ability to tell one's story confirms that person's identity (134). The Invisible Man's narrative proves that he can locate the events of his life on a broader scale. Single incidents gain significance only in the context of our whole life. That is why the construction of the narrative marks the climax of the Invisible Man's illumination. According to Taylor, self is a "being capable of articulation" (*Sources of the Self* 375). The Invisible Man achieves self-consciousness by telling his tale.

The Invisible Man defines himself through writing. All along he has been defined by others, having practically no voice. People brand the Invisible Man one way or another, without allowing him to express his own thoughts and feelings. Composing the narrative, he has found his own voice. In the Prologue the Invisible Man asks an old slave-woman what freedom is. For her freedom is "nothing but knowing how to say what I got up in my head. But it's a hard job" (9). Freedom consists in the ability to articulate one's thoughts. The Invisible Man gains real freedom by writing down his story. The control over his text gives the Invisible Man full self-control, releasing him from the manipulations of others. Constructing in writing his own tale without depending on intermediaries, or any amanuenses, he becomes fully articulate. Having destroyed the texts written for him by false friends, he sets out to create his own text. The writing down of the narrative crowns the Invisible Man's striving for autonomy. Tony Tanner maintains that the autobiographical enterprise he undertakes allows him to "step out of other people's times and schemes" (89). At the same time the Invisible Man seems to step into our sense of time. Like a yokel who knocked out a prizefighter (Ellison 11), he breaks the pattern of the reader's certainties. Turning away from history designed by manipulators of reality, he creates his own story, putting it in "black and white" (Ellison 16).

Writing his autobiography, the Invisible Man wants to tell people "what was really happening when [their] eyes were looking through" (439). The narrative is a desperate attempt to shatter at least part of his invisibility. The Invisible Man realizes that the stereotypical notions of African Americans stem to a great extent from white people's ignorance. Demonstrating in writing his humanity and individuality, he tries to establish an invisible bond with the reader and hopes to change white people's perception of black Americans. The Invisible Man exposes himself before the reader, articulating his thoughts and feelings. Being unable to forget, he feels the need to share his story with other people, both white and black. He does not want to be the only one to "dream this nightmare" (437). Taylor observes that "through language we remain related to partners of discourse either in real, live exchanges, or in indirect confrontations" (38). If American citizens do not want to talk to the Invisible Man in a conventional way, he will reach them through his writing. Storytelling is therapeutic for him. However, he is not certain about the success of his endeavor, knowing that people cannot stand the truth. They do not want to be wrenched out of their illusions, preferring instead to harbor their misconceptions. Portraying blacks as inferior, whites try to boost their own ego. White Americans transfer all that they repress onto people of color. There is yet another risk involved in his storytelling. The Invisible Man has "disarmed" himself in the process (438). Now that whites are aware of his invisibility, he can no longer treat it as a protective device. Still, the Invisible Man realizes that all the dangers outweigh the potential benefits resulting from his writing. He takes the risk, because he wants to "create the uncreated features of his face" (268). Writing his autobiography, the Invisible Man creates himself as an individual. As an invisible man he virtually does not exist in the American world. The narrative enables him to overcome his nonexistence. According to Henry Louis Gates, author of *The Signifying Monkey*, "the absence implied by invisibility is undermined by the presence of the narrator as the author of his own text" (106). Having written down his story, the Invisible Man is no longer a "disembodied voice" (Ellison 439), but the embodied voice. He gains substance through his writing. The Invisible Man gives form to his story and writing, like light, gives form to him. Without light he is formless. The Invisible Man's craving for light symbolizes his hankering after visibility.

African American autobiographical writing could be compared to a jazz composition. It involves "assertion within and against the group" (Ellison cited in Sten 87). Individual pursuit of self-consciousness goes hand in hand with self-searching in a broader sense, especially if we take into account the Invisible Man's youthful ambition to "create the uncreated conscience of his race" (268) and his mature bold statement "that, on lower frequencies, I speak for you" (439). The Invisible Man strives not only for his personal visibility, but also for the visibility of his people. The question of representation comes to the foreground in any autobiography written by a person from a marginalized group. As a man who walks with holes in his shoes,[12] the Invisible Man has every right to say "that, on lower frequencies, I speak for you" (439). Yet not all African American autobiographers find themselves in a similar (dis)position. Stan Butterfield notes that a personal success in American society usually meant an increasing alienation from the masses of black people (94). The Invisible Man's predecessors were to a varying degree aware of the dilemma. At various stages of his life the Invisible Man himself is confronted with a similar predicament, although he is not always conscious of it. By disassociating himself from the Brotherhood he manages to avoid Booker T. Washington's success. He also chooses a different model of autobiographical writing.

If we are to accept Butterfield's division of African American autobiographies into those that oscillate between the black and white world and the revolutionary voices from prison that flatly reject the white world, then the Invisible Man's text might be seen as a bridge between the two modes of writing. Opting for diversity and approaching the world "through love and hate," the Invisible Man first of all gives priority to humanity, be it black, white or any other color. It is true that he creates his narrative underground, in isolation from both worlds. Still, his isolation is never fully complete.[13] Nor is Louis Armstrong the only influence that leaves a tangible imprint on his writing. Ellison himself makes it a point to place his text within a larger literary framework that reaches not only beyond African American literature, but also beyond Anglo-American literature towards the world literature: "Part of that reaches as far back as Dostoyevski's *Notes from the Underground World*" (Ellison, Introduction XV). He also distinguishes between his relatives: Langston Hughes, Richard

Wright and ancestors: Ernest Hemingway, T.S. Eliot, William Faulkner (An Interview with John Hersey 42). "Putting his invisibility in black and white," the Invisible Man builds upon literary traditions across the racial divide, looking back to those before him and anticipating the voices that are still to come.

The Invisible Man's speeches are a prelude to his writing. The personal experience of invisibility inspires the Invisible Man as an orator. At the same time most of his speeches make him more visible and boost his racial consciousness. The first speech is a failure. It is patterned after Booker T. Washington's Atlanta Exposition Address. White guests mock the Invisible Man, hardly listening to him. In his carefully memorized speech the Invisible Man supports the idea of brotherly love. Obsequious as he is, he subconsciously articulates suppressed thoughts and emotions, accidentally swapping the phrase "social responsibility" for "social equality" (33). Unlike the battle royal speech, the second speech is purely spontaneous and improvised. However, overtones of the first speech still reverberate in the second one. The Invisible Man extols the long-standing tradition of black humility, trying to discourage black people from violence. Again he invokes the example of a great Southern conciliator — implicitly Booker T. Washington. Despite some similarity, the second speech is nonetheless different. Witnessing the eviction, the Invisible Man finds his racial consciousness. So far lower class blacks have been invisible to him, just as he has been invisible to whites. Now he recognizes them as his people: "And why did I see them now as behind a veil that threatened to lift" (207). The scene transports him back to the South. On previous occasions the Invisible Man has tried to pass for a Northerner. During the eviction he identifies himself as a Southerner. The Invisible Man is not only an orator, but also becomes a leader. He organizes the crowd's energy, moving people to constructive action.

Delivering the third speech, the Invisible Man achieves a certain degree of visibility — both literally and figuratively. He stands in the spotlight, whereas the audience is blurred into an invisible mass. Everyone can see him, but he cannot distinguish between individual faces of his spectators. There seems to be a veil between the audience and himself. The Invisible Man brings it down and manages to establish contact with people. Questions from the listeners and their applause prove that they are captivated by what he says. They display interest in his feelings. The enthusiastic response of the audience infuses the Invisible Man with strength and self-esteem. At the beginning he planned to weave his speech around the Brotherhood ideology; in the end he drops all ideological references. The speech ends with a personal confession, of belonging to the African American community. The Invisible Man calls himself the "citizen" of "the country of [their] vision" (261–262). The very experience of being seen in a meaningful way gives the Invisible Man a sense of arriving home[14] (261–262).

Sharing his feelings with the audience, he makes himself visible and gains a sense of belonging. The third speech is a complete success. However, the Invisible Man struggles in its initial phase. At first he is not certain whether he will get through to the audience. Standing on the stage, he feels isolated. During his speech the Invisible Man opens his mind, before the crowd, but he preserves a separate identity. He will not allow it to merge with a group. His assertion within and against the group is conspicuous in the last speech — during Tod Clifton's funeral. He disassociates himself from the rest of the crowd, wondering whether all the people participate in the funeral because they were Clifton's friends or because they want to see a spectacle. Detached as he is, the Invisible Man does not remain unaffected by the responses of the crowd. Listening to the funeral chanting, he listens to something within himself. The song releases a wave of emotion in the Invisible Man. On this occasion he can distinguish between the individual faces of people, studying them to find out what is hidden underneath. The eulogy for Clifton is unlike any of his previous speeches. It verges on music. Its rhythm renders the Invisible Man's anger, sorrow and frustration.

Invisibility, Tricksterism and Performativity of Human Identities

Invisibility is not only a source of inspiration and illumination. It also opens the door to the world of tricksterism. Tricksterism is a technique of survival in a hostile environment. Being confronted with a more powerful opponent, a trickster cannot rely on traditional methods of struggle. Tricksterism does not entail an open confrontation. In order to outsmart an enemy, a trickster has to resort to unconventional tactics like wit, deceit, masking and signifying. Invisibility is a prerequisite of tricksterism. If African Americans are unseen, then in a sense they have an edge over whites. It is difficult to fight against an invisible enemy. Most of the time whites were not at all aware of the enemy's existence. White people's knowledge was incomplete, which gave African Americans an element of surprise. They could capitalize on their invisibility. The Invisible Man compares a slave to an ingenious scientist who has perfectly mastered the science of survival. Simulated obsequiousness was one of his weapons. Suddenly it dawns upon the Invisible Man that one does not need to head for success "upward" since one can also go "downward" and " around in a circle" (Ellison 385).

Black people could not succeed if they embraced the idea of success espoused by whites. African Americans' road to success was different. Obstacles surmounted on their way prevented them from playing by the rules of whites. They had to adopt different measures in their striving for success. The hallmarks of Afro-American success were different as well. Sometimes sheer survival was already a success. The Invisible Man's remarks correspond to Gates's observations: "What did/do black people signify in a society in which they were intentionally introduced as the subjugated, as the enslaved cipher? Nothing on the x axis of white signification, and everything on the y axis of blackness" (47). Horizontal and vertical positions are culturally determined. On the horizontal axis of white signification blacks were reduced to submission and servitude. On the vertical axis they could successfully channel their invisibility. Gates traces the origins of Afro-American tricksterism to the mythologies of Yoruba cultures. The chief trickster was called Esu. The African American tradition replaced Esu with the Signifying Monkey. The relationship between whites and the black trickster parallels that between the Lion and the Signifying Monkey. The Lion, although more powerful, is outsmarted by the Monkey because he cannot decipher the Monkey's figurative language. He reads it literally, not figuratively. African tricksterism was transplanted onto the American soil, finding its way into Afro-American oral tradition and into everyday life of African Americans. The Signifying Monkey is one of many African American tricksters. Brer Fox, Brer Rabbit, Brer Bear, Jack the Rabbit, Jack the Bear are others, to name just a few. Joel Chandler Harris wrote down trickster tales in his collection *Uncle Remus Stories*. Charles Waddell Chesnutt, the author of the *Conjure Woman* collection, expanded the narrative plot of trickster tales and introduced human characters instead of animals.

The very origins of *Invisible Man* go back to a trickster tale which Ellison was told in 1939 by Leo Gurley. Back then a twenty-five year old Ellison was in Harlem, compiling folklore material for the Federal Writers' Project (Levine 405). The tale told the story of Sweet-the-Monkey who "could make hisself invisible" (405). "Sweet-the-Monkey" is his nickname. His real name is not mentioned. He lives in Florence, South Carolina, "one of those hard towns on colored folks" (in Levine 405). Literal invisibility becomes for Sweet-the-Monkey a source of protection and a tool of mischievous subversion. Capitalizing on his invisibility, he steals from white people, often under the cover of the night.[15] At one point "he even cleaned out the damn bank" (406). On most occasions, however, he enters various places just for the sake of trespassing and breaking the rules of segregation: "most of the time he broke into places he wouldn't take nothing. Lots a time he just did it to show 'em he could" (in Levine 406). The places he enters are off limits to black people. It is not without significance that Sweet-the-Monkey robs the bank, subverting in this way his position of an object of property and becoming its subject. Banks were and still are inaccessible to African Americans in more ways than one. First of all, the capital accumulated there is controlled entirely by whites. Secondly, African Americans have historically been barred from tapping the resources managed by those institutions. They still find obstacles on the way whenever trying to secure loans, credits etc. There is also another shade of meaning to Sweet-the-Monkey's bank robbery. Usually perceived as petty criminals, African Americans were not thought capable of any large-scale operations. Performing his acts of subversion, Sweet-the-Monkey proves his resourcefulness and "shows 'em he could."

The Invisible Man encounters different examples of tricksters in the course of the novel. All of them remain invisible to the outside world. They usually can see more than the people around them do. Realizing that they are unseen by others, tricksters take advantage of their invisibility. It is the blindness of their immediate environment that allows them to succeed in their craft. The Invisible Man's grandfather reigns supreme among all other tricksters. Living in slavery, he is virtually forced to become a trickster. Slave masters treat slaves as a part of their domestic livestock, expecting full subordination. At the same time they create the myth of felicitous life on the plantation in order to justify the system of bondage. Promoting paternalism, whites want to believe that slaveocracy is the only right and just system. Blacks are to confirm whites in their misconceptions. Just as they are to corroborate their mistaken beliefs about blackness. The Invisible Man's grandfather has managed to decipher white mentality. Whites want him to be obedient and respectful, so he feigns obedience and respect. Instead of showing white people his true face, he allows them to see only what they expect to see. The grandfather tries to pass on the legacy of tricksterism to the next generations, urging them to undermine [Whites] with grins, agree 'em to death and destruction" (19–20).

Preserving a dual personality, the grandfather has never lost his alternative self. He dissimulated before the outside world, but remained true to himself internally. The grandfather's servility blinded whites, yet it never undermined his own humanity. As the Invisible Man finally concludes, these are only his liberated children that became dubious about their humanity (438). The grandfather strikingly resembles the protagonist of Chesnutt's short story "The Passing of Grandison." Both disguise their real feelings, resorting to masking and signifying. Their tricksterism assumes a variety of forms. They do not limit themselves to verbal tricksterism, but employ mimicry and gesture in order to fool whites. It is white people's arrogance that makes them so vulnerable to tricksterism. Ellin Horowitz claims that the grandfather adopts the "ancient Chinese strategy of absorbing the conqueror" (81). To avoid destruction, he allows whites to "swoller" him until they "bust wide open" (13–14).

Bledsoe[16] represents a different mode of tricksterism. The Invisible Man's grandfather practices tricksterism to protect himself, whereas Bledsoe becomes a trickster to grab power. A craving for power underlies all his actions. The grandfather's tricksterism does not target the black community, while Bledsoe's tricksterism turns against it. He would go to any lengths to attain his position: "I'll have every Negro in this county hanging on tree limbs by morning if it means staying where I am" (128). Bledsoe shares in the spiritual blindness of the white world. He becomes blinded by his lust for power. The Invisible Man is no less invisible to him than he is to whites. Being the president of the black college, Bledsoe is not really interested in uplifting the race. He proves skilful in manipulating everyone around him. Yet all his manipulations are aimed at bolstering his own status. Bledsoe does not present the racial situation as it really is, sheltering whites from the plain, unvarnished truth about the plight of sharecroppers inhabiting the black belt. They are to remain out of white people's sight. Not to disturb the conscience of white people, he introduces them only to respectable, cultivated blacks. The imagery employed in the novel exposes Bledsoe's duplicity. Half of his face is shaded when we can see him sitting in his office. Bledsoe has two faces — one for whites, the other for blacks. In the presence of whites he is always an embodiment of composure. Before the meeting with Norton, he fashions his image like a sculptor, looking in the mirror to smooth his features and hide his anger. Bledsoe speaks openly to the Invisible Man about his manipulative tactics, exulting in the power he has over whites. White trustees think that they are in control, when in reality they are manipulated by him. Preaching humility to black students, Bledsoe wants them to be as accommodating towards whites as possible. With all his emphasis on humility, Bledsoe bears certain affinity to Booker T. Washington. Ellison probably meant to jab irony at the black leader. However, we cannot entirely identify Bledsoe with Washington.

Treacherous as Bledsoe is, he stays far behind Rinehart, who is a master of treachery. Rinehart is both literally and figuratively invisible. In order to carry out his fraudulent tricks, he needs to efface himself, to remain as inconspicuous as possible. He cannot be seen by all of his victims at the same time. Projecting different images of himself, he practices tricksterism on many levels. Rinehart jumps into different forms, thriving on fluidity. His multiple personalities give him only a semblance of freedom, but no real identity. Alice Bloch calls Rinehart a "universal Negro" (267), because he embodies stereotypes ascribed to African Americans: a gambler, preacher, lover, runner (Ellison 376).

Rinehart is nothing but a swindler cashing in on people's credulity. The grandfather's tricksterism helps him endure white exploitation, whereas Rinehart's tricksterism becomes a tool of exploitation. As Tony Tanner points out, his heart is all "rind" (87). Deceiving everyone around him, he strips himself of his humanity. Ellison compares Rinehart to the protagonist of Melville's Confidence Man, who tricks passengers aboard the Mississippi steamship into giving him money. According to Ellison, Rinehart personifies chaos: "He has lived with chaos for so long that he knows how to manipulate it" (48). Ellison goes on to explain that "rinehart" was a "call used by Harvard students when they prepared to riot"

Invisibility in African American and Asian American Literature

(Ellison, cited in Gottesman 48). What follows the Rinehart episode is the breakout of the riot in Harlem. The Harlem demonstrations end in chaos and destruction. For Ellison, Rinehart also represents America and change. The 1930s, the period of economic depression and instability are an ideal time for Rinehart to unleash his treachery. Tanner contrasts Rinehart with Bledsoe, Jack, Norton and Emerson, drawing our attention to the fact that Rinehart is "most at home in the subterranean world" (87). Bledsoe, Jack and others feel most comfortable on the surface, while Rinehart prospers underground. They bask in the spotlight. Rinehart remains largely unseen. Jack is afraid that he might fall outside history. Rine slips under the surface of history, hoping to remain undetected.

Towards the end of the novel Tod Clifton becomes something of a trickster. Before turning to tricksterism, Clifton himself was tricked by the Brotherhood. Having discovered that the Brotherhood treats him like a marionette, he breaks with the organization. Instead of allowing others to exploit him, Clifton starts to manipulate his own image. At the beginning the Invisible Man does not understand Clifton's decision. He believes that Clifton has negated his humanity by quitting the Brotherhood. It does not occur to him that Clifton has left the Movement to keep his humanity. The Invisible Man is disgusted by the doll show, just as he is repelled by Mary's "Negro Bank." According to the Invisible Man, black people should fight the stereotypical portrayal of African Americans as entertainers degrading themselves for money. Portraying blacks as lighthearted, whites were trying to cleanse their feeling of guilt. The Invisible Man does not realize that Clifton's apparent self-betrayal is really an act of self-preservation. As a member of the Brotherhood he was manipulated by the top brothers, who did not really see him. Stepping out of the organization, Clifton reverses the pattern. Now he pulls the strings and gains full self-control. Manipulating his own image, Clifton reclaims agency. Eventually, however, his tricksterism ends tragically.

Initially, the Invisible Man does not fully recognize tricksterism. His grandfather's words seem quite enigmatic. Yet he appears to have subconsciously decoded at least part of his message. The Invisible Man feels like a traitor whenever playing by the rules. Intuitively he senses that he does not show whites his true face. Only a real disguise makes the Invisible Man fully aware that invisibility is a key to the world of tricksterism. After becoming literally invisible, he discovers the potential of invisibility I was and yet I was unseen" (383). The potential of invisibility can be fully fulfilled especially in the Northern United States, where everyone is more impersonal than in the South (377).

The Invisible Man comes to see how pliable human identity really is. Suddenly he feels certain plasticity about himself. In the South everyone had their identity thrust upon them. In the North there seems to be much more freedom of movement. One can shape one's own identity, create oneself anew by projecting different images of oneself. The Invisible Man begins to understand that he can manipulate his identity.

Like all the authors analyzed here, Ellison emphasizes the performativity of human identity. Nowhere is it more visible than in the Rinehart episode. The Invisible Man becomes aware that all identities are performed only after donning his disguise. At first the Invisible Man passes unconsciously. Having finally realized that he is mistaken for Rinehart, he notices that something strange is happening to him. His relation to reality is changed. Not only is the Invisible Man an enigma to the outside world, but also the outside world becomes a puzzle: "faces were a mysterious blur" (365). Wearing a disguise of dark glasses and a white hat, he appears estranged from reality, which is suddenly defamiliarized, loses its shapes: "It was like looking into the depths of a murky cave" (367). Even people he has known for a long time seem different. The Invisible Man starts to have doubts about himself and about others. On the one hand, he finds it difficult to dissociate himself from his real self. On the other hand, he notices that he looks different and behaves differently, saying things he never really intended to say. The whole experience triggers a wave of doubts about human identity. Seeing how easy it is to pass for someone else, the Invisible Man begins to ponder over the nature of human identity. How palpable is it if one can change it so easily? Tanner draws parallels between the Rinehart episode and the scene from H.G. Wells's novel *The Invisible Man*, published in 1897. In one of the scenes Wells's Invisible Man dresses up to piece together his new identity. Let us look in detail at other points of convergence and divergence between both texts.

Unlike Ellison's Invisible Man, Wells's Invisible Man wants to abuse invisibility in order to seize power over the lives of the people around him. For the Invisible Man, a disguise and literal invisibility are simply a source of protection, not a launch pad for dishonest manipulations. Wells's Invisible Man bears more resemblance to Rinehart than to the Invisible Man.

While the Invisible Man is first of all figuratively invisible, Wells's Invisible Man literally disappears. Ellison's Invisible Man gains a semblance of literal invisibility only after dressing up. Wells's Invisible Man literally disappears thanks to a scientific formula. After his death his body becomes visible again. It turns out then that he is an albino, the fate which the Invisible Man hopes to avoid: "Colorlessness" and "turning slowly from black to albino" (434–435). In this passage Ellison speaks of figurative colorlessness. Still, there is a scene in the novel in which the Invisible Man passes a shop window with an advertisement that promises to whiten black skin (199). In his outrage at the very idea the Invisible Man stops short of smashing the window. It is difficult to speculate whether Wells's *Invisible Man* had any impact on Ellison's novel. Ellison himself emphasizes that "science fiction was "the last thing [he]aspired to write" (Introduction XII). Still it is difficult to overlook the connection between the two novels.

Although the Invisible Man is not initially fully aware of tricksterism, he identifies himself with trickster figures throughout the novel. Tricksters fascinate and scare him at the same time. Their defiance and fortitude produce conflicting emotions in the Invisible Man. The encounter with a New York trickster Peter Wheatstraw makes him think about Jack the Rabbit and Jack the Bear. In hospital the Invisible Man identifies with Buckeye the Rabbit and Brer Rabbit. When asked who Buckeye the Rabbit was, he is elated at finally discovering himself (184). Yet he finds it too dangerous to identify with a trickster figure in public. If a trickster is to remain effective, he must keep his identity hidden. An act of self-identification would inevitably lead to the undoing of a trickster. Subconsciously the Invisible Man hits upon the main principle of tricksterism. Ellin Horowitz observes that the Invisible Man regains his memory by taking refuge in the folk tradition (84). Following the shockwave therapy, he cannot remember anything. Only the mentioning of Buck the Rabbit brings back memories from his childhood.

The Invisible Man makes several attempts at tricksterism. The first attempt comes before he has grasped the full potential of invisibility. Immediately after joining the Brotherhood, the Invisible Man plans to employ trickster tactics. In the initial phase of his affiliation with the organization he intends to enact a double personality, to be someone else internally and someone else for the outside world. He plans to preserve a cautious attitude to the Brotherhood ideology, while pretending before the brothers that he completely agrees with them. This first and not yet fully conscious attempt at tricksterim founders. The Invisible Man's initial reserve towards the Brotherhood turns into enthusiasm. Getting engrossed in the work for the Movement, the Invisible Man forgets about his plan and begins to live out the role. His second attempt at tricksterism is conscious and fully executed although it does not bring the desired results.

The Invisible Man rejects Rinehart's example but he embraces his grandfather's tricksterism. Tricking everyone around him, Rinehart is an ultimate fraud. Like his grandfather, the Invisible Man plans to turn his tricksterism only against an enemy. His treachery is to shield the black community against the manipulations of Brotherhood leaders. If whites insist on the invisibility of black people, they will have to pay for it. African American invisibility will backfire on them. For a while the Invisible Man thinks that wearing a mask and hiding their real emotions, blacks can be much more effective in undercutting white supremacy. Since white people refuse to see African Americans, African Americans should make themselves heard, uttering what whites desire to hear most: "yassuh" (384, 386).

Confirming Brotherhood leaders in their misconceptions, the Invisible Man is going to put their vigilance to sleep. They will feel his invisibility. It seems that as an invisible man he can wreak much more damage. The Invisible Man wonders whether the word treachery applies to him at all. If people question his integrity, how can he be treacherous? Accidentally, his plan plays into the hands of Brotherhood leaders. Ignoring the tension simmering in Harlem, the Invisible Man does not foresee that the dissatisfaction of black people will eventually reach boiling point, culminating in a self-destructive riot. The riot allows the Brotherhood to eliminate uncontrollable members of the Harlem community.

Even though the Invisible Man fails in his Brotherhood tricksterism, he still remains something of a trickster. In the Prologue he refers to himself as a thinker tinker, who has a "theory and a concept" (11). Living in the building rented exclusively to whites and draining white electricity resources, the Invisible Man plays a trick on the white world. In line with his reasoning, invisibility releases him from the rent. Since the society refuses to recognize him, he does not have to assume social duties, but can practice civil disobedience. As a gadgeteer, who finds practical application for his theories, the Invisible Man places himself in the tradition of Ford, Edison and Franklin (11). He rises above the color-line and reaches for cross-racial identifications. On the one hand, he compares himself to the three white Americans. On the other hand, he identifies with an African American trickster Jack the Bear. The Invisible Man hibernates, awaiting the awakening of his vitality. Louis Armstrong's music demands action from him, but he feels incapable of action. Yet being in this dormant state, the Invisible Man knows that he is not going to be inactive forever, because hibernation allows him to gather strength for a future period of renewed activity (16). When the right time comes, he will spring to action. Descending underground, the Invisible Man literally lives out his invisibility. Confining himself in a cellar, he extricates himself from society and its restrictive definitions. The Invisible Man stays underground to mentally dissect everything without any interference. His hibernation is not a state of complete inactivity. The mind keeps the Invisible Man restless, preventing him from becoming totally detached. It is during the hibernation that he creates the narrative. Only after breaking everything down into parts, can the Invisible Man put together a comprehensive picture of his whole life. Hibernation is the time of limited physical activity but intense mental exploration, which leads to the construction of the narrative. Hibernating underground, he finally succeeds in tricking the white world.

While the Invisible Man appreciates the power of tricksterism, he understands that it cannot be an ultimate end for African Americans. Useful as it is, tricksterism does not bring black people any closer to visibility, in a sense entrenching them even further in their invisibility. The Invisible Man does not feel like saying yes "against the nay-saying of [his] stomach"(433). He becomes fed up with affirming whites in their mistaken notions about blackness. All his experiences make him wonder whether his grandfather did not err about saying yes despite the urge to say precisely the opposite. He concludes that reality has changed since his grandfather's times (426). Survival was a priority for the Invisible Man's grandfather. For the Invisible Man and other African Americans survival is no longer a chief goal. The efforts of the new generation are directed at winning an equal place in the American democracy. The grandfather's strategy stands in opposition to Brother Tarp's approach. The grandfather yesses whites, whereas Brother Tarp says no and is punished for it. He says no until he breaks the chain and finds his way to freedom. As Thomas Vogler points out, Tarp is the Invisible Man's spiritual father and brother (146). Having become tired with nodding assent, the Invisible Man resolves

One: Different Faces of Invisibility

to be always faithful to himself. Still, he does not dismiss the grandfather's words completely, speculating that there must be some deeper meaning in his message. Saying yes, African Americans were to rise above violence, to affirm the founding principles of the United States (433). Maybe their yes was a sign of greater maturity and understanding that human relations should be based upon the principle of equality and reconciliation.

The Invisible Man finally decides to emerge, because he wants to be active in a much more profound sense. Invisibility does not entirely release him from responsibility. Approaching life through love and hate, the Invisible Man understands that he cannot withdraw from society forever. In the Prologue he declares "I believe in nothing if not in action" (11). The hibernation needs to come to an end if he is to remain true to that declaration. After retreating into the hole, the Invisible Man has isolated himself for too long. Although invisible, he has to be socially active and has a socially "responsible role to play (439).

He has known all along that one day his hibernation would be over. Staying underground indefinitely would amount to partial denial of his humanity. Being a part of mankind, he cannot remain in his self-contained, self-created world, but has to come back to other human beings. It is true that the decision to emerge entails certain risks. It is difficult to keep from plunging (432). The Invisible Man admits that "the old fascination with playing a role returns" as he is drawn upward (437). Enriched with his reflections and his experience, he is no longer so prone to get lost on the stage of social theatrics. He must take a risk and test himself in the real world, in the world that is "ornery, vile and sublimely wonderful" (435). However, it is the only world he can return to. Life underground taught him to be cautiously optimistic. Having done a lot of mind-searching, the Invisible Man assigns himself "no rank or limit" (435). All definitions are somehow confining. Instead of clinging to one view of the world, he embraces the world of infinite possibilities. First he was for society, later against it (435). Now he keeps his mind open, reserving judgment for later. Ultimately, the Invisible Man emerges, because underground he is even more invisible than on the surface.

Ellison reappraises invisibility, but he by no means suggests that African Americans should settle for it. Invisibility becomes a focal point for contradictions in his novel. On the one hand, it is a burden. On the other hand, it carries dormant potential. Black people can capitalize on their invisibility, yet they should never be diverted from the final goal, which is visibility. Writing the narrative and in this way utilizing his invisibility, the Invisible Man moves at the same time closer towards visibility. The efforts of black people alone are, however, not enough to achieve visibility. In order to become fully visible they need to encounter cooperation on the part of the white world.

Two

THROUGH INVISIBILITY TOWARDS VISIBILITY
Sam Greenlee's *The Spook Who Sat by the Door*

"Tokenization goes with ghettoization" (Gayatri Spivak, *The Postcolonial Critic*, 61).

In Sam Greenlee's *The Spook Who Sat by the Door* (1969) invisibility becomes a weapon in African American struggle for visibility. It is no longer a peaceful civil rights struggle but military struggle. Unlike his predecessor the Invisible Man, Dan Freeman, the protagonist of *The Spook Who Sat by the Door*, has no desire to integrate or peacefully assert his rights. Like other militant nationalists of the 1960s, Freeman envisions military guerrilla warfare as a solution to African American invisibility. Sam Greenlee,[1] himself a member of the black cultural nationalist movement shows sympathy for the fervor of the black militant nationalists but at the same time he hints at certain flaws of the movement. Invisibility functions in the novel primarily on two levels: Freeman's literal invisibility and the literal invisibility of his paramilitary organization — the Freedom Fighters. Freeman's invisibility hinges mainly on mimicry. The Freedom Fighters are invisible because of the tactics which they employ in their military operations. Their underground guerrilla warfare is aimed first of all at winning visibility for people stranded behind "invisible walls of the ghetto." The invisible people from the ghetto come to the foreground in Greenlee's novel. They are invisible in a double way: both to whites and to the black middle class. A large part of *The Spook Who Sat by the Door* is dedicated to the frictions within the black community.

Unlike the Invisible Man's grandfather, Dan Freeman becomes literally invisible, not simply to survive, but to advance the cause of his people and bring them to visibility. Manipulating whites: first in the CIA and later in the social organization, Freeman succeeds where the Invisible Man failed in his affiliation with the Brotherhood. Ironically, white people help him to execute his plan. Clinging to their stereotypes of African Americans, they are unlikely to decipher his intentional manipulation of those stereotypes. Hence white people make African American mimicry much easier than it would otherwise be. Having thrust invisibility upon African Americans, they did not suspect that it may backfire on them one day. Feigning loyalty and consciously impersonating stereotypes attributed to African Americans, Freeman not only puts white vigilance to sleep, but also wins their support for the initiatives that enable him to launch the ghetto rebellion. White people create their own enemy by giving Freeman his CIA training, which he later uses to organize the Black Freedom Fighters movement.

According to Freeman, all black people are predisposed to make good spies, because they constantly need to watch out for a false move.[2] In order to succeed or sometimes even to survive, they were often forced to live out the stereotypes ascribed to them. Still, it did not prevent them from remaining internally whole and true to themselves. CIA training helps Freeman to put the finishing touches on the cover that he has been piecing together for years. If applied constructively, invisibility can be both a protective device and a vehicle for the ultimate goal — visibility.

Invisible Freedom Fighters and Black Nationalism of the 1960s

Freeman's invisibility goes hand in hand with the invisibility of his paramilitary organization. The Black Freedom Fighters are "an underground revolutionary movement" (97). Operating under the cover of the night, they are literally invisible for most of the time. After each operation they disappear. Freeman does not begin from scratch, but builds on an already existing organizational structure of the ghetto gang — the Cobras, who are an underground organization "visible only in their moments of violence, closed off to the outside world otherwise" (106). The Freedom Fighters put into action the Invisible Man's words and "make invisibility felt if not seen" (Ellison 384). They may be unseen, but like all other oppressed characters discussed in this study, they can see sharp and clear, even at night. Their equivalent of second-sight is "night vision" (219). To protect it they wear dark glasses during the day and stay in a darkened room one hour before sunset. The night gives the Cobras yet another layer of invisibility. Greenlee is by no means the only African American author who reflects on the special relation that Afro-Americans have with the night. The protagonist of Walter Mosley's *Devil in a Blue Dress* (1990) — Easy Rawlins also sees the night as his ally. He would like to become literally invisible to slink out through cracks in a prison wall:

> All I did was sit in darkness, trying to become the darkness ... I dreamed in my wakefulness that I could become the darkness and slip out between the eroded cracks of the cell. If I was nighttime nobody could find me, no one would even know I was missing [Mosley 74].

During the war Easy also hopes to be shrouded by the night: "Just make believe you is the night" (195). After a skirmish with Ras the Invisible Man descends underground, emerging only at night.[3]

Remaining invisible to the outside world, the Freedom Fighters become visible to themselves. Their action frees them from fear and self-doubt. Apart from teaching the young recruits the techniques of combat, Freeman acquaints them with their own history, infusing his people with pride in their own blackness. All along he stresses the need to excavate black pride that is buried deep within. His sentiments are in tune with cultural nationalism of the 1960s. In their poetry Amiri Baraka, Nikki Giovanni, Sonia Sanchez and many others were no longer asking for their rights. They were demanding them. Celebrating blackness, African Americans openly manifested pride in black culture. Cultural separateness was the reason to celebrate, not lament.

It is not without significance that underscoring the importance of black pride, Freeman refers to a sharecropper tradition. Most nationalists looked back to their past, trying to recover African American heritage and rediscover their own history. For centuries they were effaced from white history books. In the 1960s they were working hard to undo the damage done by white historians. One of the spiritual gurus of the 1960s Maulana Karenga[4] distinguishes between historians and history writers: "history writers who simply record what the people in power dictate and historians who write that which reinforces our self-concept" (47). Freeman recalls how he had to "descend to the bowels of the library ... passing the books written by the 'name' American historians in his search for the truth about his people" (108–109). He passes on his knowledge to people from the ghetto, telling them of slave revolts and of distinguished figures deleted from the official American history: Sojourner Truth,[5] Denmark Vesey[6] and Nat Turner. Other nationalists of the time also invoked renowned African Americans of the past and present, for example Nikki Giovanni,[7] celebrates in her poetry such figures as Martin Luther King, Malcolm X, Sojourner Truth, James Brown,[8] Aretha Franklin.[9] All these attempts at reappraisal of African American history and its main actors were to empower African Americans, to instill them with pride and self-esteem. The recurring message was that they should treasure their blackness and derive strength from it rather than see it as a source of self-denigration. In her poem "The True Import of Present Dialogue: Black vs. Negro" Giovanni asks her people if they can reject negative associations of blackness and move beyond what they were imbued with by the white world (Giovanni 19–20).[10]

Like most other black nationalists, Freeman emphasizes their African origins, sensitizing people from the ghetto to the severed link with Africa.[11] Despite stressing their African origins, Freeman does not try to recapture the link with people still living in Africa. The founder of the Organization of Afro-American Unity (OAAU)—Malcolm X[12]—called Africa a "motherland," encouraging African Americans to travel back to Africa or reconnect with it through some other means of communication ("Basic Unity Program" in Van Deburg 110). Emphasizing the diasporic meaning of their blackness, members of OAAU identified with black people all over the world, seeing them as allies in the struggle against their oppression. Malcolm X blamed whites for alienating African Americans from black people in other countries. He argued that white people would like Afro-Americans to see themselves as totally isolated and without allies ("Basic Unity Program" in Van Deburg 110). In the 1966 Position Paper on Black Power, SNCC[13] leaders compared their situation to the situation of other colonized people of Africa and Latin America ("Position Paper on Black Power" in Van Deburg 126). Stokely Carmichael—former SNCC and Black Panther leader—came to promote Pan-Africanism and organized the All-African People's Revolutionary Party ("First of All and Finally Africans" in Van Deburg 203). The chief goal for Pan-Africanists was the unification of

Two: Through Invisibility Towards Visibility

Africa as one state, in which all Africans could seek refuge. Although Carmichael's focus was on Africa, he wanted to forge an alliance with all non-white people, drawing parallels between African and Asian struggle against oppression ("Pan-Africanism — Land and Power" in Van Deburg 205).

Freeman's ideology owes a good deal to cultural nationalism, but first of all it is rooted in revolutionary nationalism. No wonder, then, that freedom is his main postulate. His last name is no coincidence either. Time and again he repeats that nothing will stop him from being free. To illustrate the continuing captivity of his people, he cites from spirituals: "Go down Moses and set my people free" (111). During the days of the Underground Railway spirituals were signal songs calling black people to freedom. In the 1960s black people may have no longer been literally enslaved, yet they were not entirely free either. Freeman promises his fighters to take them to the freedomland. Real life revolutionary nationalists were equally emphatic in speaking about the captivity of their people, arguing that they still had to be liberated. The Black Panthers' minister of information Eldridge Cleaver wanted some territory liberated in Babylon ("On Meeting the Needs of the People" in Van Deburg 244). In *Separatist Economics*, "A New Social Contract," Roy Innis — a CORE[14] director — drew a parallel between "Jews caught in Egypt" and African Americans in the United States (Innis in Van Deburg 177). In his 1970 speech to the Congress of African People Amiri Baraka called African Americans slaves, reproaching them with their inability to free themselves. Freedom is a reverberating theme of many revolutionary nationalist manifestos. "Freedom from oppression" makes a refrain of the above-mentioned OAAU program co-founded by Malcolm X. The first sentence of the "Black Panther Party Platform" reads "We want freedom" (in Van Deburg 249).

Freeman shares other nationalists' craving for self-determination. The common belief was that black people should not wait for white people to liberate them, but liberate themselves. All decisions concerning the lives of African Americans should be taken by African Americans. This yearning for self-sufficiency manifested itself in various practical solutions: from economic independence to a variety of separate nation theories. It is difficult to state unequivocally where Freeman fits on this scale, but self-determination is definitely the basic tenet of his ideology. Self-determination that is at stake is not only political self-determination, but first of all spiritual self-determination. To be truly free, African Americans first of all need to reclaim their own selves. Self-determination rhetoric among nationalists was a manifestation of separatist tendencies in the nationalist movement. Although Freeman does not openly endorse a separate economy or does not push towards the creation of a separate black nation, he shudders from any form of integration. To a certain extent he is inconsistent in his separatism. At the beginning of his mission, while still in college, he hopes that being African American will not entail poverty. After moving to the final stage of his plan's execution, while already back in the ghetto, he concludes that black people will always be underprivileged but their exclusion from the world of privilege does not automatically doom them to the life of misery and self-pity. Freeman's separate nation ideology is not fully transparent. Despite acknowledging the existence of two separate nations, he does not appear to strive for a politically autonomous entity. Unlike some other nationalists, he does not aim at transforming the system but simply at liberating himself from it. He does not explain, however, to what extent his people are to be autonomous. Even though the military execution of his plan is first-rate, his political agenda remains largely wishy-washy, if existing at all. It seems that he does not know exactly where the events will take him and where he will end up.

Greenlee does not accept the black nationalist ideology indiscriminately. Unlike other nationalists, he does not reject all whiteness, but carefully defines whiteness, naming groups responsible for his oppression. He exposes and critiques various faces of whiteness: conservative whiteness (with its discourse in the media), liberal whiteness (with its tokenism) and emissaries of white power: police and the National Guard. Greenlee's protagonist Freeman does not seethe with hatred towards all whites, ranting about the "white devil," but draws a very distinct portrait of his oppressors. He cautions his friends against hatred towards whites. According to Freeman, hatred is self-destructive, leading nowhere and detracting Afro-Americans from taking concrete steps against oppression. Articulating the oppressive faces of whiteness, Freeman differs from those nationalists who lashed out against whiteness across the board without clearly defining their target and without proposing any tangible measures that would chip away at white power. Just as he warns against indiscriminate hatred for whites, he also opposes random or unnecessary violence. All Black Freedom Fighters' attacks are meticulously planned and executed. When asked whether he enjoys waging a war against whites, Freeman answers flatly: "No" (129).

The Black Freedom Fighters share most similarities with the Black Panthers Party. Both organizations emphasize action. They take the Invisible Man's motto "I believe in nothing if not in action" to the next level (Ellison 11). The Panthers stress that unlike other movements, they "take action," rather than "sit back and talk" ("Armed Black Brothers in Richmond Community" in Van Deburg 243). They see the police as armed guardians of the imperialist system, representatives of power structure: "the white cop is the instrument sent into our community by the Power Structure to keep Black People quiet and under control" (ibid). It is all too clear to Eldridge Cleaver and to other black people who stands behind the National Guard and whom they protect — the white establishment and white politicians, who perpetuate the system. Cleaver wants to expand the attacks from the instruments of oppression to the source of oppression: "we are moving beyond racist pig cops to confront the avaricious businessmen and the demagogic politicians" (Cleaver in Van Deburg 257, 248). Cleaver did not necessarily mean to attack them on the military front, but on the economic one: by transferring means of production to the black community. The Panthers were much more visible in black communities than the Black Freedom Fighters. They could boast much stronger ties with African Americans in the ghetto. Apart from launching military operations, they took initiatives that offered immediate help to people living in the ghetto, for example food programs like breakfast for children, recreational areas like People's Park, etc. The fictional Black Freedom Fighters could not embark on such ventures, because then they would lose a protective mantle of their invisibility. Both organizations defined themselves as revolutionary. Yet if the Panthers spoke about toppling the government, Freeman remains vague about the end result of his revolution.

The Panthers' revolution is to a greater extent modeled after the Chinese prototype. One can notice striking resemblances in nomenclature: People's government, People's Housing, People's Transportation, People's Industry. Since this is a comparative study and in the next chapter I relate Asian American nationalism to black nationalism and Yellow Power to Black Power, I find it essential to stress at this point that black nationalism of the 1960s owes part of its ideology to the Chinese Revolution and

Maoism. According to Edward C. Smith, the Black Panthers found Maoists more appealing than contemporary Russian revolutionaries because:

(1) Russian revolutionaries meddled excessively with the politics of other countries.
(2) China itself was not white.
(3) They also associated China with fallen civilization of North Africa (Smith 75–76).

Freeman's ideology is relatively free of explicitly anti-imperialist postulates. Distinct as he is from the communists, he still reads the theories of Giap and Mao Tse-tung (61). Mostly, however, he is interested in the warfare tactics of various, often politically adverse, guerrilla organizations: guerrilla fighters in Algeria, in the Philippines, the guerrilla war against the Malayan Communists, the tactics of the Viet Cong (61).

Freeman's plan of action against white supremacy is two-pronged. He wants to exert pressure on the American government by tarnishing its image in the world. Retaliatory actions against African Americans will bring the maximum of spotlight both to the victims and to the oppressors. The white government will need to choose between shedding the blood of black people and preserving its positive image abroad.[15] Freeman hopes that through hit and run attacks he will force whites to stop interfering with African American affairs. Interestingly, civil rights activists aimed at a similar effect as Freeman, although they employed different tactics. If they were visible in their peaceful struggle, Freeman is invisible in his military operations. Civil rights activists fought for the right to integrate, while Freeman struggles for the right to separate. The U.S. engagement in the Cold War and its pro-democracy operations in Asia inevitably played some role in the 1960s debate on civil rights (Gotanda 146). The American government could not pretend to the role of democracy's savior abroad without creating a semblance of equality at home. The second front on which he plans to attack is economy. By engaging white forces throughout the country, he hopes to drain white economic resources and force whites to choose between their military engagement at home and abroad.

Ingenious as Freeman's plan may seem at first glance, it is studded with inconsistencies. These inconsistencies are apparent to his young recruits, who voice their doubts without any reservations. Although aware of the loose ends in his logic, Freeman does not seem to be aware of the fact that he can recruit only a limited number of members for his organization. Sometimes he speaks of the Black Freedom Fighters as if they counted all twenty-five million black people who live in the United States. He also seems to overlook the fact that once his organization spreads to other cities, it may begin to lose its protective shield of invisibility.

Freeman's idea of transformation is limited to African Americans alone, and does not embrace all oppressed people of color. Some black nationalists aimed at changing the system both for oppressed black people and for marginalized people of other races. Freeman's views on African American participation in the Vietnam war strikingly diverge from those of black nationalists and black civil rights leaders. African Americans on both sides of the political spectrum agreed that black people should not fight in Vietnam. Black nationalists saw the war in Vietnam as a colonial war and as one more manifestation of American racism against people of color. Malcolm X argued that African Americans should identify with people of color all over the world, since racism is an international phenomenon. According to Malcolm X, America proceeded to colonize people of color abroad in a similar fashion as it colonized African Americans at home. Expressing similar views to Malcolm X, Nathan Hare maintained that African Americans had no conflict of interest with the Vietnamese or Cambodians (Hare cited in Flowers 57). It was erroneous to assume that the Pentagon and African Americans had common enemies. The Black Panthers declared that African Americans should be exempt from military service altogether, insisting that conscience did not allow them to confront other people of color on the battlefield. Additionally the Panthers argued that they had no obligation to fight for the racist government that victimized them ("Black Panther Party Platform and Program" in Van Deburg 250). Black nationalist poets also weigh in on the debate. Nikki Giovanni notes in the above cited poem "The True Import of Present Dialogue: Black vs. Negro" that black people fight all over the world for the United States, the United Nations, the North Atlantic Treaty Organization, the South East Asia Treaty Organization, but they still need to militarily confront whites in defense of their own interests (Giovanni 19–20). In the "final solution" Sonia Sanchez claims that the right to fight in Vietnam is the only right that American leaders offer to black people (Sanchez 18). Martin Luther King concurred with African American nationalists on the issue of Vietnam. As a champion of peaceful struggle, he saw it as the utmost hypocrisy that white leaders expected African Americans to embrace nonviolent means in their struggle for civil rights, while they unleashed the horror of war and violence in foreign countries. King also maintained that war operations abroad detract the U.S. from the fight against poverty at home (McCarthey 129). Both nationalists and integrationists pointed out that the American government treated Vietnam as a testing ground for chemical weapons, just as it used Hiroshima and Nagasaki to test the atomic bomb.

Freeman is fully aware that the war in Vietnam is part of the American colonial and imperial enterprise. The catchwords: "freedom" and "democracy" are only a cover for its imperial ambitions. The Vietnamese and other colonized Asians find themselves in a similar position as African Americans. African Americans are the oppressed minority at home whereas the Vietnamese are the victimized people of color abroad:

> American white folks have more nerve than anybody; they call them gooks and us niggers, out there in Vietnam and in Korea when I was there. And they don't see why the gooks and niggers should not kill one another for whitey's benefit [102].[16]

Still, he believes that during their military training they can acquire skills which African Americans can later use in their struggle against racism in the United States: "There's a certain poetry in whitey training us to mess with him. Every black cat in Vietnam is a potential asset for our thing" (102). There was no poetry in Vietnam. Freeman does not take into account that not every black man is cut out to be a fighter and is as mentally resistant as he is. Having served in Korea during the police action, he probably underestimates the horror of Vietnam. There is no poetry for Little Cole from Thulani Davis' *1959* who comes back home mute.

A contradiction in the nationalist movement lies in the fact that while identifying with oppressed people abroad, some black nationalists displayed hostility towards immigrants from Asia. I am bringing this up here for several reasons. First of all this is a comparative study and the second half of this project is devoted to Asian American invisibility. A large portion of the final chapter revolves around immigrant invisibility. I am also interested in tracing various patterns of internal invisibility among oppressed groups. In Chapter Three I speak about the pitfalls of centrism and multiple oppressions stemming from the centrist approach. Oppression in itself is not a shield against ethnocentricity. Supporting all black ventures, some nationalists were convinced that immigrants posed a danger to their economic interests. Their presence in black neighborhoods was undesirable. The emphasis on racial purity was not without significance either. As I point out in Chapter Four, civil rights victories led to the relaxation of strict immigration policies. Many Afro-Americans might have found it objectionable that the government admitted substantial numbers of newcomers while not being able to take care of minorities already living in the United States.

Immigrants were not the only oppressed group targeted by black nationalists. African American women also found themselves on the defensive. Criticizing black chauvinism, Giovanni says "They have made Black women the new Jews"[17] (Giovanni cited in Georgoudaki 158). Giovanni's statement is of special interest to me in the context of the previous paragraph. As I emphasize in Chapter Four, immigrants began to enter black neighborhoods in large numbers in the 1970s when they were taking over businesses from the Jews who were moving out at the time. African Americans saw Jews as exploitative of black communities. With Jews gone from their neighborhoods and whites unavailable as an immediate target, someone else became a culprit. Black nationalists attempted to create an identity around which all African Americans were to rally. They envisioned a subordinate role for black women who should submit to male community leaders rather than express their individual perspective or advance their own interests. The 1960s' rhetoric expounded by certain groups of white people must have inevitably exerted an impact on black men's backlash against African American women. In his 1965 report presented to Johnson's administration Assistant Secretary of Labor Daniel Patrick Moynihan defined African American families as matriarchal and therefore out of step with the rest of American society. Rather than blame the disenfranchisement of African Americans on the policies of respective governments, Moynihan and other white sociologists found fault in the alleged dysfunctionality of black families. Throughout his report Moynihan underscores the lack of the father in Afro-American families. Underachievement in black males was blamed on women. Moynihan claims that since African American women are chief supporters, African American males lack motivation. In "Mama's Baby, Papa's Maybe" Hortense Spillers observes that the African American family system can be defined as neither patriarchal nor matriarchal. To explain the structure of Afro-American family she takes us back to slavery times. In the slavery system children did not belong to the mother, but to the slave master. As a result kinship lost its meaning. If African Americans had been granted the right to kinship, it would have altered property relations, since the child would have belonged to the mother. African Americans were not allowed to exercise any ownership — not even of their own offspring. Deprived of a biological mother, every child still followed the condition of the mother. Such legislation was essential for slave masters to maintain their property rights because a lot of them fathered black children. Motherhood is no longer sacred in slavery. The system is not matriarchal, among others on account of the fact that a woman could not claim her own child. It is not patriarchal either because a father — often a slave master — is anything but a father in the full sense of the word.

Accentuating the denigration of their own manhood, African American nationalists overlooked and underplayed the long history of African American women's degradation. They saw themselves as the greatest victims. Strangely enough, Malcolm X's OAAU identified men as sole victims before the Emancipation ("Basic Unity Program" in Van Deburg 112). According to OAAU, women and children became victims only recently — in the 1960s. Although many women were active in the nationalist movement, most African American male activists identified a black nationalist as a man. Women found themselves effaced. They were doubly invisible both to whites and to male members of their communities. Maulana Karenga defined a black nationalist as "a man who saves his brothers from a leaking boat" (Karenga cited in Flowers 78). Amiri Baraka concluded that "Nature has made women submissive" (Baraka cited in Flowers 79). In "Quiet Happiness" Don L. Lee could be accused of sexism as well. He creates an image of a pure African American woman and dreads women who do not live up to his standard. Angela Davis comments on the stance of her male colleagues by saying: "I became acquainted very early with the widespread presence of an unfortunate syndrome among some black male activists — namely to confuse their political activity with an assertion of their maleness. They saw — and some continue to see — black manhood as something separate from Black womanhood" (Davis cited in Flowers 78). Sam Greenlee is a rare exception among black nationalists. As mentioned earlier, he celebrates some African American women in the volume of his poetry *The Blues for an African Princess*. Several of his poems are dedicated to distinguished African American women, including female black poets. While many of his colleagues resented the success of African American women, Greenlee gave them their due credit.[18] His last volume of poetry so far *Be-Bop Man/Be-Bop Woman* (published in 1995) shows that women have a permanent place in his agenda. Assuming a partner-like approach, he treats them as an integral part of African American movement, not outcasts, but insiders.

Although Dan Freeman is not as appreciative of African American women as Greenlee, he does not target any oppressed groups. Still, he engages in the apotheosis of black manhood, treating women in the novel instrumentally. Women who are involved in his organization play a rather subordinate role to their male leaders. Yet he realizes that they can make a vital contribution to their struggle since in many situations they are more invisible than men: "we can use women; they can often go places and do things men can't do" (96). Freeman uses women throughout the novel: "he used Dahomey Queen [his black prostitute friend] three times a week" (61). In the last phase of his mimicry — when he impersonates the playboy of the Midwest, women constitute part of his cover. Apart from giving him personal satisfaction, numerous sexual relations help him to project an image of a carefree, frivolous dandy with "nothing [on his] mind except chicks, clothes and whisky" (241). His real love is Joy, whereas other women are just playthings for him. Turning Freeman into a male fetish, Greenlee risks reinforcing the stereotype of African American virility and hypersexuality. Although there is no denigration of African American women in the novel, most of the female characters drawn by Greenlee are hardly positive. All of them are all too eager to succumb to Freeman.

Freeman himself is not only invisible as a black man, but also as a leader. The rule upon which his organization operates reads "No one is indispensable" (107). When one member of the organization is lost, another immediately has to step in. Once discovered, Freeman will simply disappear, just the way his fighters disappear after each attack. He will again retreat into invisibility. Although the ties between members of the organization are close, Freeman shudders at the thought of hero-worship, careful not to detract his followers from the real goal — undermining of white supremacy. With his zest for life, he rejects the idea of martyrdom. According to him, real heroism lives in life, not in death. Freeman's concern parallels the observations of the real-life nationalist Stokely Carmichael: "Now everyone is wearing Malcolm X T-shirts and Malcolm X blah, blah, blah. But Malcolm today would be more important to us alive than dead, although in death he has become more famous" ("Pan-Africanism — Land and Power" in Van Deburg 210). According to Carmichael, African Americans begin to fully appreciate their leaders when they are dead. Freeman is much more suspicious of the very idea of leadership. It is effective only if it leads to effective organization.

While Freeman is really committed to the nationalist cause, many of his nationalist counterparts were keen on forwarding their own interests. Contrary to popular belief, the nationalist endeavor was not a proletarian venture, but predominantly a lower middle class enterprise. In "The Paradox of the Afro-American Rebellion" Cornel West observes that the ideology of black nationalism helped many of its black petite bourgeoisie followers to assuage their feelings of guilt (53). In a similar vein, Manning Marable notes that black nationalism was especially beneficial to black entrepreneurs who could capitalize on the "buy black" catchword ("Beyond Identity Politics" 320). It is true that organizations that most resemble the Black Freedom Fighters, for example the Black Panthers, were mostly composed of the black working class. However, considering Freeman's utmost revulsion for the black middle class, it is quite ironic that so many people whom he scorns had a similar political affiliation. Another matter is that not all members of the black middle class involved in the nationalist cause had the same motives. His own class status is somewhat uncertain, a point on which I am going to elaborate in the last section of the chapter. Freeman does not identify with any political faction. Like the Invisible Man, he believes that all definitions are restrictive. Therefore he avoids labeling.

Power in itself is not Freeman's motivation. Still, the Black Freedom Fighters' action is empowering mostly to the fighters themselves. The benefits to the larger black community are questionable. Freeman indeed does succeed in making whitey look like a fool, for example by humiliating the National Guard colonel or by blowing up the mayor's headquarters, but invisible warfare launched by the organization brings a backlash against people in the ghetto. Before starting his rebellion, he is conscious of the foreseeable consequences of his actions, "of the hell they would create for their people in the struggle for their freedom" (109). Whose freedom? In theory, Freeman fights for the freedom of all African Americans. In practice his operations are liberating to those immediately involved in the struggle, enhancing their sense of pride, defiance and manhood. Although the Black Freedom Fighters' guerrilla struggle in many ways backfires on the black community, it is not completely out of step with the sentiments of people living in the ghetto. Their desire to strike back springs to the surface during the riots. Like the Invisible Man, Freeman does not advocate rioting, yet he hopes that it will reinvigorate the black community and ensure support for his movement and well-organized military struggle.

Freeman's craving for freedom reaches an obsession point when he kills his best friend to protect the whole operation. The distance of the sympathetic third-person narrator is clear at this point of the novel. Committed and earnest as Freeman is to the liberation project, he falls in the trap which caught many other nationalists. The nationalist fervor blinds him to broader ramifications of his actions. His personal longing for freedom overshadows for him other factors at stake. The community pays a heavy price for his fight for freedom and the goals which he hopes to achieve are barely feasible. Still, it is difficult to judge his choices. He knows better than anyone else that the civil rights project rewarded the chosen few, leaving millions of others stranded in the ghetto. The desperation of African American nationalists and their disenchantment with a futile promise of the American democracy told them to look for solutions elsewhere and try alternative remedies to the despair of their people.

Invisibility of the Black Ghetto

> The dark ghetto's invisible walls have been erected by the white society. (Kenneth Clark, *The Dark Ghetto* 11)

> A whole history remains to be written of *spaces*— which would at the same time be the history of *powers*— from the great strategies of geopolitics to the little tactics of the habitat. (Foucault, "The Eye of Power" in *Power/Knowledge* 149)

The invisible of the ghetto receive more attention in Greenlee's novel than any other section of the black community. For most of the time they remain unheard and unseen by the rest of the American society. As long as they keep in their place, whites do not concern themselves with their fate. Only when the African American anger springs to the surface, do white people begin to see them, fearing that they may fall victim to their anger: "Negroes are visible only when convenient or menacing" (Greenlee 135). The black ghetto becomes visible when it threatens to spill out and encroach upon spaces reserved for non–African Americans.

The physical location of the black ghetto and other inner city ghettos does not reflect their marginal position in American society. The metaphor margin-centre no longer holds here. It is reversed. Whites flee to the suburbs, while minorities are usually stuck in inner city areas. It is ironic that sociologists like Kenneth Clark should identify African Americans as an outgroup, since they are located inside the city. Launching the rebellion, Freeman wants to change spatial dynamics and "turn the city inside out" (Greenlee 97). The traditional textualization of space is not always applicable to the location of marginal spaces. Althusser argues for example that what is inside the space is visible, whereas what is outside the space is invisible (Althusser cited in Smith and Katz 73). The present layout of the city changed those relations. Minorities remain invisible and yet they are located inside the space — inner city — the centre. Neil Smith and Cindi Katz claim that location makes people visible in their differences. Pretending that ethnic ghettos do not exist, the white apparatus of power tries to make even those differences invisible.

While location is dynamic and permeable, the white establishment conspires to naturalize spatial relations, to render certain spaces immutable, hidden and natural. *The Spook Who Sat by the Door* shows that location is never a matter of accident, but always a part of a shrewd and calculated design. Physical location is always conditioned by social location and the other way round. Doreen Massey very astutely illustrates the link between space and the social realm: "Space is socially constructed and the social is spatially constructed" (146). Positions are never fixed and set in stone but always permeable and dynamic.

The ghetto perpetuates all other problems adherent to it. Douglass Massey and Nancy Denton argue in their famous book *American Apartheid* that "crucial resources and benefits are distributed through housing markets" (151). Incarcerated in the ghetto, African Americans are cut off from those resources. Segregation facilitates other forms of discrimination. People usually secure their jobs through friends and personal contacts, rarely through newspaper advertisements or the like. Since African Americans seldom venture outside the ghetto confines, they have their friends among other poor Afro-Americans. Hence they are in no position to obtain desirable employment. Most businesses in which African Americans could get a job are located outside the ghetto. The job situation in the ghetto was exacerbated by the gradual migration of businesses out of the area in the 1950s and 1960s. As more and more African Americans were migrating North in the 1950s (1.5 million) and 1960s (1.4 million), some businesses were moving south or to the areas on the outskirts of the city (Denton, Massey 44–45). White people's flight to the suburbs began in the 1950s, having been spurred by a variety of factors. Following the World War II years, American families were experiencing the baby boom. Seeking more and more space, they turned outside central cities, towards inexpensive land in the suburbs (Denton, Massey 44). Increasing numbers of black people inside the cities were another factor that pushed white inhabitants away from the urban core. Suburbanization triggered urban restructuring geared to the needs of the suburbs. Newly constructed highways connected the suburbs to daytime offices of people who worked there during the day and left the city by night. Communities of color found themselves caught in the middle of urban restructuring. In the 1950s and 1960s local elites ensured the removal of black-inhabited apartments to make room for financial centers. Black people were moved to newly constructed public housing projects characterized by extremely high density and close proximity to other black neighborhoods, away from white sections of the city. Denton and Massey point out that "urban renewal almost always destroyed more housing than it replaced" (56). In *Making the Second Ghetto* Arnold Hirsh defines urban restructuring of the 1950s and 1960s as the construction of the "second ghetto," the first ghetto having been constructed in the 1920s (252). The Federal Housing Administration reinforced the construction of the ghetto through its mortgage and loan policy. Most of the loans and mortgages were granted to white suburbs and very few to inner city neighborhoods (Denton, Massey 54).

    The policy of consecutive Republican governments starting with Nixon led to further degradation of the already destitute inner city ghettos. Prior to Nixon's administration one also could notice certain positive shifts in public housing policies and legislation. In March 1968 the Kerner Commission identified segregation as a primary cause of the problems haunting the ghetto, including the riots (Denton, Massey 59). The Commission advised the construction of federal housing outside the ghetto.

April 1968 saw the passing of the Fair Housing Act, which outlawed redlining in the sale and rental of housing. Nixon retracted from the road leading to dismantling of the ghetto and eventual integration. The acme of inner city collapse occurred during Reagan's administration (James Lee xiv). His policies dealt the most serious blow to people stranded inside urban ghettos. It is at the time of Reagan's administration that the exodus of business from inner cities and the withdrawal of funding reached the greatest proportions.

The third-person narrator of *The Spook* emphasizes the link between the location of the ghetto and its isolation from the job market. He speaks of the unemployed who "stubbornly" look for jobs "on the periphery of the city" while their "more realistic black brothers" spend their time in the bars and poolrooms of the ghetto (144). The separation of the ghetto from the job market is thematized several times in the novel — among others in Freeman's conversation with an elderly "immigrant"[19] from the South. Reminiscing on the times when African Americans in the North had no problem with finding employment, she pines over the effect of automation and relocation of factories to Southern states. She also notices the puzzling correspondence between the crest of African American migration to the North and the outmigration of Northern businesses to the South (196). African American migration began in the 1890s and peaked between 1950 and 1960, when 1,457,000 African Americans migrated North (Denton 27, Holmes 442). Robert A. Holmes draws our attention to the differences between European immigration and migration of African Americans from the South (444). Both entered the cities at a different moment. European immigrants encountered a developing economy, whereas African Americans confronted an already automated production, for which they were unprepared.

Desperate for recognition, black people see riots as their last chance to stake a claim to visibility and audibility. This is how the narrator of *The Spook* introduces the riot scenes in the novel: "tonight these people were not invisible. Tonight whitey knew they existed ... it was past time to let the white man know they existed" (Greenlee 154, 203). According to Ralph Ellison, "Riots are the language of the unheard" (*Shadow and Act* 38). Rioting infuses black people with pride, defiance and a sense of action. Clark argues that it is also a sign that they have not yet given up hope that things can change (18). Greenlee suggests the reverse. African Americans riot because they have nothing to lose.

Two: Through Invisibility Towards Visibility

The invisible inhabitants of the ghetto resemble people from Du Bois's metaphor cited in the Introduction. They are also imprisoned behind "*invisible* but horribly tangible plate glass" that is "between them and the world" (*Dusk of Dawn* 649, 650, emphasis added). Hopelessness pushes black people to rioting. It is their last-ditch attempt to become heard and seen.

Rioting also constitutes the only form of retaliation against the white world. Unleashing destruction of white property, African Americans rebel against the system which positions them as objects of property, rather than subjects. Cheryl Harris points out that whiteness has come to be perceived as a marker of property. Targeting white property, African Americans lash out at one of the most distinct hallmarks of whiteness. The white apparatus of power sees property destruction as the most disturbing feature of black rioting. This is true both of the riots in the 1960s and the 1990s, during the Rodney King Rebellion. The human stories that lie behind the riots are of no significance to white authorities.

The black ghetto may be invisible to the white world, but the white world with its hypocrisy is all too visible to black people. Its opulence taunts them to escape the ghetto never to return again. As Clark points out, the mass media intrude inside the ghetto, revealing life unfolding outside its walls (12). Those who escape rarely go back to the world which they left behind. Freeman's girlfriend Joy escapes the ghetto never to return again. She associates the ghetto with crime, fetor, drugs, promiscuity, prostitution, hypocritical preachers and degenerate police. Unlike Joy, Freeman cannot leave the ghetto behind.

Blaming the riots on the communists and nationalists, white authorities in *The Spook* refuse to see them as a spontaneous outburst against the abominable conditions in the ghetto. Signing away all responsibility, they fail to acknowledge their own role in the creation and perpetuation of the ghetto. To justify the existence of the ghetto, politicians and the white media look to the realm of sociology. The above-mentioned Moynihan report is the best example. The rhetoric consistent with Moynihan report kept recurring in the printed media, especially in model minority articles which juxtaposed the achievements of Asian Americans with an apparent lack of achievements of African Americans. Asian Americans were elevated to the status of model minority, whereas African Americans received a stern rebuke for lagging behind despite living in the United Sates much longer than people of Asian descent. Proponents of the model minority thesis produced a very selective analysis shorn of any deeper sociological reading. Virtually all of those articles promoted rugged individualism, the attribute of anyone who succeeded in the United Sates. Robert Lee maintains that the model minority myth helped whites to promote racial liberalism, in line with which individual effort should preponderate over any measures taken by the state (160). Model minority articles contrasted the black ghetto with the communities inhabited by Asian Americans: Chinatowns, Little Tokyos, Koreatowns etc.

Freeman can see through the rhetoric used by white politicians and the white media to justify the existence of the ghetto. He retorts to his black friend who condemns the riots: "You come on like *Time* magazine. The conditions they force us into cause the crime, then they use the crime to justify the conditions ... run twice as fast to get half as far; whitey sitting there with his hands on the controls of the treadmill laughing his ass off" (176).[20] Freeman overtly parodies one of the news reports: "the daily News suggested that Negroes prove themselves worthy of full citizenship by becoming model non-citizens first" (171–172). The word "noncitizens" is highly ironic, because how can they be "model citizens" if even after the passage of the 1964 Civil Rights Act they are denied rights stemming from American citizenship. Freeman dismisses Dawson's espousal of law an order, arguing that the ghetto is always in a state of permanent disorder: "the ghetto's always been a jungle[21] ... we're keepers of the zoo. You can't cage a whole race of people without asking for trouble" (175). He responds to one set of sociological theories with another — mainly with social determinism according to which human behavior is conditioned by the social environment. He also notes that whites discover black crime only when it spills out. Otherwise they display no concern for black-on-black crime.

The criticism of whiteness is all embracing in *The Spook Who Sat by the Door*. Unlike conservative whites who questioned the intellectual potential of African Americans and their right to equality, liberal whites emphasized that all human beings are equally predisposed and it is only up to them to utilize their potential. The exemplification of the discourse supported by liberal whiteness comes up during the conversation between Freeman and Senator Hennington. The senator is the best example of a politician who wants to cure the effects without addressing the causes of the black ghetto's misery. Time and again the senator uses the phrase "culturally deprived," failing to notice African Americans' material deprivation. His accentuation of cultural deprivation tones in well with the discourse of model minority articles. White politicians and the media presented African Americans as culturally deficient. In this case culture did not denote artistic achievements but values attributed to a given group of people. Senator Hennington speaks of juvenile delinquency and illegitimate pregnancies. His solution — the propagation of contraception. He can see only a tiny part of the picture, missing the whole framework in which dramas of the ghetto unfold.[22] Unemployment, overcrowded housing, the neglect of city inspectors remain unnoticed. People like Senator Hennington would like to explain everything through culture, taking racial discrimination out of the picture altogether.[23]

Apart from the already mentioned critique of the white media, Freeman comments on their coverage of the riots. Most television networks treat riots as nightly entertainment. Television coverage gives viewers much more than simply entertainment. The view of the riot-torn ghetto provides them with a sense of having made it in the American society, of being on the other side, the safe side of their residential neighborhoods. At the same time there is always a fear that the ghetto might encroach upon their turf.

To keep the black inhabitants of the ghetto in check, the white apparatus of power reaches for a whole medley of weapons. Drugs are among the most effective. Dejected, unemployed, disheartened by the indifference of the outside world, many African Americans become an easy prey of drug dealers. Inundating ghettos with drugs, whites manage to neutralize people who otherwise might turn belligerent to show their dissatisfaction. According to Freeman, the police are relieved with the spread of addiction in the ghetto because drug addicts pose a threat to themselves and each other but they will not intrude into the white territory. Freeman's views on the issue are supported by sociological studies of the drug problem in the ghetto. Cornel West points out that the flood of drugs speeded up the flight of the black middle class and upper working class to the suburbs (52). People who stayed began to fear each other, while the police remained indifferent. Politicians also remained quiet on the issue, secretly rejoicing over the pacification of the ghetto.[24]

People from the ghetto are not only invisible to whites but to other African Americans as well. Not all African Americans are necessarily interested in dismantling the ghetto. Some of them also have a vested interest in perpetuation of the ghetto. As mentioned earlier, a number of black businessmen cashed in on the "buy black" catchword, treating the ghetto as an outlet for their products (Marable 73). Black politicians have more to lose from the integration of the ghetto than any other section of the black community. If ghettos were dismantled, they would lose an essential electorate base. Once black people were truly integrated and race was no longer an issue, they would be much less likely to vote along racial lines. Instead they would identify with interests of a particular neighborhood. In the 1960s black congressman William Dawson failed to support a black councilman Robert Taylor[25] in his attempts to place public housing projects outside the ghetto (Massey, Denton 214). The project would take a substantial portion of votes out of the ghetto. It is probably not a coincidence that the black accommodationist policeman in *The Spook* is also called Dawson. Unlike Freeman, Dawson gives priority to his personal success over the welfare of his people. Dawson's line of reasoning is followed by many other members of oppressed groups. It becomes especially visible in *Native Speaker* discussed in Chapter Four.

Freeman spares no criticism to black leaders who hedge their own positions instead of representing interests of the community:

> They don't give a damn about any niggers except themselves and they don't really think of themselves as niggers ... You ought to hear the way they talk about people like us. Like, white folks don't really have much to do with the scene. It's that lower-class niggers are too stupid, lazy, dirty and immoral.... Their definition of integration is to have their kids the only niggers in a white private school [56].

Needless to say, Freeman's distrust for middle-class integrationist leadership is in line with the sentiments of other nationalists, including black nationalist poets. In *Sacred Cows ... And Other Edibles* Giovanni pokes fun at black leaders: "God bless them ... someone in the Black community five years after their death will still be voting for them" (Giovanni cited in Georgoudaki 160). She says that the black community often finds the idea of leadership more important than ideas themselves. Black leaders are the sacred cows and any attack against them is automatically treated as an attack on all black people. Sonia Sanchez compares the black middle class to puritans who dissociate themselves from lower class African Americans.

Invisibility of black people from the ghetto to black leadership happens within a larger pattern of internal invisibility discussed in the novel. Frictions between lower class[26] African Americans and the black middle class come to the foreground in *The Spook*. Members of these groups are invisible to each other. The disfranchisement of lower class African Americans helps the black middle class to sustain an elite status. If there are no African Americans beneath them, then they are no longer an elite. This reverse power dynamics is visible in the attitude of black middle class students in the CIA school towards Freeman. They see him as a threat, as a living testimony to the fact that somebody from the basement could move up, penetrate their exclusive club and maybe even take their wives: "He must be put in his place ... he should know that he was among his betters" (14). They see Freeman as an impostor. He is a double "alien" (14), invisible both to the white instructors and the black middle class students. For the black middle class Freeman becomes an object of ethnographic interest. They "eyed Freeman uneasily" (14). While white literature usually registers white-upon-black gaze, Greenlee speaks of black-upon-black gaze. For the black middle class Freeman is no less an "other" than he is an "other" for white people. The imagery employed to depict the black middle class symbolizes their aspiration to meet white standards. Most of them are light-skinned and dress after a white fashion. A strong critique of the black middle class recurs in Greenlee's poem "Credentials," in which the I-speaker accuses the black middle class of despising lower class African Americans but at the same time profiting from their struggle for the rights of black people. According to the I-speaker of "Credentials," members of the black middle class may condemn the uprisings in Watts, Newark and Detroit, yet they still benefit from them.[27]

    The black middle class is as invisible to Freeman as he is invisible to the black middle class. At the beginning he sees the black middle class and civil rights leaders as a homogenous group. Only after recruiting members of the black middle class, does he discover that he cannot slot all of them into one category. Overall, however, he believes that the black middle class exploits other blacks, capitalizing on their disfranchisement. If in many cases this is true, he probably goes too far claiming that people from the ghetto pay for their privileges. Freeman himself repeatedly emphasizes that "whitey" is responsible for "the scene." The outmigration of the black middle class is not the reason for the poverty in the ghetto. Only the change of federal policies can alter the situation. H. L. Gates asserts that "black prosperity does not derive from black poverty: Those who succeed are those whose community, whose families, prepared them to be successful" ("Two Nations" 252). There is no denying that the black middle class is not responsible for conditions in the ghetto. Yet if more African Americans showed Freeman's involvement in the affairs of the ghetto, that might make some difference.

As I emphasize throughout this study, the white apparatus of power bears the brunt of responsibility for creating fissures inside the black community. Freeman knows full well who breeds discord among African Americans: "Damn near the deadliest people in the world ... but killing each other all these years instead of the people who put all that fear[28] and anger inside them" (100). In many cases it is also fear that tells the black middle class to keep away from the ghetto. Just as the Invisible Man in the 1930s is afraid that any contact with black-belt peasants will bring him down in the eyes of whites, the black middle class of the 1960s fears that any association with African Americans from the black ghetto will compromise their middle class status. Some middle class African Americans despise people from the ghetto, because whites are quick to identify lower class African Americans with all black people across the board.[29] In many cases it may not be reverse power dynamics but simply the fear of being brought back to the place which they hope to wipe out from their memory. Tensions inside the black community are not limited exclusively to frictions between different classes, but take place within the same group as well. Black on black crime inside the ghetto is the best example. Here again external factors weigh in, bringing people incarcerated in the ghetto to the point of desperation and setting them against one another. Unable to compete with the outside world or vent their disenchantment on that world, they find an easy target in their own people.

White people are not alone in opposing racial desegregation. Black Power representatives also oppose it (Denton, Massey 215). Their separatism is at odds with the idea of integrated neighborhoods. In their view, desegregation would jeopardize African American distinctness, posing a further threat to their unity and solidarity. Miscegenation would thin out the black race.

Forty years after the publication of *The Spook Who Sat by the Door* the black ghetto still remains very much invisible both to whites and to many blacks as well. The ghetto is practically effaced from the political agenda of the U.S. The invisibility of the black ghetto becomes most conspicuous during the election season. It is a taboo subject both for black and white politicians. While African American politicians question redlining policies in employment and education, they do not mention the ghetto. During the 2004 Democratic presidential debate Reverend Al Sharpton attacked his opponent Howard Dean for failing to hire African American and Hispanic staff members. Yet no one even touched upon the persistence of the ghetto. If the white apparatus of power is responsible for the invisibility of the ghetto, African Americans also find themselves bound by multiple, often contradictory locations, especially in relation to each other.

Dan Freeman's Literal Invisibility and Mimicry as a Linchpin of Literal Invisibility

African Americans remain invisible to white people, but they can see whiteness in full color. Like other characters discussed here, Freeman is gifted with second-sight. Acquainted with white people's perceptions of African Americans, he can become literally invisible and employ literal invisibility as a weapon against his oppressors. He allows whites to see only what he wants them to see. Like Rinehart in *Invisible Man,* Freeman has many different faces. However, unlike Rinehart's treachery, his tricksterism does not target the black community. Putting on various masks and manipulating white stereotypes of black people, Freeman takes the edge off white watchfulness. While his immediate audience can see only part of his performance, his broader audience (the readers) is granted a full-sight view.

Freeman's literal invisibility and literal invisibility of many other marginal figures hinges on mimicry. Lacan compares mimicry to "the technique of camouflage practiced in human warfare" (Lacan cited in Bhabha 85). The terms "camouflage" and "warfare" ideally describe Freeman's mimicry. Sceptical of traditional warfare tactics, Freeman launches an undercover warfare on the people responsible for his oppression. Bhabha defines mimicry as "recalcitrance," "double articulation" (86). People whom Freeman tricks can see only one side of his articulation, unaware of this recalcitrant side. In "Postcolonialism, Anthropology and the Magic of Mimesis"

Graham Huggan expands on the findings of earlier scholars: Adorno, Taussig,[30] Bhabha and draws a clear distinction between mimicry and mimesis (91). While mimicry is a "mischievous," "disruptive imitation," mimesis is a "symbolic representation" (94–95). Huggan notices a clear difference between "mimicry of the white man" and the "mimicry of the white man's mimetic representation" of marginalized people (94). Mimesis approximates the latter.[31] Although I refer to Freeman's subversive performance as "mimicry," there is no denying that it comprises the elements of both. It is definitely "disruptive," "mischievous," and "recalcitrant." Yet at the same time it is not a mere imitation, but rather an interpretative representation of white people's portrayal of African Americans. He painstakingly creates a series of personas that he dons for the outside world. The disruption becomes conspicuous when Freeman interrupts the conservative general's oration on intellectual inferiority of African Americans and their athletic superiority. He chimes in: "and we can sing and dance too" (63). Huggan claims that mimicry subverts someone else's agenda, whereas mimesis creates its own" (101). Freeman both subverts his white oppressors' agenda and pursues his own. Still, if we are to acknowledge Huggan's distinction between mimicry and mimesis, then Freeman's performance has more in common with mimicry, since, as I mentioned earlier, his alternative agenda is not fully articulated, but full of loopholes.

Discussing Freeman's mimicry, I would like to further problematize the term *slippage*. Bhabha's definition of slippage —"almost the same but not quite" (89) implies an unconscious or unintentional lapse, something that is beyond the control of a mimic person. Freeman's case shows that slippage can be deliberate as well. In Freeman's rendition, slippage is no longer an inadvertent and awkward lapse, an uncomfortable slip, but a meticulous strategy of deceit. Nowhere is this more apparent than in his affiliation with the CIA. Working for the CIA in Washington, Freeman projects an image of an aspiring black man who wants to meet white standards, but still drops a stitch here and there, creating an impression that he is somewhat a misfit. He wants to dress well, but does not know how:

> He was dressed in quiet bad taste, his suit *a bit too* light, his cuffs *a bit too* deep, lapels *a bit too* wide, shoulders *a shade too* padded ... His suit was *a bit too* cheap and his wristwatch, of eighteen-carat gold, *a bit too* expensive. He walked with a gangling shuffle, his head tilted *slightly* toward one shoulder [67, emphasis added].

Two: Through Invisibility Towards Visibility

Everything in his posture is a little bit overdone or incomplete, not significantly, just enough to throw whites off guard, give them a feeling of superiority and stave off any suspicion.

Realizing that most white people cannot stand a black man who is one hundred percent up to the job, he repeatedly feigns incompetence and uncertainty. In their superciliousness whites with whom he mingles want African Americans to look to them for confirmation. They have to feel that black people need them. During his affiliation with the CIA he also "makes an easy job look difficult," often reaching for a mask of ignorance and naivety (59). Freeman is a live embodiment of the traits ascribed by whites to African Americans. At the CIA school he exaggerates some of those features, but it arouses no one's suspicion that he speaks with a very heavy accent and has extremely narrow vocabulary despite graduating from premier universities. The reason why no one finds it strange is because whites with whom he interacts cherish their stereotypes to such an extent that they would blind themselves to obvious facts rather than correct their vision of reality.

For most of the time Freeman's slippage is deliberate. Still, on some occasions he makes an unintentional slip as well, although he takes great pains to avoid this. Anxious not to make a false move, he moulds his features like a sculptor. Like Bledsoe, he looks in the mirror to check his facial expression:

> He checked his mask in the mirror for *slippage*, this was not the time to arouse suspicion. The face that returned his stare in the mirror was sincere, serious, concerned and just a bit worried that it might lose a five-figure salary because the natives had been restless last night. His mask was perfect [180].

There is an unintentional slippage when he orders French wine with French accent, compromising for a while his mask of ignorance. Yet no one notices because no one expects him to order wine with French accent (60). As I pointed out at the very outset, white people create his cover as much as he does. They approach him with an already fixed set of presumptions and his task is to "impressionistically support the stereotype" (32). As David Palumbo-Liu states in "Assumed Identities," "we expect certain types of behavior from certain people, and these expectations may persist despite any evidence to the contrary" (767). Therefore the "color-blind" general does not notice when Freeman turns pale, having listened to his overtly racist comments on African American intellectual inferiority. The gravest unintentional slippage occurs when Freeman leaves a propaganda tape on the table in his apartment. On the same day he also forgets to check whether anyone is inside before he makes a confidential phone call. Should he make such a phone call from his apartment, especially after being warned by his one-time prostitute friend? Does he not suspect that his phone may be tapped? But then, is there any space safe if you need to be on guard even at your own home? Freeman makes all these mistakes when he is under pressure, anxious to warn his comrades of an approaching search in one of their safe-houses. No mask is ever one hundred percent perfect. It always has some holes. These holes threaten to become larger at the time of increased tension, tiredness, indisposition. No one's impersonation can be fault-free. It is difficult to draw a stiff line between one's private and public self. The private self can always encroach upon the public self, putting in jeopardy a scrupulously assembled performance.

As in *Invisible Man*, mask imagery recurs throughout the novel. Time and again the third-person narrator uses the word "mask" to depict Freeman's mimicry (182, 186). He flashes his smile even when no one is in the room. His acting may be supreme, but it is not good enough to fool his girlfriend who turns him in. Confident as he is, Freeman sometimes does not trust his own acting skills either.

Freeman's mimicry happens in three distinct stages: the first — at the CIA school, the second — during his affiliation with the CIA proper and the third — when he works for the social foundation whose ostensible purpose is to forge a link between people from the ghetto and the white world. Its real purpose is to keep the black lower class in check. We could compare Freeman's association with the foundation to the Invisible Man's association with the Brotherhood. While the Invisible Man fails in his attempt at tricking the Brothers, Freeman successfully manipulates white members of the board. Both organizations prey on the black community, treating African Americans instrumentally. Both want to keep African Americans under tight reign and prevent them from claiming real power. Representing interests of the white elite, the Brotherhood treats African Americans as pawns in their political game. The priority for the foundation is to forestall any spilling out of the ghetto. African Americans are to remain "corralled" inside an inner city area. Rather than openly manifest their disenchantment at the American system, they are to stay quiet and patiently endure their fate of inner city inmates.

Composed mainly of white liberals, the foundation is still a patchwork of political interests. At least to a certain extent it embodies attitudes prevailing at the time in the American society. White people involved in the foundation come from various political backgrounds: Burckhardt — a white conservative businessman, Thompson — a liberal professor of sociology and Stephen — a self-concerned liberal member of the white middle-class. Burckhardt openly demands unquestioning obedience from the black lower class. At the time of the riots he is scared to death that the ghetto might intrude into white districts. No member of the foundation is interested in either integrating the ghetto, changing the power dynamics or improving the conditions inside the ghetto. Stephen — the white chairman of the board — displays interest solely in his salary. What first of all matters to him is a Ford grant that would allow the purchase of a new car. When riots break out, he does not show any concern for the situation in the ghetto, but fears for the reaction of other board members. Freeman says that Stephen "is like a dog" (182). Professor of sociology, Thompson, treats African Americans like guinea pigs for his research. In his theories he resembles contemporary sociologists of the 1960s. Like most of his colleagues, Thompson does not trace the disadvantages of African Americans to institutional racism, but to the social and cultural deprivation of black people. Sensing the Professor's sociological bent, Freeman casts himself as a father figure that will inspire juvenile delinquents from disintegrated families. Like many other white characters, Thompson is presented as blind. To get through to him, Freeman "looks deep into his contact lenses" (90).

Working for the foundation, Freeman impersonates a black middle-class upwardly mobile black man "with nothing but chicks and sports cars on his mind" (241). For the outside world he is just like many other middle class African Americans whom he hates so much. Freeman from previous incarnation disappears to give way to new "J. Pressed and Brooks button-downed Freeman" (77). Gone is the shuffle, ill-fitted dress and tilt of the head. Now he walks like a well-trained athlete and chooses his clothes with meticulous care. Even his drinks change. Scotch gives way to martini on the rocks. His apartment in Chicago is part of the new cover as well. No one suspects that "tame, smug, self-satisfied Freeman" might be up to any mischief (104). His impersonation is so convincing that some African Americans begin to see him as a sell-out. White people would like all African Americans to turn into black dandies desiring nothing but material success. The middle class helps to assuage white fears of blackness.

Virtually all middle class African Americans wear masks. Smiles never disappear from their faces. The only difference between Freeman and his middle-class colleagues is that he impersonates a black middle-class man to carry out his plan, while those around him slip into middle-class roles for personal comfort or simply to stay afloat in the American reality. Yet they are never fully secure in their middle-class positions. Smiles cover the panic that they may slide down the social ladder. Most of them face two alternatives: play the game without any questioning or quit altogether. To keep their place in the hierarchy, they usually need to perform twice as well as whites.

Contemptuous as Freeman is of the middle class, he openly admits enjoying parts of his middle-class life. The luxury and the lavish life-style appeal to him. He is just as attracted by luxury as anyone else, being pulled in opposite directions.[32] On the one hand, he tells other guys from the ghetto that it is not so bad to be poor. On the other hand, some elements of his cover appeal to him.

During the third and second stage of his mimicry Freeman is visible and invisible at the same time. As a social worker he is like an "invisible agent" shifting easily between the ghetto and the white territory in order to gain and pass sensitive information (188). He is visible and invisible in social circles — at integrated parties and other social events, where people begin to see him as an eligible bachelor. The paradox of his simultaneous visibility and invisibility is nowhere more conspicuous than at the time of his affiliation with the CIA. Freeman's main task was first of all to be seen. He is a living proof of "fair employment policies of the CIA." As long as there is one black person working for the agency, it is integrated: "He was given a glass-enclosed office in the director's suite. His job was to be black and conspicuous as the integrated Negro of the Central Intelligence Agency of the United States of America" (47). The fragment again bears resemblance to Du Bois's metaphor of African Americans incarcerated behind plates of glass. However, unlike the black people from Du Bois's metaphor, Freeman does not scream for recognition but quietly pursues his agenda.

Two: Through Invisibility Towards Visibility

On the surface he becomes what people around him expect him to be. In reality he is the best under cover agent in the CIA, "moving through Washington *like an invisible man*" (60, emphasis added).

Freeman's affiliation with the CIA exposes white hypocrisy at its worst. White conservatives are forced to put their prejudice on the shelf and take him on to create appearances of equality, while white liberals consider his presence in the CIA a success of their integration policies. Howard Winant points out that the white liberal racial project makes a pretence to racial justice, yet at the same time it avoids commitment to it "for pragmatic reasons" (105). In *Possessive Investment in Whiteness* George Lipsitz elaborates on Winant's statement by illustrating how whiteness hides its privilege behind the mask of innocence and clear conscience. Lipsitz claims that Title VII of the 1964 Civil Rights Act gestures towards fair employment practices, while at the same time it introduces stipulations which effectively sap its own force: "The Equal Employment Opportunity Commission established by the act that lacked its own enforcement mechanism, such as cease-and-desist orders, and could offer only "conciliation" as a remedy to aggrieved individuals" (40). Title VII was drafted in such a way as to protect seniority rights of white workers, failing to extend such rights to people of color. As a result African Americans bore the brunt of economic transformations that occurred in the 1970s and 1980s.

The above-mentioned Senator Hennington is an embodiment of white liberalism that guards its own hedges and wears the mask of equality. "Pragmatic political reasons" cited by Winant become visible during Hennington's political campaign. The senator's political agenda does not offer any substantial changes in racial relations. Instead of taking concrete measures that would target racial discrimination, he plans to win over black voters with a campaign of cheap media tricks — "cloak and dagger Civil Rights," as he puts it (6). The term "cloak and dagger" very aptly illustrates liberals' approach to civil rights. It is much more a masquerade than any serious attempt at challenging the existing status quo. For "pragmatic political reasons"— not to antagonize white voters, the senator refuses to tighten cooperation with black civil rights leaders and incorporate their views into his program. He is not interested in the African American perspective. The senator's arrogant attitude becomes apparent in his conversation with Freeman. Realizing that the senator is one of those whites who know best what is good for African Americans, Freeman says nothing but yeses him. Flattered by Freeman's feigned ignorance and naiveté, the senator tells his boss that he has heard a lot of helpful tips from him. The scene is a good illustration of the Invisible Man's statement: "Yes! Yes! Yes! That was all anyone wanted of us, that we should be heard and not seen and then heard only in one optimistic chorus of yassuh" (384). Thirty years after the events described in *Invisible Man* take place, whites could no longer afford not to see African Americans. Yet they still did not care to listen. Freeman makes the most of this limitation.

Freeman's mimicry stands in sharp contrast to the black middle class's imitation of whiteness. While his mimicry is subversive, their imitation has only one goal — a materialistic success. They "ape Mr. Charlie" (13), having "sold their nigger soul for a mess of materialistic pottage" (14).[33] Their conversation revolves around their incomes, professions, schools they attended, expensive car brands, alcohol labels etc. They savor their middle-class status, deluding themselves into thinking that they have escaped. According to Freeman, African Americans can never fully escape and "spin a middle-class cocoon thick enough for [whites] not to penetrate" (52). There is a slippage between their power and the power of people whom they aspire to emulate.

At the CIA school Freeman is very much a pariah, yet for most of the novel he is a link, a go-between, a middleman between communities, not only between whites and blacks, but also between opposite factions of the white political spectrum and at one point between whites and Asians. In the CIA he is used as a liaison between a conservative general and a liberal senator (60). As a result their relations considerably improve. As a social worker in the Chicago foundation Freeman is a link between white people and the black ghetto. Having secured the trust of both communities, he safely shifts between the ghetto and the white turf. Himself a descendant of ghetto dwellers, once a member of a youth gang, now turned a middle-class black man with ostensibly white tastes, he seems to be an ideal choice for a mediator between the two communities. Freeman has the confidence of black people, because unlike other members of the black middle class he does not cut himself off from the black lower class, but wants to preserve the connection. Still, it takes more than sheer willingness to win the trust of underprivileged African Americans — especially members of youth gangs. While they distrust many other social workers, they show no apprehension in their contacts with Freeman. It is thanks to his easy-going, approachable style that he manages to win people's hearts. In a sense he is a middle-man only nominally, because in reality he has his feelings invested squarely on one side. Freeman's translation between both communities is not exactly faithful to the original. Rather than present events to whites as they really are, he sells them his own interpretation. It does not mean, however, that he enjoys deceiving white people. Acting out white stereotypes of African Americans, he risks further ossifying of those stereotypes. Eager as he is to tell whites what he really thinks, he is afraid that his words would fall on deaf ears. Many tried it before with no apparent results.

Freeman's mediation is not limited to his most immediate environment. At one point he becomes a black man who translates between the "Western" world and the "Orient." Working for the CIA, he accompanies his boss on his frequent trips to Asia. During one of those trips he smooths over an incident between the president of the United States and Hindu officials. Apparently unaware of the sanctity of the Taj Mahal for the Hindus, the president gives a roar at this sacred site. Hindu representatives turn pale in bewilderment and indignation. Freeman steps in and saves the situation. His translation cuts both ways. He not only explains the president's actions to the Hindu press, but also translates the other way round, enlightening the president on the significance of the Taj Mahal. The president looks at the Taj Mahal and the rest of the Hindu culture through the prism of Western stereotypes about the east. Since to him the site is exotic, it does not occur to him that to Hindus it may be holy. He understands the significance of the Taj Mahal only after it is translated into his own culture, without envisioning the place as significant in itself.

Even though Freeman is more knowledgeable than the president, he also has his stereotypes about the east and exoticizes it. A considerable part of the "Orient's" textualization revolves around the sexuality of Asians. Asian women were seen as lascivious and approachable, while the men either as eunuchs or as sexual predators posing a threat to white womanhood (Leong xvi, R. Lee 10). Freeman has no such preconceptions about people living in Asia. Still, like many other Westerners, he sees the sexuality of Asians as essentially different from that of Westerners: "He found out that in Asia he was not as hip in bed as he had imagined and took a postgraduate course in bed, oriental style" (62). As Edward Said points out, the "Orient was often seen as a place where one could look for sexual experience unobtainable in Europe" (Said 190) and by extension in the rest of the Western world. Freeman does not exactly search for such experience in Asia, but to his surprise he finds it there. As a result, he "learned to make love in several languages" (62). Freeman aspires to the role of a mediator who embraces "oriental" trends. Having purchased clothes in Hong Kong and Bangkok, he dispatches them to his apartment in New York. It bears mentioning at this point that the New York apartment is no longer part of his cover, but part of his private self, because it is his secret getaway, a repository for all parts of his identity that do not match his cover.

There may be practically no unintentional slippage in Freeman's performance before the outside world, but there is always an internal slippage. The question of Freeman's own visibility to himself gains prominence in the novel. How visible to himself is he? In order to remain effective, an invisible agent must remain true to himself internally. Even though Freeman keeps a separate identity, he is not sure whether he is still able to say who he is. Putting on different masks and playing practically before everyone, he wonders if his cover has not at least partially merged with his identity. All his masks in a sense become part of him.

An inner slippage also occurs whenever he wants to speak out but cannot. Freeman keeps a poker face before practically everyone — both whites and blacks. His private self is always shadowed from people around him — even his most immediate environment. On the one hand, he derives a certain measure of satisfaction from successful execution of his plan. On the other hand, constant impersonation leaves him tired and lonely. There is an unscalable wall of silence between Freeman and the outside world. Unlike the Invisible Man, Freeman cannot tell others "what was going on while [their] eyes were looking through" (Ellison 439). The third person-narrator does the telling for him.

How effective is Freeman's strategy? Can one reach visibility through invisibility? Although Greenlee at many points highlights the loopholes in Freeman's philosophy and strategy, overall he wants us to believe that his tactics in many ways do work. A series of well-organized rebellions infuses whites with fear and makes them recognize the Freedom Fighters as a force to be reckoned with. Will Freeman's underground war bring any substantial changes for African Americans? The black middle class begins to lose its integrated jobs — presumably because of the rebellion. African

Two: Through Invisibility Towards Visibility

Americans in the ghetto support guerrilla operations although they are the ones who pay the heaviest price. In the long term they have potentially most to gain. There are two competing currents in *The Spook Who Sat by the Door*: an espousal of black nationalism embodied by Dan Freeman and the narrator's voice of caution, showing sympathy towards the nationalist cause, but at the same time looking at it with a sober eye. It is not without significance that we, as readers, approach the text with a hindsight of thirty-nine years following its publication, thirty-nine years which saw a significant dilution of the Black Power and nationalist movement. Greenlee chooses to close his book on a strong separatist accent. In the closing lines of the novel Freeman listens to the sounds of the guns and to Billie Holliday's song "God Bless the Child."[34] Unlike the Invisible Man who emerges to the surface to literally claim his visibility, Freeman will need to stay underground. His cover gone, he will have to disappear and once again seek refuge in invisibility. Freeman and his predecessor — the Invisible Man approach their invisibility differently and utilize it differently. Both choose diverging roads towards visibility and they envision African American future in a different way. Yet neither sees invisibility as an end in itself, but as a means to an end — visibility.

Three

Performing Towards Visibility
Maxine Hong Kingston's *Tripmaster Monkey*

> "Everything is so invisible and I'm just bringing it into visibility"
> (Kingston, *Conversations with Maxine Hong Kingston*, 189).

In *Tripmaster Monkey* Maxine Hong Kingston does much more than just bring Asian Americans and especially Chinese Americans into visibility. She tells us what happens in the process of their striving for visibility. If Dan Freeman from *The Spook Who Sat by the Door* envisions militant nationalism as a weapon against white supremacy, Wittman Ah Sing — the protagonist of *Tripmaster Monkey*—opts for cultural nationalism. Asian American activists of the 1960s and particularly cultural nationalists looked up to black nationalists, sharing with them many common goals. Asian American invisibility stands in sharp contrast to Afro-American invisibility. Still, both invisibilities are firmly anchored in the blindness of the white world. In *Tripmaster Monkey* Kingston not only illustrates Asian American invisibility but also problematizes the very notion of visibility. What kind of visibility are Asian Americans striving for and what are the best ways leading towards it? Reaching for human connections on multiple levels, Kingston rejects conventional identity politics espoused by Wittman Ah Sing. All movements built upon conventional identity politics to a certain degree replicate the structures of dominant systems. Any attempt at recentering, at moving from margins to the centre entails its own pitfalls. Kingston illustrates what happens in the course of staging and performing Chinese American identity. Like all the authors studied here, she does not focus solely on the invisibility of her own people to whites but sheds light on the tensions within Chinese American community.

Three: Performing Towards Visibility

Wittman Ah Sing hopes to achieve visibility for himself and for his people through theatre. A theatrical performance and real life performance of Chinese American ethnic identity become Wittman's chief weapon in his striving for visibility.[1] We may recall that performance and mimicry belonged to Dan Freeman's arsenal of weapons. However, in both cases performance is employed in a different manner. Unlike Wittman, Freeman does not reach for a theatrical performance.[2] Utilizing his invisibility and impersonating stereotypes attributed to Afro-Americans, Freeman successfully fools whites, catching them off guard. Wittman, on the other hand, shudders from real life imitation of white stereotypes ascribed to Chinese Americans. He meticulously fashions an image of himself, which is an antithesis to white expectations of Chinese Americans. Both manipulate "authenticity" and ethnicity to their own ends. While Freeman is "authentic" to white expectations of black people, Wittman is "authentic" to the vision of Chinese Americans concocted by Chinese American nationalists. Freeman engages in real life mimicry, whereas Wittman incorporates elements of mimicry into his play.

Staging a play, Wittman tries to dismantle white stereotypes of Chinese Americans.[3] The very medium that he employs — theatre — reverses the condition of visibility and invisibility. Those who are usually invisible enter the stage to claim spotlight and their visibility. As is the case during the Invisible Man's speeches, the audience remains largely invisible. The narrator informs us that "Whenever Chinese Americans performed, they wanted to be seen"— literally and figuratively (13). Producing their own plays, they had an opportunity to tell the American public about themselves by themselves. All along the American society conspired to render Chinese Americans invisible — either by physically barring them from the United States, expelling them, confining to the ghettos or in the end by trying to completely assimilate them and make them as indistinguishable as possible. Being no longer distinguishable, they are no longer a threat. Their presence on the American stage at least partly counterbalanced white attempts to render them invisible, absent from the American society. Wittman's goal is to "spook out prejudice" (324), "to awaken the audience" (277) and wrench it out of its false dreams about his people.

Before choosing theatre[4] as an artistic medium, he contemplates fiction. Yet in the end he settles for theatre among others to avoid "racinated descriptions:" "The actors will walk out on the stage and their looks will be self-evident. They will speak dialects and accents, which the audience will get upon hearing" (34). The play allows his people the maximum of self-representation. In his predilection for theatre Wittman mirrors Asian American artists of the 1960s and the 1970s — people like Philip Gotanda, Wakako Yamauchi and Frank Chin. Wittman himself bears a striking resemblance to Frank Chin, a point on which I am going to elaborate later. The choice of theatre was not random but a shrewd and calculated move, enabling Asian American artists to make the most of their limited resources. Karen Shimakawa points out in *Asian American Body on Stage* that by staging theatrical productions, Asian American activists could access large numbers of people in a relatively short time and with minimum expense (67). Participating in a live performance, spectators share in the process of creation, being to a greater extent involved in an artistic venture. Hence they identify more closely with characters impersonated on stage. Because of the immediacy of the theatrical experience the artists found it much easier to win over the hearts and minds of people. Karen Shimakawa highlights the moment of recognition which should happen in theatre (68). Watching the spectacle unfold and discriminating between the persona of an actor and that of a character, spectators ideally should become aware that all identities are performed and socially constructed. The attraction to theatre is a point of convergence between Asian American and Afro-American artists of the period.[5]

Asian American Invisibility versus African American Invisibility

Afro-Americans and Asian Americans may have adopted similar strategies in their struggle for visibility, but this does not change the fact that they are invisible in different ways. Both groups grapple with different stereotypes. In many ways Asian Americans find themselves more displaced in the Unites States than Afro-Americans. No one questions the right of Afro-Americans to live in the United States, whereas it is not entirely uncommon for an American of Asian descent to hear: "Have you got a green card?," "Do you speak English?," "When did you arrive?," "How do you like this country?" or "Go Back to Asia." A black person, on the other hand, is unlikely to hear "Go back to Africa." The label "alien"[6] has haunted Asian Americans all along. From the very beginning of their presence in the United States they were seen as undesirable. The Exclusion Acts of 1882, 1884, 1886, 1888, 1902, 1907, 1917, and 1924 physically barred Asian Americans from entering the country (Lowe 180, Gotanda 136, 137). The 1882, 1884, 1886, 1888 and 1902 Acts referred to Chinese Americans. As a result of the 1907 Gentlemen's Agreement, Japan agreed under pressure to decrease the number of immigrants arriving in the United States, Hawaii, Mexico and Canada (Gotanda 137). The 1917 Act covered people from South Asia, Southeast Asia and the Islands of the Indian and Pacific Oceans. The 1924 Act barred Japanese Americans and other Asians from immigration to the United States altogether. Its legal framework encompassed "aliens ineligible for citizenship." At that time no people of Asian descent could apply for citizenship. Despite the bans on Asian American immigration, Asian Americans still kept entering the United States illegally, risking their lives during perilous journeys to America, or the "Gold Mountain." Only the 1943 Magnuson Act abolished the ban on Chinese American immigration and the 1952 McCarran Walter Act on Japanese American immigration (Gotanda 139, 145).

Exploiting Chinese American work, whites still conspired to efface them, to make them as invisible and unobtrusive as possible. They were deemed good for work, but inapt for personal contacts with whites. Chinese Americans worked among others on the railroad, in agriculture (for example in the wheat fields of California, on sugar plantations in Hawaii), in the canneries, laundries and in the mining industry (Chan 25–45). Although they contributed as much as any other ethnic group to building the country, they were denied the rights granted to other inhabitants of the United States. Until the 1952 McCarran Walter Act Asian Americans could not become citizens of the United States. Following the Civil War the door to citizenship opened for Afro-Americans. If non-white, you had to wait to earn your right to become a citizen. The 1790 statute (Act of March 23, 1790: 1 Stat. 103) gave the right to naturalization only to white people (Gotanda 140). African Americans were found worthy of American citizenship only in 1870, when the Nationality Act extended naturalization rights to black people. It was ninety-four years after the founding of the American state and two hundred and fifty-one years after the first slaves were brought to the American continent.[7] Chinese Americans began traveling to the United States in large numbers in the early 1850s, Japanese Americans in the 1880s (Chan 25). They had to wait for their right to citizenship for around a hundred and fifty years until 1952. The McCarran Walter Act not only made it possible for Asian Americans to become citizens of the United States, but also eliminated "the white persons" caveat of the naturalization law (Gotanda 145).

Asian Americans never were legally slaves.[8] This does not mean, however, that they were free from persecution and discrimination. The threat of lynching, violence or robbery was very real whenever they found themselves outside the precincts demarcated for them. In *Tripmaster Monkey*, one of the episodes in Wittman's play presents a riot scene in which the white mob raids a grocery store and is about to lynch a Chinese man (Kingston 298).[9] Although whites did not enslave Asians in the United States, they subjected them to forms of discrimination not very far removed from slavery. Following the collapse of slavery, whites began to use Asian Americans as cheap labor ("coolies"), exploiting them to the limits of human endurance.[10] Gary Okihiro observes in "Is Yellow Black or White?" that cooliesm proved very convenient to white Americans, who could replace slaves with cheap workers from Asia. They did not need to jockey for their votes, so they could pay them less than Afro-Americans and they also could use them as a bargain card against African Americans (Okihiro, *Margins and Mainstreams* 44).

Asian American alienation from the American state is not a thing of the past, but very much part of Wittman's reality in the 1960s. Asian Americans still remain largely unacknowledged and taken out of the picture. Despite being a fifth-generation Chinese American, Wittman is often treated like a fresh immigrant, a "wetback" (227), who needs a green card to stay legally in the United States.[11] He feels overlooked in the white and black American world, where racial tensions between blacks and whites come to the foreground and other marginalized racial and ethnic groups are frequently left out. He tells us:

> I have a nightmare that ... someday Blacks and whites will shake hands over my head. I'm the little yellow man beneath the bridge of their hands and overlooked. Have you been at a demonstration where they sing:
> > Black and white together
> > Black and white together
> > Someday-a-a-ay [308].

Reducing racial relations in the United States to the black and white binary, whites took Asian Americans out of the equation, banishing them outside the perimeter of the United States. Afro-Americans faced discrimination and persecution, but they had a firm foothold on American soil. They also enjoyed and still enjoy much more leverage on the political scene. In the above quoted passage Wittman mentions a civil rights demonstration which he attended.[12] Although part of the civil rights movement, Asian Americans played a clearly subsidiary role. Being outnumbered by Afro-Americans, Asian Americans ended up to a great extent invisible on the political scene (Espiritu 33). Yen Le Espiritu notes that "when the Peace and Freedom Party was formed on the basis of black and white coalitions, Asian American activists felt excluded because they were neither black nor white" (33). In the 1960s most Americans still looked at racial relations in their country from the perspective of slavery times. Native Americans already "taken care of," there were whites, blacks and the "problem" to resolve. Blacks made the problem, whites vouchsafed the solution. Having said all that, we need to remember that Wittman makes the above cited statement in 1962, before the 1965 changes in the immigration law and before the influx of large numbers of Asians. However, the increase in the Asian American population did not subvert the black and white binary which has dominated American politics. Only recently has the dynamics been changing. Asian Americans are still left out of the picture when it comes to electoral politics, but Latinos are now seen as a force to be reckoned with. More and more often white politicians court Hispanic voters.

Rather than acknowledge that Asian Americans belong to the United States and to the West, many white people still place them in the East, looking at them through the prism of Orientalism.[13] Hence they are seen as exotic, inscrutable and alien. Defamiliarizing Asian Americans, whites miss the fact that they lead lives very much like their own. Wittman says sarcastically that in order to be recognized as Americans, they would need to make a Chinese American soap opera. For most white people, divisions between the East and West are set in stone.[14] Wittman quotes from Kipling to render their attitude towards Asian Americans: "East is east and west is west and never twain shall meet." Like other Asian Americans of the time, Wittman rebels strongly against being called "oriental": "Once and for all: I am not oriental. An oriental is antipodal. I am a human being standing here on land which I belong to and which belongs to me. I am not an oriental antipode" (327). The term "oriental" carries all the stereotypical notions of Asians automatically extended to Asian Americans. If Westerners were believed to be rational, moral, mature, restrained, masculine and courageous, Easterners were attributed precisely the opposite features, being portrayed as irrational, immoral, immature, hypersexed, feminine and cowardly. As Edward Said asserts in his famous book *Orientalism,* the East was a mirror reflection of the West.

Asian American and in this case Chinese American alienation from the United States is two-fold. First, Asian Americans are often literally perceived as strangers — non–Americans. Secondly, even if acknowledged as citizens of the United States, they are still seen as radically different in terms of culture. Whites approach Asian Americans with a fixed set of presumptions, picturing them as "inscrutable"[15] and "exotic." These two adjectives represent the most popular stereotypes about Asian Americans:

> They've got us in a bag, which we aren't punching our way out of. To be exotic or to be not-exotic is not a question about Americans or about humans ... I'm common ordinary. Plain black sweater. Blue jeans ... We do ejaculations. We do laffs. And they call us inscrutable ... We need to be part of the daily love life of the country, to be showed and loved continuously until we're not inscrutable anymore [*Tripmaster Monkey* 310].

Wittman's sentiments correspond closely to Kingston's own views:

> To say we are inscrutable, mysterious, exotic denies us our common humanness, because it says that we are so different from a regular human being that we are by nature intrinsically unknowable. Thus the stereotyper defends ignorance ... To call a people exotic freezes us into the position of being always alien ["Cultural Misreadings" 57].

Depicting Asian Americans in terms of exoticism or non-exoticism, whites treat them as a separate species judged by a separate set of standards that do not apply to the rest of mankind. Asian Americans are denied not only their Americanness, but also their humanity. It is essential that Kingston uses the word "freezes" to depict the nature of stereotyping. Certain groups are indeed frozen in distorted images of themselves. Some stereotypes reach the status of immutability. Homi Bhabha calls it "fixity" (66). In "The Other Question: Stereotype, Discrimination and the Discourse of Colonialism" Bhabha speaks about stereotype in the singular, treating it almost like a monolith and in this way compounding its power. I believe that it is much safer to speak about the immutability of some stereotypes rather than the "fixity" of stereotype in general. In my study I would like to accentuate the fluctuating nature of certain stereotypes. Despite the per-

Three: Performing Towards Visibility

sistence of some stereotypes, the portrayal of both Asian Americans and African Americans has changed. With the changing times new stereotypes sprang up to replace the old ones. By approaching stereotypes on a case by case basis rather than fusing them into a monolith and labeling them "stereotype," we can much more effectively dismantle the process of stereotyping and pinpoint its inconsistencies. It is also much more empowering for the stereotyped if they can distinguish between individual features of the oppressive forces instead of treating them as some malevolent shapeless power. To enhance the visibility of the oppressed, we need to increase the visibility of the mechanisms of oppression as well.

As I have been emphasizing throughout this study, the invisibility of marginalized racial groups hinges on the construction of whiteness as a racial category. All these negative definitions of Asian Americans help whites to build a positive sense of their own self. Like other authors discussed here, Kingston unveils mechanisms governing white subjectivity. She underlines that Asian American invisibility is deeply rooted in white blindness. White people do not see Asian Americans as they really are not because they are not able to see, but because they do not want to see. Wittman argues: "We're not inscrutable at all. We are not inherently unknowable ... They willfully do not learn us and blame that on us that we have essential unknowableness" (310). Again there is a striking correspondence between Wittman's views and Kingston's impressions: "How dare they call their ignorance our inscrutability" ("Cultural Misreadings" 56). Like Ralph Ellison, Kingston emphasizes that white blindness is not an inborn imperfection, but a conscious failure, an easier way out of an uncomfortable situation. Rather than get to know Asian Americans as they really are, whites prefer to render them "inherently unknowable." Blind to the concerns and misgivings of non-white people, whites feel safe in their ignorance, signing away all responsibility. Isolating others and viewing them from the safe distance of the ivory tower, white people create a wall of impermeability around themselves. Awareness might make a chink in white supremacy, so cautiously guarded. Wittman calls white ignorance "willful innocence" (310). To illustrate the ignorance of white people, he quotes from Baldwin's *Notes of a Native Son*. In the episode cited by Wittman the narrator speaks about his experience in the Swiss Alps, where villagers have never seen a black man. Both Wittman and the narrator of *Notes* question the innocence of white people, who frequently claim that they were born into their supremacist positions. Their reasoning runs along these lines: It is only a matter of historical accident that we speak from the position of power, while black people or Asian Americans do not. What else can we do but bear the burden of our fathers and play the roles passed on to us by earlier generations?[16] Such claims shade whites from qualms of conscience and from responsibility for their actions.[17] Assuming a defensive position and treating their privilege as a matter of historical accident, they naturalize it, creating an unbridgeable gap between themselves and the oppressed.

Apart from elaborating on the social invisibility of Chinese Americans, Wittman points out that they are also culturally invisible to a greater extent than African Americans. In their ignorance white people are quick to associate Chinese Americans mainly with Chinese cuisine, Chinatown restaurants and "Oriental" souvenirs. The mainstream society effaces Asian American contributions to building the country and their achievements in arts and literature. Some of those achievements are just as invisible to Wittman himself. It becomes clear when he says:

> So what do we have in the way of a culture besides Chinese hand laundries? ... Where's our jazz? Where's our blues? Where's our ain't-taking-no-shit-from-nobody street-strutting language? I want so bad to be the first China Man bluesman of America [27].

He neglects different historical and social specifics of Asian and Afro-American experience. Wittman's views on differences between cultural achievements of Afro-Americans and Asian Americans are very much in line with Frank Chin's reflections on the subject: "American language, fashions, music, literature, cuisine, graphics, body language, morals and politics have been strongly influenced by Black culture. They have been cultural achievers, in spite of white supremacists' culture, whereas Asian America's reputation is an achievement of that white culture — a work of that racist art" (*Aiiieeeee* XXV). Unlike Wittman, Chin is much more aware of the role that white repressions and Chinese American history played in stifling their cultural expression. Still, he probably goes too far, claiming that all Chinese American cultural manifestations stemmed directly from white repressions.

After arriving in the United States, Chinese American immigrants could not concentrate to such an extent on cultural production, because first of all they had to focus on sheer survival and breadwinning — getting a job and earning money which they usually sent to their impoverished families in China. The Chinese families frequently went into debt to pay for their relatives' journey to the "Gold Mountain." Part of the money which Chinese immigrants earned in the United States had to be set aside for paying the debt and paying for their journey back home (Takaki 35). The lucky few who had their families with them thought mainly about providing for them.[18] Facing deportation, battling Exclusion Acts and widely spread anti Asian sentiment, they were not always interested in making themselves visible to the mainstream.

The threat of violence was very real for Chinese immigrants. Historian Sucheng Chan distinguishes three patterns of violence against Chinese Americans: attacks against individuals, outbursts of violence against Chinatown communities and, finally, organized attempts to oust the Chinese from certain towns (48). Some of those violent outbreaks against Chinatown communities took place in Los Angeles in 1871, in Chico in 1877 and especially drastic acts of violence occurred in Rock Springs, Wyoming in September 1885 and in Seattle, Washington from October 1885 to February 1886.[19] As non–American citizens, the Chinese could not count on the protection of the American law. Although Afro-Americans were legally citizens of the United States, they could barely count on the protection of the American law either. Violent accidents against African Americans and Asian Americans were directed both at individuals as well as the whole residential communities in the towns and the cities. The Atlanta riots of 1906 are a well-documented example.[20] Still, there were no efforts to drive African Americans out of the United States.[21]

Unlike Afro-Americans, Chinese Americans did not know the language, which was a drawback in itself and it certainly made any cross-cultural production all the more difficult. For a long time labeled as "aliens ineligible for citizenship," Asian Americans had other things on their minds than the creation of jazz. Once finally accepted as legal citizens, they still had to battle the stigma of alienness. No wonder, then, that they focused on economic advancement instead of engaging in bohemian or subversive movements. Rebellion is a privilege and Asian Americans did not feel secure enough to afford it.[22] Afro-Americans lived in the United States for much longer than Chinese Americans or other Asian American ethnic groups. Wittman may claim that Chinese Americans were in the United States "all the time before Columbus," but the truth is that most Asian

Americans did not live in the country for as long as African Americans did. Both groups had different mentalities. Despite facing formidable barriers, Asian Americans found it easier to adopt an immigrant mentality, because unlike African Americans, they did not need to confront the memory of slavery. Even though most of them were forced to immigrate to the United States by an inimical situation in their respective homeland countries, they were not dragged to the American continent in chains, as most African Americans were. The priority for Asian Americans was to move up in the American society as fast as possible. Hence they did not necessarily envision artistic profession as the best career choice for their children. Ah Sings' actor family was by no means the most representative model among Chinese Americans. Wittman is aware of all these factors, yet he does not take into account how they influenced his people.

Wittman not only looks up to Afro-Americans for their cultural achievements, but also gives them as an example of successful self-definition. He partly blames Chinese American invisibility on Chinese Americans themselves, because according to him they failed to define themselves:

> Who *are* we? Where's our name that shows that we aren't from anywhere but America? We're so out of it. It's our fault they call us gook and chinky chinaman. We've been here all this time, before Columbus, and haven't named ourselves. Look at the Blacks beautifully defining themselves. 'Black' is perfect [326].

Asian American nationalists admired the cultural distinctness of black nationalists and the Black Power movement. Looking for the right name for his people, Wittman says that they cannot be yellow, but for a while there was a Yellow Power movement parallel to the Black Power movement. Originally the term "yellow" like "oriental" carried negative associations. It might, for example, strike a chord of "yellow peril." Asian American activists reappropriated "yellow" and resignified it. In 1968 Asian American students organized an "Are You Yellow" conference at UCLA (Espiritu 32). The conference revolved around the construction of their collective identity, the Yellow Power movement and the war in Vietnam. 1970 saw the birth of the new pan Asian organization, which called itself "Yellow Seed." In the end Asian American activists gave up the "yellow" label, because they concluded that the term was not all embracing enough.[23] Defining themselves as brown, the Filipinos felt excluded. Asian American emerged as the term embracing all Americans of Asian descent.

Three: Performing Towards Visibility

Naming themselves Asian Americans, they rejected labels thrust upon them by the white world and reclaimed agency, reaching for their own name. The term "Asian Americans" gave them more clout politically. Representing themselves as a group, they found it much easier to push through certain issues.

All these attempts at naming themselves reflect a search for panethnic unity, to use Yen Le Espiritu's term. Yet Wittman searches for the distinctive name for Chinese Americans. According to him, they are more invisible than Japanese Americans who have a catchy name: Americans of Japanese descent. He wants for his people the name that will highlight their potential and their contributions throughout the history of the United States: "I'm trying to give us a Sierra-climbing name, a tree-riding name, a train-building name" (326). At the same time Wittman rejects other names. Some of those names were used by Chinese Americans themselves, for example: "Han Ngun" or "Tang Ngun" or "China Men" (326). The problem is, however, that they meant something else to Chinese Americans and something else to the white world.

While Chinese Americans used the term China Men neutrally or with a positive coloring, some whites used it in a deprecating manner.[24] China Men does not underscore Chinese Americans' Americanness sufficiently enough. It perpetuates their status of an alien in the eyes of other Americans. Wittman also rejects the name Celestials, pointing out that Chinese Americans never called themselves this way. Whites referred to them as Celestials, hoping that they would "go to heaven rather than stay in America" (327).

Wittman sees Chinese American as the best name for Americans of Chinese descent. However, his Chinese American has no hyphen. In his view, the hyphen allows whites to put more stress on their Chinese heritage rather than their Americanness. Treating race like an essence, many white people believe that they can discriminate between what is Chinese and what is American in Chinese Americans. Wittman speaks about an experiment in which he participated at college. He was paid fifty dollars an hour and the task was to slot various personality traits under Chinese or American. The experiment stirs up the feelings of outrage in Wittman because he reads it as a clear attempt to mark Chinese Americans as essentially different, to intensify their double-consciousness, their sense of being apart from the fabric of American society. He regrets going ahead with the experiment instead of shredding the questionnaire sheets (328). The test corresponds to a scene from Wittman's play — the performance by the Siamese brothers Chang and Eng, or Chang-Eng, as they are also called. The brothers are attacked by the circus mob that wants to see the "hyphen" by which they are supposedly joined. Chang shouts at the audience: "We know damned well what you came for to see — the angle at which we're joined at.... You want to know if we feel jointly. You want to look at the hyphen. You want to look at it bare" (293). The reproach is directed not only at the imagined spectators of a freak show within the play, but also at Wittman's audience. The reviews of the play suggest that non Chinese American spectators approach Wittman's play as a non American and non Western production. They expect to see in Wittman's play the exotic, Chinese flavor, the ethnic hyphen, which in their eyes makes Chinese Americans and all other Asian Americans different from them. They want to "look at it bare" (293). The expectations of Wittman's audience embody the expectations of the American audience in general. All ethnic artists and especially writers were supposed to expose themselves before the American public. Therefore autobiographies written by Asian American authors attracted more attention than other genres.

Kingston plays around the hyphen issue, problematizing Chinese American identity. The white mainstream sometimes treats Chang-Eng as one person, sometimes as two separate people. To underscore this ambiguity Kingston speaks of them "Chang-Eng are," or "him/them" (292). Chang is much more attached to his Chinese heritage, while Eng is assimilated to a greater extent. When Eng is drafted into the U.S. army, Chang manifests his individuality by claiming that he is not going to join. White Americans' approach towards Chang-Eng illustrates their attitude to all Chinese Americans. Depending on what suited them at a given moment, they treated Chinese Americans as Chinese or as Americans.[25]

Wittman's characterization of Asian American invisibility against the background of Afro-American invisibility is not nearly complete. His portrayal may give an impression that Asian Americans were utter underdogs in comparison to Afro-Americans. The American world in the 1960s may have been in many ways black and white, but Asian Americans did not lag behind in all areas. Asian Americans may have been more invisible politically and much more invisible culturally, but they were ahead of Afro-Americans in other fields. Reflecting on her childhood in the 1950s, Amy

Three: Performing Towards Visibility

Ling says: "Being 'yellow' was perhaps not as bad as being 'brown' or 'black,' but, without a doubt, it was not as good as being 'white'" ("Whose America Is It" 28). "Being yellow" certainly sheltered Asian Americans from stereotypes which seriously impeded the lives of black people. Asian Americans did not have to grapple with the criminalization of their race. Quite the opposite. While Afro-Americans were portrayed as lazy good for nothings, Asian Americans were usually presented as paradigms of industriousness and efficiency. Hence they stood a greater chance of finding employment. Wittman is unsuccessful in his search for a job, but he cannot blame his successive failures squarely on his race. Part of the reason is that he is a playwright and his profession is not very marketable to begin with. Additionally, Asian American artists were discriminated in their search for a job, usually finding themselves employed only as props in films and theatre. His hardly conventional job aspirations are a detracting factor as well. He wants to be among others a fail-safe detonator and a reader of the tribe. At some point he flatly admits that he has no desire for employment. It is true that at the time when Wittman is staging his play — 1963 the model minority myth was not yet fully fledged. The action of *Tripmaster Monkey* unfolds before a spate of articles extolling the achievements of Asian Americans began to appear in the American press — before the publication of "Success Story, Japanese American Style," (*New York Times Magazine* Jan 9, 1966), "Success Story of One Minority in the United States" devoted to the purported success of Chinese Americans (*U.S. News and World Report*, Dec 26, 1966), "Success Story: Outwhiting Whites" dedicated to the success of Japanese Americans (*Newsweek* June 1971).[26] Yet certain elements of the discourse were already present at the time. Robert Lee traces the beginnings of the model minority discourse to the 1950s and the logic of the Cold War (145). The model minority myth went hand in hand with the rhetoric of assimilation and accommodation, which according to Lee was to assuage white fears of red scare, black-white miscegenation and homosexuality.[27] Wittman himself is not entirely blind to the discourse either. In his monologue at the end of his play he brings up stereotypes that are the flip side of the model minority myth. Beneath all these stories about the success of Asian Americans there still lurks the assumption that they do not achieve their success by fair means. Asian Americans are seen as cheats who "make a dollar out of fifty cents" (Kingston 332).[28] Race is treated like an essence and Asian Americans are believed to possess the qualities that predispose them to make profit. Hence they "are good at figures," but bad at the liberal arts (332).

Staging Chinese American Identity/Invisibility

Wittman's play is an attempt to counter the stereotypes of Chinese Americans. He hopes to "take people's gaze off" and become really seen (Rilke cited in Kingston, *Tripmaster Monkey* 305). Like all invisible men discussed here, Wittman uses his invisibility constructively. It becomes a springboard for action, lending a spark to his creativity. Like the Invisible Man, Wittman "makes music of his invisibility." However, Wittman's artistic venture is very much a collective enterprise. He draws other people together in the process of creation. All invisible men analyzed here strive not only for their own visibility, but also for the visibility of their people. Yet Wittman's fellow Chinese Americans actively participate in his artistic undertaking: "Players ... improvised a ritual that made the playwright's sketch up-to-date and relevant, and showed him what happens next." Wittman is proud of the fact that his play allows his actors to improvise and fully unfurl their creativity (277). They become visible not so much through Wittman's agency, but through their own acting. Objects which members of the community bring to the set represent individual and collective histories of invisibility. Now they help them in their striving for visibility. Invisibility becomes a tool bringing them closer to visibility:

> A backscratcher from a Singapore sling, a paper umbrella from an aloha mai tai, a Buddha bottle with a head that unscrews — *make something of it. Use it.* From these chicken scraps and dog scraps, *learn what a Chinese American is made up of* [277, emphasis added].

These bits and pieces make up the discourse on Chinese Americans. The juxtaposition of items that do not necessarily go well together highlights the contradictory and fragmentary nature of the discourse on Chinese Americans, who are denied the wholeness or completeness of representation, emerging through ill matched scraps that never add up to the full picture. The above quotation corresponds closely to the fragment of *Chickencoop Chinaman* by Frank Chin:

> Chinamen are *made*, not born, my dear. Out of junk-imports, lies, railroad scrap iron, dirty jokes, broken bottles, cigar smoke, Cosquilla Indian

blood, wino spit, and lots of milk of amnesia [*Chickencoop* in *Aiiieeeee* 52, emphasis added].

Both Chin and Kingston draw our attention to the construction and constructedness of Chinese American images. Chin is more explicit than Kingston in pinpointing the inconsistencies of the discourse. He speaks overtly about "lies" and "milk of amnesia." White amnesia helps whites to efface Chinese Americans from American history and glide over the contradictions of the discourse. They never see Chinese Americans in a sharp light, but always through the haze of their illusions. Chin uses a gendered term "chinamen," while Kingston refers to all Chinese Americans, irrespective of their gender. Unlike in Chin's text, in Kingston's text there is a strong commandment directed at Chinese Americans and at whites. To whites she says: "learn what a Chinese American is made up of." Discard your illusions and see Chinese Americans in sharp light. See also the nonsense of your own illusions. To Chinese Americans she says: "Make something of it. Use it" (277). Channel your invisibility constructively. The protagonist of Frank Chin's *Chickencoop Chinaman*— Tam Lum — is a failed artist. Invisibility stifles his artistic potential. Unlike Lum, Wittman transcends his invisibility and draws inspiration from it. Isabella Furth very aptly observes, saying that "he makes of his scaffold a stage" (63).

As I pointed out at the very outset, Wittman's play involves mimicry, a disruptive play on stereotypes.[29] He consciously incorporates some of those stereotypes into his play only to expose them, to show their absurdity. Unlike Freeman, Wittman uses mimicry to awaken the audience, not put it to sleep. In one of the scenes the audience watches a gambling match between a Chinaman and a Mexican. Rudyard Kipling is the witness of the event and a commentator for white tourists. Being a loser in the game, the Chinaman reaches for the Mexican's winnings and for a gun. The shot rends the air, yet ironically everyone stays alive but the Chinaman. Kingston knows better than leave the reader with Kipling's comment. She chimes in herself on the scene, saying tersely: "You would think that that Chinese guy had killed somebody instead of having gotten killed himself" (300). Playing upon the white stereotypes of Chinese Americans, Wittman hopes that the audience will see through the inconsistencies of their own inventions. In this way he wants to deconstruct the discourse from within. The scene overlaps nicely with his later comment: "All we do in movies is die. Our actors have careers of getting killed and playing dead bodies" (322). The recurring theme of death embodies a white desire to get rid of Chinese Americans, to leave them out of the picture and out of their lives. Once again it becomes visible how whites struggle to blot out Chinese Americans, to inscribe them as invisible. Employing mimicry in his play, Wittman makes the process of inscription visible, peeling away one layer after another. Wittman's mimicry is doubly disruptive if we take into account that Chinese Americans were stereotyped as masters of imitation.[30] Imitation is central to mimicry. Chinese Americans not only expose the stereotypes attributed to them, but also use the technique frequently ascribed to them as one more stereotype of their behavior. Still, the actors in Wittman's play do not make their meaning plain only through mimicry or indirectly. They speak out their grievances overtly as well, for example during the earlier mentioned episode when Chang shouts at the audience or during an attempted lynching scene.

Mimicry is only one of the devices employed in Wittman's play. Accentuating the Americanness of Chinese Americans, Wittman reaches for cross-cultural references, making syncretism and intertextuality integral parts of his art.[31] Embedded in Chinese American tradition and American popular culture, the play includes an opium war in the West, Shakespearean merry widows, Jade Snow Wong[32] christening a warship, Edith and Winnifred Eaton,[33] Lantern Festival in the City of Big Lights (Tai Ming Fue). A great portion of the action takes place in the landscape of the frontier, to which Chinese Americans belonged as well. An opium war episode unfolds in line with the convention of a western. Still, it involves not only John Wayne but also a Chinaman and a kung fu gang that jumps to his defense. Wittman reinserts Chinese Americans in the history of the old West, honoring their presence on the frontier. The scene that wins the biggest applause of the audience is a cancan dance performed by veteran Chinese American actresses who used to dance it during World War II. Each of them has a flag of an ally country on her pants. Before spinning their dance number, they sing "Dear Land of Home." All these references to various symbols of American culture are to make the audience aware that they are no less American than Americans of other ethnicities. They cherish their distinct cultural heritage, but at the same time they are also attached to American popular culture. Wittman hopes that the audience will begin to see a person of Chinese American descent as a yet another average American and the other way round. Similar motiva-

Three: Performing Towards Visibility

tion guides Wittman when he first thinks about creating fiction. He plans to seduce the reader into identifying with Chinese American characters by withholding the revelation of their ethnicity until the end of the novel (34). He aims at a parallel result in his play, but he no longer needs to introduce his characters as non-white, because they speak for themselves.

The Chinese American heritage is as much part of Wittman's play as is American popular culture. However, the parts of Chinese heritage that find their way into Wittman's play are not chosen at random but carefully selected. Wittman sifts through Chinese tradition, looking for stories that will make his people beautiful, heroic and adventurous. Very much in line with American trends, the whole play vibrates with the spirit of adventure. The story told Wittman by an elderly Chinese American immigrant is not included in the body of his play. Mrs. Chu tells him the story of Chinese women immigrants who hanged themselves in a deportation camp. After hearing the story, Wittman is disappointed because he hoped for a story that would cast Chinese Americans as heroic victors (234). If mimicry is a reenactment of stereotypes about Chinese Americans, the tales which he incorporates into his play are a clear and sharp reversal of those stereotypes.

Chinese heroic epic tradition is an essential component of his play. He brings up such classics of Chinese epic as *The Three Kingdoms*, *The Art of War*, *Journey to the West*. His intention is to sensitize the audience to the fact that his people also have a tradition of heroism. Throughout *Tripmaster Monkey* Wittman refers to the episode of *The Three Kingdoms* in which three friends forge a life-long alliance and take an oath of friendship in a peach orchard. At this point we can again notice close correspondence between Wittman and Frank Chin. Both look up to Chinese heroic tradition, putting emphasis on martial valor, male friendship and masculine code of honor. Engaging in the ethos of masculinity, they attempt to reverse the stereotype of Asian men as effeminate, cowardly, treacherous and passive. Both strongly revolt against Charlie Chan and Fu Manchu stereotypes. Despite bearing certain resemblance to Chin, Wittman is nonetheless Kingston's child. No wonder, then, that he does not transfer all Chinese myths straight from Chinese culture to American culture, but adapts them to the American reality. More than one publication has been devoted to the Kingston-Chin debate. While Chin stands guard over the authenticity of Chinese myths, Kingston transplants them onto American soil, adjusting them to her own experience and the experience of other Chinese Americans. Reflecting in *The Woman Warrior* on her own storytelling, the narrator admits that her stories may be "twisted into designs" (189). This ornamentation earned Kingston from Chin the name of a fake author.[34] That is the way Chin labels her in the introduction to *Big Aiiieeeee*, "Come All Ye Asian American Writers of the Real and the Fake," published in 1991 and in his earlier piece, "This Is Not Autobiography," published in 1985. Like Kingston, Wittman is to a greater extent aware that Chinese myths and tales are not immutable, but permeable and ever changing. Treating China and its history like a monolith, Chin himself falls into the trap of Orientalism. Wittman, on the other hand, is much more aware of the changing reality. Making first drafts of the play, he comes to the conclusion that it misrepresents both Chinese American and Chinese reality, because: "story boats and story houses where a professional can talk are as gone at Lake Anza and the Bay as they must be gone from China" (41). His art is to capture the Chinese American experience.

The tale of Empty Scrolls illustrates Wittman's desire to create a uniquely Chinese American identity and art. In the story patterned after *Journey to the West* (Chu 181) Tripitaka, Monkey, Piggy and Mr. Sandman travel to the West (India), where they receive scrolls from Indians (Hindus). Having discovered that the scrolls are empty, they demand an exchange. Yet it turns out that "the empty scrolls had been the right ones all along" (42), which means that they should not accept ready made texts but had to create their own. If we treat the story figuratively, the travelers could just as well be Chinese Americans. Rather than take cues from the outside world, they need to fill the empty scrolls with their own stories and their own experience. That is what Wittman is striving for in his play. No wonder, then, that it is not woven around a unified plot but unfolds through a series of vignettes. The Chinese American history in the United States is full of raptures. It is not a smooth onward progression. Just as in the case of the Invisible Man, it entails traveling back and forth rather than moving forward in a straight line (Ellison 385). Exclusion laws, expulsions, zoning ordinances, lynchings make for the fissures in Chinese American experience. The episodic structure of Wittman's play fully renders the tumultuous history of his people.

To what extent does he succeed in making his people visible? They certainly achieve greater visibility. However, they do not become fully visible. Although the audience likes the play and the reviews are positive, they still reflect stereotypes about Asian Americans. As Karen Shimakawa points out "Asian Americans never walk onto an empty stage" (17). It is already filled with stereotypes and the audience is unwilling to relinquish them:

> "East meets West." "Exotic." "Sino-American theatre." ... "Sweet and sour." They wrote us up like they were tasting Chinese food. "Savor beauteous Nanci" ... That's like saying that LeRoi Jones is as good as a watermelon. "Yum yum, authentic watermelon." ... they have ways to criticize theatre besides sweetness and sourness. They could do laundry reviews [Kingston, *Tripmaster Monkey* 307, 308].

These reviews are almost precisely the reviews which Maxine Hong Kingston received after the publication of *The Woman Warrior*: "East meets West," "The Twain did meet among the ghosts." "East and West collide inside a human mind" ("Cultural Misreadings" 60). Any reference to Chinese American heritage in the play suffices to earn Chinese Americans the label "exotic," and to place them in the East. Contrasting Asian American invisibility with Afro-American invisibility, Wittman says that no one would write a review "America meets Africa" for Lorraine Hansberry's *Raisin in the Sun*. Kingston contrasts her own reviews with the reviews of *Roots* by Alex Haley: "I did not read any reviews of *Roots* that judged whether or not Alex Haley's characters ate watermelon or had rhythm" ("Cultural Misreadings" 57). Some reviewers look at the play through the prism of Chinatown restaurants and laundries. At the end of *Chickencoop Chinaman* its protagonist Tam Lum comes to the conclusion that in order to find the acclaim of the mainstream, he would need to write a cookbook, because Chinese Americans are associated mainly with Chinese food. Wittman concludes that to be seen as ordinary Americans, they would need to make a soap opera rather than stage a play. He acknowledges that even then they might be found "exotic" or the audience might be disappointed to find out that they are not exotic (309). To a certain extent they find themselves in a no win situation. Kingston speaks about the "double-bind of stereotyping: "damned-if-you-do-and-damned-if-you-don't" ("Cultural Misreadings" 56). How can they counter stereotypes and stop being exotic if the mainstream insists on their being exotic and at the same time blames them for it? The audience brings to the theatre its preconceptions and these preconceptions inevitably exert an impact on how it receives the play. The spectators like the show, but they do not manage to uncover all the meanings of Wittman's disruptive play on stereotypes. Nor do they correctly interpret references to the Chinese heroic epic tradition. Does mimicry entail, then, the risk of ossifying stereotypes? All reviews of Wittman's play are very selective. They provide us with impressions of the whole play, not its particular fragments. Therefore we do not know how the audience interpreted the episodes involving mimicry. Another matter is that despite all its attributes, theatre as a medium also has its limitations. Unlike the written text, theatre gives much less space to explain what is going on. Ultimately the audience is left with the raw performance, while the reader of *Tripmaster Monkey* is assisted by the third person narrator.

The play not only makes Chinese Americans more visible to the outside world, but also brings them closer together, strengthening communal ties. Invisibility is also a uniting force. They stage a play because "they had a need to do something communal against isolation" (141). Launching the stage production, Wittman wants to revitalize his community, to rekindle the spirit of brotherhood: "Community is not built once and for all, people need to imagine, practice and recreate it" (306). In order to flourish, communities need to be nurtured. Entering the narrative structure of the play, all of Wittman's actors are involved in a communal identity performance. As James Dowd argues in "Aporias of the Self," "our selves are as much group projects as they are the constructions of individuals" (259). Celebrating individuality and on many occasions speaking unfavorably of the Chinese American community, Wittman still sees himself as a member of that community and wants to rectify it. The play gives its actors the feeling of safety, infusing them with a sense of belonging. Poring over the lines of the play, they linger well into the night, unwilling to leave the safe space of their communal ground: "The night was growing late, yet people who had to go to work graveyard or in the morning were taking up lines of a play that *the savage world beyond the black windows didn't know or care about*" (285, emphasis added). They derive much more than just a feeling of safety from their communal identity performance. There is only one step from acting to action. The play also gives them a sense of being active, of actively participating in shaping their identity. Being involved in the play, they create a counterbalance to "the savage world behind the black windows" and during the final performance they invite it inside, ready to disarm it with their art. Like Ellison, Kingston stresses the importance of action: "They came because what Boleslavsky said is true: 'Acting is the life of the human soul receiving its birth through art.' Everyone really does want *to get into the act*" (276, emphasis added). The Invisible Man says: "I believe in nothing if not in action" (11). Wittman argues that one should always plan for success, not for failure, never stooping to anything that would breach the rules of ethics (207).

Although Wittman's play features primarily Chinese Americans, it also includes people of other races and ethnicities. Being all-inclusive, it becomes a prototype for a hyper-panethnic community, going beyond the definition of panethnicity given by Yen Le Espiritu (2). Panethnic movements usually comprise people of the same race. These people may have different histories and different experiences of discrimination, but all of them belong to the same race. Pan is the Greek word for all (Espiritu 2). Including people of all races, Wittman extends the meaning of the word "pan," making his play truly all-inclusive. Wittman wants to redefine the mainstream, including everyone who is excluded in the hope of integrating Americans' public and private life: their jobs, education, transportation as well as their relationships. His project is in tune with his plan to "blacken and yellow characters." Lomans and Tyrons are no longer white, but of different colors. What happens in Wittman's play rarely takes place in real life. As in *The Spook*, people of non white racial groups are usually integrated as token figures, mere props in the show, not main actors. An all-inclusive racial make-up of his play is also in line with his principles: "Think Jew, dress Black, drive Okie," "Be more Japanese and French," "Do the right thing by whoever crosses your path. Those coincidental people are your people" (208, 209, 223). Idealistic as Wittman is, he has problems with living up to his principles. He may be all-inclusive in his play, but he is hardly all-inclusive in everyday reality.

The Pitfalls of Recentering

Staging the play, Wittman drags his people out of the wings and brings them to the centre, where they can speak out in the open. An epigraph from Rilke illustrates the act of staging and recentering: "they crept along the wings and spoke what they had to, only not to irritate you. But you drew them forward, and you posed them" (Rilke cited in *Tripmaster Monkey* 304). As I pointed out at the beginning, recentering carries its own dangers and Kingston, unlike her protagonist, is all too aware of them. Striving for his own visibility, Wittman renders other people invisible in the process. His own oppression blinds him to other kinds of oppression. Although he launches a scathing critique of whiteness, he is not exhaustive in his criticism. Wittman targets the centre and its ideology very selectively, attacking only racial discrimination and not even here is he fully comprehensive. He not only fails to identify certain patterns of discrimination, but at some points imitates the centre himself. Many of the universal dogmas find their way into Wittman's ideology. While the mimicry employed in his play is disruptive, his mimicry[35] of the centre is not. I would like to return now once again to the politics of location. In their essay on spatialized politics Neil Smith and Cindi Katz claim that the "core identity" cannot be left "intact" (78). Wittman disempowers whiteness only on some fronts, but on many others leaves it untouched.

It is at this point that we can see the closest correspondence between Wittman Ah Sing and Frank Chin. It is also at this point that we can notice the greatest distance between the third person narrator and Wittman. Kingston not only makes Chinese Americans visible, but also responds to the charges of Chinese American nationalists — primarily Frank Chin.[36] Like black nationalists, Asian American cultural nationalists espoused conventional identity politics, aiming at the recapturing of essential, authentic ethnic identity. Conventional identity politics, unlike transformational identity politics, assumes the preexistence of fixed identities (Bondi 86). Fighting against essentialist practices of white people, they themselves became embroiled in essentialism. Conventional identity politics precludes the possibility of building broader alliances among the oppressed. Difference in itself is not a prerequisite for the acceptance of other people's differences. Excessive accentuation of their own difference blinds proponents of identity politics to the similarities which they may share with people who are marginalized in a different way.

Emphasizing their masculinity, American nativity and heterosexuality, Asian American cultural nationalists effaced Asian American women, fresh immigrants, diaspora and homosexuals. Jeffery Paul Chan, Frank Chin, Lawson Fusao Inada and Shawn Hsu Wong put stress on masculinity, American nativity and heterosexuality in the first Asian American anthology *Aiiieeeee* published in 1974. It is understandable that they aimed at dismantling stereotypes about Asian Americans. Still, they did not limit themselves to dismantling them, but attacked authors who chose a different path. The editors of *Aiiieeeee* expected all Asian Americans to accept their vision of Asian America. Ironically, the tenets promoted by them were also the linchpin of whiteness. By incorporating so many of white dogmas, Chin compromises the value of his ideology as a "counter-discourse," to borrow the phrase from David Palumbo Liu (*The Ethnic Canon* 17). Stephen Sumida points out that struggling against centrism in American society and in the canon of American Literature went hand in hand with the creation of another centre around which Asian Americans were supposed to rally (805–806). Such practices undermined internal heterogeneity within Asian American studies of the period.

Both Wittman and Frank Chin accentuate their American birth. They draw a distinction between Chinese Americans and fresh immigrants. In *Aiiieeeee* Chin defines Asian Americans as "American born and raised" (VII). He distinguishes between "American by choice" and "American-born" (X), Asian Americans and "Americanized Asians" (XV). By making such distinctions, he treats ethnicity as something authentic, something to be born into rather than adopted and performed. Chin creates his model of Asian Americanness upon exclusion and othering, not inclusion. Like whites, he reserves the right to exclude "others." Chin does not take into account that all Americans were once fresh immigrants. His much celebrated Chinese American progenitors, constructors of the railroad were also fresh immigrants, excluded by white Americans, who often boasted their lineage of several generations. Emphasizing his American roots and cutting himself off from newly arrived immigrants, he wants to debunk the stereotype of Asian Americans as foreigners, permanent outsiders. This does not change the fact, however, that he mimics whites in their othering and discriminating practices. As a result fresh immigrants ended up being invisible in a double way: both to whites and to Asian Americans whose ancestors had settled in the United States a long time ago. Chin does not see himself as a discriminator. He tries to clarify his position on the issue by saying:

> I'm not shunning immigrants. I'm stating a fact that I am not Chinese. I am not shunning Albinos, elephants, dwarves, and midgets either. But call me one and I'll just have to set you straight [Chin cited in Shengmei Ma 29].

Saying that he does not shun immigrants, he still indirectly equates them with dwarves and midgets. Truly Asian American, Chinese American, he reigns supreme among all those "other" beings. In his hierarchy they clearly rank below.

Apparently unaware of his own mimicry of whiteness, Chin goes as far as to call "Americanized Chinese writers" for example Lin Yutang and C.Y. Lee "white supremacists" (X). According to him, they deserve the label, because in their works they live out the stereotype of "the good, loyal, obedient, passive, law-abiding" totally assimilated citizens who make it in the American society on white people's terms. Rebellious as he is, Chin proves very selective in his attack upon whiteness and its tenets. Rather than dismantle the structures of oppression, he in many instances replicates them. His hardly comprehensive critique of whiteness may stem from the fact that he treats it as a monolith, a homogenous bastion. To be fully successful in his analysis of whiteness, he would need to differentiate between its constituents. In the 1976 Afterword to *MELUS* Chin says, "[I] have no idea what whites think is beyond whiteness into the universal mode" (14). Universal as it pretends to be, whiteness rests upon other universals, to which Chin prefers to remain blind. Patriarchy, apotheosis of masculinity and heterosexuality are no less part of whiteness than racial oppression is. Chin critiques only those aspects of whiteness which immediately concern him, not noticing the rest.

Like Chin, Wittman believes that fresh immigrants undermine his Americanness, because whites are quick to extend the stereotype of a fresh immigrant to all Asian Americans across the board. Hence his hostility towards fresh immigrants. For him they are aliens: "they think they can come over here and take advantage of us Americans.... Good thing we don't have any more people to come from China" (267). Wittman utters these words in 1963, when the gates were just about to open for more people to come from Asia.[37] Himself treated as an alien by the mainstream society, he cannot sympathize with people who are even more alienated than he is. Wittman is afraid of being engulfed by the sea of aliens who pose a danger to his Americanness. Already treated very much like an alien, he may entirely lose his mark of distinction. His five generations of American descent may dissolve completely. In one of the scenes Wittman and the family disparagingly referred to as "f.o.b."—Fresh Off the Boat—pass each other in a tunnel: "[they] tried to pass each other both on the same side, then both on the other, sidestepping like a couple of basketball stars. Wittman stopped dead in his tracks, and shot the dude a direct stink-eye.

Three: Performing Towards Visibility

The F.O.B. stepped aside" (5). They walk in each other's direction, yet they almost collide in their tracks rather than meet in their ways. Working hard to pass each other, both seem to be aware that they belong to two different worlds. Wittman assumes an air of superiority, waiting for the immigrant to make way for him. Conscious of Wittman's hostility and his subservient status, the "f.o.b." steps aside, making room for the fifth-generation American. Neither speaks to the other, but we have access to Wittman's thoughts. He formulates a very negative view of what he perceives almost as fresh immigrants' essential difference: their noticeably different clothes, behavior and smell (5). At the same time Wittman realizes that his parents have a different attitude to immigrants, pretending to recognize in them their relatives from China. Just as Wittman is intent on underscoring his Americanness, they are unwilling to let anyone know that "they lost their Chinese" (193).

A clash of nationalisms takes place during Wittman's conversation with a newly arrived kung fu fighter, whom he includes in his play. Wrapped up in his nationalistic fervor, Wittman makes no effort to understand the mentality of a fresh immigrant. He tries to Americanize the kung fu fighter, urging him to forget the Chinese Revolution and Chinese history. According to Wittman the Kung Fu fighter is going to remain a fresh immigrant if he does not swap Chinese Revolution for Independence Day (282). Wittman himself time and again alludes to his Chinese roots, for example when he shows his wife Tana a Chinese memory village and a scroll with names of his ancestors. The kung fu fighter is invisible to Wittman. It does not occur to him that a fresh immigrant may be more attached to his old land than to the new one. There was a contradiction in cultural nationalists' attitude to immigrants. On the one hand, they identified with third world countries and its oppressed people like the Vietnamese. On the other hand, they set themselves apart from refugees of those countries. Although various panethnic organizations welcomed fresh immigrants to their movement, they forced them to accept their vision of Asian America, hardly ever giving newcomers an equal say in the debate on their policies (Espiritu 16).[38]

The nationalist accentuation of nativity has since drawn much criticism. While in the 1970s Asian American studies focused on American birth and rootedness, from the 1990s the trend has shifted and Asian American studies are no longer circumscribed by the borders of the United States. It is essential to point out that scholars of both periods find themselves confronted with diametrically different historical circumstances. At the time when the action of *Tripmaster Monkey* unfolds Asian Americans born outside the United States were still a minority. The 1965 changes in the immigration law[39] triggered an influx of immigrants from Asia. Currently Asian Americans born outside the United Sates are no longer in the minority but in the majority. Scholars like Shirley Geok-lin Lim, Arif Dirlik, Cynthia Sau-ling Wong, Lisa Lowe, David Eng have contributed to the recovery of diaspora. Trying to dispel the myth of a sojourner, Frank Chin said "We came here to settle" (Afterword to *MELUS*, 17). David Eng, on the other hand, wonders whether the discourse of settlement really captures the situation of Asian Americans. Considering their tumultuous history, their literal and figurative exclusion, persecution and exile, it might really be questionable whether the discourse of settlement with all its usual connotations really applies in this case. Their hard work and aspiration to settle did not make them settlers on even par with other ethnic groups in the United States. Eng underscores the importance of external locations in the formation of Asian American subjectivity. He asks "Where is Asian America? Can Asian America finally be located?" (204). We could answer this question with a quote from Arif Dirlik:

> Asian America is no longer just a location in the United States, but is at the same time a location on a metaphorical rim constituted by diasporas and motions of individuals. To understand Asian Americans it is no longer sufficient to comprehend their roots in U.S. history or, for that matter, in countries of origin, but a multiplicity of historical trajectories that converge in the locations we call Asian America, but may diverge again once again to disrupt the very idea of Asian Americanness [13].

The multiplicity of geographical locations goes hand in hand with the multiplicity of other locations, accounting for greater heterogeneity within Asian American studies. Frank Chin's model of authentic Asian American identity was displaced by multiply located identities. This celebration of multiple locations cannot, however, draw Asian Americans away from issues which still need to be settled within the political and geographical landscape of the United States. Cherishing heterogeneity, Asian Americans face common challenges, which they can confront only by joining forces.

Wittman's relation to his Chinese American ethnicity is problematic. Neither Wittman nor Chin seems to be aware to what extent they perform their ethnic identity. We could juxtapose Chin's definition of authentic identity with Judith Butler's definition of performative identity. According to Butler, identity is "a stylized repetition of acts," a "performative accomplishment which the mundane social audience, including the actors themselves, come to believe and to perform in the mode of belief" (*Gender Trouble* 141). Unlike proponents of conventional identity politics, Butler maintains that "there is no preexisting identity by which an act or attribute might be measured" (141). Butler's findings parallel James Dowd's observations. In "Theatrical Self: Aporias of the Self" Dowd argues that "a self resembles a wardrobe: we pick up bits and pieces of identity along the way and, as long as these elements fit and are suitably stylish, we will wear them for the time being" (246). Dowd's metaphor is a good illustration of Wittman's self-stylization. Against the advice of his ancestors Wittman wears green to highlight the yellow color of his skin, to make it visible. However, before he begins to perform his yellow skin by wearing green, he first needs to discover his "racial skin" (44). It does not happen until someone tells him that Chinese Americans look yellow in green clothes. Communal identity performance which happens in Wittman's play mirrors his own identity performance, which is full of contradictions.

Wearing green to play up his ethnicity, he still does not want to be prescribed or confined to it by other people. Therefore he will not go to the prom with the only Chinese American girl in the class and will not sit beside the only Chinese American woman in the audience. Wittman finds himself in a narrow bind, because for most people the Chinese American heritage is at odds with the idea of Americanness. On the one hand, he cherishes his heritage. On the other hand, he bends over backwards to underline his Americanness. Therefore he is very upset with himself after saying: "We came from the Tropic of Cancer." It seems to him that the statement goes against his promise of identifying as born in the United States. He is also very inconsistent in his attitude to other Chinese Americans. They are to a great extent invisible to him. Embracing popular culture and some mainstream trends, Wittman is still ready to jump on anyone who appears to be a little more assimilated than he is. He calls Nanci "banana," because she comes from a rich Chinese American family that is out of touch with Chinatown. He himself has a love-hate relationship with Chinatown. It embodies for him the ghettoization of the society. Still, he is critical of Chinese Americans who have drifted away from Chinatown completely.

Yet another contradiction in Wittman's ideology lies in his accentuation of heroic epic and warlike tradition. Like other members of the 1960s Asian American movement, he is a staunch pacifist and a draft dodger. Yet on many occasions he fashions himself in the image of a warrior: a samurai or sayonara soldier" (12). Frequent references to the heroic epic tradition go against his pacifism. Does Wittman Ah Sing really sing the tale of peace or war? As mentioned earlier, by stressing the war heroism of Chinese legendary characters, he wants to debunk the stereotype of Chinese Americans as passive, cowardly and feminine. Hence he says in his monologue: "To say 'I' was to say 'I fight.'" In Wittman's view all Chinese Americans are warriors and descendants of Gwan the Warrior (319).[40] In this way he tries to encourage other Chinese Americans to be more proactive in asserting their rights. They should not let whites deprive them of their subjectivity and of their fighting spirit. The above cited sentence strikes a chord of Frank Chin's statement:

> In Confucianism, all of us — men and women — are born soldiers. The soldier is the universal individual. No matter what you do for a living — doctor, lawyer, fisherman, thief— you are a fighter. Life is war. The war is to maintain personal integrity in a world that demands betrayal and corruption ["Come You All" 6].

Although fighting is used here figuratively, the war in Chin's and Wittman's heroic stories is real. Reaching for war and violence, they try to dismantle the master's house by using the master's tools" (Lorde cited in Moy, "Asian American Visibility" 191). King-Kok Cheung characterizes the position of Chin and his camp by saying that they "risk remaking themselves in the image of their oppressors" ("The Woman Warrior vs. Chinaman Pacific" 244).

The third person narrator[41] notes that Wittman's employment of the heroic tactics in his play may detract from the horror of a real war (306). Kingston herself searches for a more dramatic language of peace, not war: "I'm trying to find the peace language ... I'm trying to find a way to show acts of peace that are as dramatic as acts of war" (*Conversations with M.H. Kingston*, ed. Skenazy 222). She reflects on her own writing *The Woman Warrior*, wondering whether she could not have used different strategies in the book. In particular, Kingston mentions the scene, in which she stands up to a racist employer: "it took no more than a paragraph to write that. Can the same scene be done more dramatically? So that when a reader reads it, it stands out more than the story of getting on the horse and riding into battle?" (*Conversations* 222).[42] Just as Frank Chin reaches for the metaphor of fighting to depict Chinese Americans' struggle and the struggle of other human beings, the narrator of *The Woman Warrior* sees herself figuratively as a fighter, for example when she says: "the swordswoman drives me" (56). She brims over with fighting spirit, the spirit which tells her to confront and transcend the barriers erected by the racist society. She alludes to women warriors once again in *Tripmaster Monkey*: Nanci and Tana, who gain a sense of liberation out of their impersonation of women warriors (148). Kingston is aware that liberation through fake or real war is only illusory. The roles of women warriors may give women a sense of liberation, but will not give them real power. Still, she acknowledges that stories of women warriors can be liberating for women, just as they were for her when she was a girl and when she was writing *The Woman Warrior*.

Both Wittman and Chin use war and violence to reclaim their battered manhood. While trying to claim back their masculinity, they fall into the trap of sexism. Rather than let women see reality through their own eyes, they would like them to accept it on their terms. Attacking Chinese American women writers whenever their version of reality does not accord with his, Chin encroaches upon their freedom of artistic expression. In the Introduction to *Aiiieeeee*, Chin writes of Chinese American women's writing and in particular of Jade Snow Wong's writing:

> The mere fact that four out of five American-born Chinese-American writers are women reinforces this aspect of the stereotype.... Wong by writing about herself in the third person, further reinforces the stereotypical unmanly nature of Chinese Americans [xxx, xxxi].

Does he expect women to be manly in their writing or does he want to silence them completely? He lashes out at Kingston for tampering with Chinese myths. Kingston answers his attacks by saying that she sees no reason why she should embrace stories which advocate submission of women and the patriarchal: "it's absolutely clear to me that we have the freedom to create alternate myths, and for Frank Chin, as a male, there is a monolith, one monument of a myth" (*Conversations* 203). Liberating as the original Chinese myths are to him, they are hardly liberating to women. Chin himself is critical of the Chinatown patriarchal, but only when it is oppressive to Chinese American men. And then, he sees Louis Chu's *Eat a Bowl of Tea* as a fine example of Chinese American sensibility. However, when Kingston makes her complaints in *The Woman Warrior*, he dismisses the book as white writing that perpetuates stereotypes about Chinese Americans and contributes to an unflattering portrayal of the community. Chin sympathizes with the protagonist of *Eat a Bowl of Tea*—Ben Loy, who feels stifled by his father's domination and his expectations that he will follow the path of tradition. The demands of the community temporarily frustrate Loy's manhood. In his own writing Chin creates male characters that battle their own heritage and usually have a problematic relationship with their fathers. The father of Fred—the protagonist of *The Year of the Dragon*—is an oppressive figure and he scoffs at his son's artistic aspirations. Dissatisfied with his own father, the main character of *The Chickencoop Chinaman* Tam Lum searches for a spiritual father. In the Introduction to *Aiiieeeee*, "Fifty Years of Our Whole Voice," and in other works, Chin devotes ample space to stereotypes about Chinese American men, but he is silent on the stereotyping of Asian American women. Published in 1974, *Aiiieeeee* was supposed to represent all Asian Americans. Yet it was edited by four men who did not examine how things looked for women. Without any mentioning of stereotypes pertaining to women, "Fifty Years of Our Whole Voice" is hardly whole. The earlier mentioned fragment is a lamentation over the fact that so few Chinese American men were published. Emphasizing to such an extent male experience, *Aiiieeeee* was to provide a counterbalance to the literature by Asian American women.

Like Chin, Wittman speaks exclusively about the stereotypical portrayal of Chinese American men, never mentioning the female side of the equation. The third person narrator and women characters in the novel need to do the job for him. Aunt Dolly and Aunt Bessie reproach Wittman with his partial vision, observing that Chinese American men complain about the denigration of their masculinity, but they spare no sarcasm to Chinese American women, for example by telling sexist jokes (317). *Tripmaster Monkey* is full of sexist comments. Wittman slots most Chinese American women into one category: overworked and haggard (73). He repeatedly becomes trapped in sexist stereotypes. His view of marriage is quite conventional as well, at least at the beginning. Even though he is on welfare and his wife works, he portrays himself as the provider for the family (331). Despite his sexist remarks, Wittman does not seem to be entrenched in his views. After half a year with mildewed coffee cups all over the place, he gets a hint that his wife wants him to participate in household chores. Afraid of becoming emasculated, he fears domesticity. Therefore he resists it for quite a while. In the end, however, he begins to see marriage as a partnership and tells his wife that no one in their relationship needs to take the role of a wife.

Wittman achieves greater visibility for himself and his people, but it comes at a price. His own invisibility eclipses for him the invisibility of other marginalized people. If we assume that the goal of the invisible is not only to become visible, but also expose structures of oppression which made them invisible, then Wittman is not fully successful. As Judith Butler points out in *Contingency and Hegemony*, "The task will be not to assimilate the unspeakable into the domain of speakability to house it there, within the existing norms of dominance, but to shatter the confidence of dominance" (179). Venturing upon the critique of whiteness, Wittman makes it only half-transparent, partly replicating structures of oppression himself.

I began this chapter by relating *Tripmaster Monkey* and Asian American cultural nationalism to *The Spook Who Sat by the Door* and black nationalism. Before I wrap up, I would like to briefly compare both movements. Cultural distinction is central to both camps. However, while Asian American nationalists in the 1970s emphasized their American nativity, most Afro-American nationalists stressed their strong connection to Africa, frequently espousing separatism. Asian American cultural nationalists celebrated their distinct cultural heritage, but at the same time aimed at reclaiming their Americanness, whereas Afro-American nationalists usually shuddered from any form of integration. African Americans do not have to struggle against the stereotype of an alien in the same way that Asian Americans do. Hence the different approach of the two movements towards American nativity. An ideological discrepancy between both movements becomes conspicuous in Stokely Carmichael's statement:

> If you are in San Francisco, for example, and you see a Japanese or a Chinese ... you do not say that there goes an American Japanese or a Japanese American. You say simply that there goes a Japanese ... Yet, probably, that Japanese cannot speak Japanese at all: he may be third or fourth generation in America. ... One of the most important things we must now begin to do, is to call ourselves "African." No matter where we may be from, we are first of all and finally Africans ["Pan-Africanism — Land and Power" in Van Deburg 204].

Carmichael sounds envious of the fact that Asian Americans are not seen as Americans but as Asians by the rest of society. Such an attitude is quite ironic if we take into account that Wittman Ah Sing envies African Americans precisely the opposite.

African American nationalists did not want to be co-opted into the existing system. Their goal was to change it. Still, they did not fully undermine structures of oppression either. Like Asian American nationalists, they partly mimicked their own oppressors. Both African American and Asian American nationalists often targeted the oppressed groups: immigrants, women, homosexuals. They displayed hostility towards immigrants for different reasons. As I pointed out earlier, some Asian American nationalists believed that the presence of fresh immigrants helped to perpetuate the stereotype of an Asian American as an alien. African American nationalists, on the other hand, assumed that immigrants endangered their economic interests.

Unlike Wittman, Kingston in *Tripmaster Monkey* does not focus exclusively on her own oppression, but sheds light on multiple oppressions. Through the third person narrator she exposes the loopholes within the ideology of cultural nationalism and highlights the fractures within the Chinese American community. Contrasting Asian American invisibility with Afro-American invisibility, she goes beyond the white versus other binary, complicating interracial relations in the United States. As I emphasized at the very beginning, Kingston achieves much more than the visibility of her people. By dissecting various levels of performance, she poses a challenge to proponents of conventional identity politics, underlining the performativity of racial and ethnic identities. Wittman may not be endowed with fully fledged second sight, but he is younger than any of the protagonists discussed in this study. His search for self-consciousness has not yet reached a climactic point. In late 2003 Kingston published a sequel to *Tripmaster Monkey* entitled *The Fifth Book of Peace*, in which Wittman moves beyond the confines of conventional identity politics. He "has to break open Chinese American consciousness that he built with such difficulty" (Kingston, "The Novel's Next Step" 40). That is precisely what Kingston does in *Tripmaster Monkey*. She "breaks open" the Chinese American consciousness, making it visible and locating it on the broader map of oppression.

Four

MULTICULTURAL INVISIBILITIES
Chang-rae Lee's *Native Speaker*

"Revelations are not to be found in the far bend of the river, darkly hidden in the trees. There are no ready savages there, and never were. We make angels and devils of our own want and regard" (Chang-rae Lee, *Native Speaker*, 295).

Among the authors discussed here Chang-rae Lee offers the most intricate and comprehensive picture of racial relations in the United States. Emphasizing the relationality of racial categories, he explores not only the invisibility of marginalized people to the white mainstream, but also the invisibility of various minorities to one another. *Native Speaker* shows how all these groups interact with each other and how whiteness comes into the picture, impinging on those interactions. Just as in any other text scrutinized in this study, whiteness is stripped of its mystique. It has very clear features. However, it is no longer whiteness in relation to a particular ethnic or racial group, but whiteness in relation to various marginalized ethnicities. Making whiteness visible, Lee doe not focus exclusively on white oppression, but like Kingston, brings into light multiple oppressions. In many instances the oppressed are no less oppressive than those who exploit them. Chang-rae Lee exposes exploitation within and between various marginalized communities. Yet he makes it clear that ultimately the white mainstream is responsible for the invisibility of non-mainstream groups to one another.

Unlike other characters analyzed here, the first-person narrator of *Native Speaker*— Henry Park — moves beyond conventional identity politics. Rather than represent just his own community — Korean Americans — he tries to undermine the invisibility of all American immigrants irrespective of their race and ethnicity. In his autobiography he speaks for all of them. The last scene of the novel illustrates very well the venture upon which he embarks in the text. In the final episode, his wife — a speech therapist — teaches a class of multiracial and multiethnic students. Most of them have linguistic problems because they are new to the country. At the very end of each class she utters each student's name, "calling all the difficult names of who we are" (349). That is precisely what Henry does throughout his autobiography. He also speaks "all the difficult names" of people whom he takes upon himself to represent in his narrative. Individual histories of those people and the histories of their mutual relations make those names difficult. Instead of engaging in the wholesale celebration of cultural difference, Henry underscores unequal power dynamics between various ethnic groups. He rejects the assumptions of liberal multiculturalists, who surmise that all diverse people of the United States are equal and have equal opportunities, gliding over differences in the socio-historical experience of American minorities (McLaren 51). Liberal multiculturalists usually reduce differences between people to cultural distinctions. The accentuation of cultural difference helps them to mask discrepancies in the social, economic and political status of various groups. Espousing critical multiculturalism, Henry underlines uneven distribution of power in American society. The process of articulation is not easy for Lelia's students. Nor is it easy for Henry as an autobiographer.

Unlike some earlier Asian American autobiographers,[1] Henry does not present the United States as an ideal of democracy extending the promise of freedom and equality to all those who desire it. He is not one of those autobiographers who bask in the glory of their success, singing eulogies to the American dream. Instead he takes under the magnifying glass the system that favors the lucky few and leaves scores of others on the sidelines. His autobiography shows how immigrants can climb to the top, at what price and on whose terms. Henry's friend Jack says:

> We are just good immigrant boys, so maybe we don't care. What you and I want is a little bit of the good life. If we work hard and do not question the rules too much, we can get a piece of what they have [288].

Minorities and especially immigrants can go only so far in the American society. Some of them may lead luxurious lives, but they have no real power. Those who succeed usually do it on white people's terms. The motto lighting the path of each immigrant reads: stay in your place and

Four: Multicultural Invisibilities

do not stick your neck out too much. Then maybe you will savor a "little bit of the good life." Success is defined in strictly materialistic terms.

Success usually also amounts to the mimicry of the mainstream. White people set the standard which others are supposed to emulate. Multiculturalists may celebrate cultural differences of diverse ethnic groups, but the difference which in any substantial way diverges from the white norm is barely tolerated:

> this country has difference that ails rather than strengthens and enriches. You can see what can happen from this, how the public may begin viewing anything outside mainstream experience and culture too threatening and dangerous [274].

The action of *Native Speaker* unfolds in 1991, some sixty years after the Invisible Man says: "Whence all this passion toward conformity...? Diversity is the word" (435). What happens to diversity in a seemingly multicultural state? The American commitment to diversity is only nominal. It may flourish in the sphere of culture. Yet it no longer withholds the confrontation when real power is at stake. The above cited passage from *Native Speaker* is a critique of corporate multiculturalism, which denounces all forms of difference, including cultural difference. Each non-white section of society should adapt a white Anglo-American view and perceive Anglo-American culture as a benchmark (McLaren 49).

The career of an aspiring Korean American politician — councilman John Kwang — illustrates what happens to difference when it aspires to real power. Running for the office of New York mayor, Kwang attempts to build a broad multiethnic and multiracial coalition. Volunteers working for him include among others Hispanic Americans, Vietnamese Americans, Indian Americans, Jewish Americans and African Americans. The establishment sees to it that his aspirations go up in smoke. Reflecting on the whole affair, Henry wonders how his Korean American mother would comment on Kwang's ambitions:

> What did he want from this country? Didn't he know that he could only get so far with his face so different and broad? He should have had ambition for only his little family. In turn, she'd proudly hold up my father as the best example of our people: how he was able to discard his excellent Korean education and training, which were once his greatest pride [333].

Minorities and particularly immigrants — newcomers — should keep their expectations low. Even if they are an embodiment of white people's success and speak "Puritan English," as John Kwang does, they should not venture out of their place, but limit their aspirations to the narrow circle of their family and focus on forwarding their private lives, leaving the public sphere to those who know better. Financial success should be the acme of their aspirations. John Kwang's fate is the fate of many other Asian Americans who try their hand at American politics. Any time they become involved in the United States politics, there is an instant suspicion of foreign capital.[2] Although the events described in *Native Speaker* take place thirty years after those depicted in *Tripmaster Monkey*, Asian Americans are still seen in many situations as aliens. An air of foreignness keeps hovering over them.

Whenever someone from the marginalized group tries to inch closer to the foreground, people from the mainstream do their best to clip their wings. They often use other immigrants to keep those insubordinate in their place: "when someone like Kwang attempts anything larger, there's instant suspicion. Someone must step up and pay to send in us hyenas. We'll sniff him out. We eat our own, you know" (288). According to Henry, immigrants are drawn into the system of oppression, being not only its victims, but also perpetrators. They usually make it in the American society by observing the rules and by exploiting on behalf of those who exploit them.

Lee gives examples of exploitation within Korean American community and mutual exploitation of immigrants from different other marginalized ethnic groups. He does not present the United States as a promised land but as an "orphanage": "It's an orphanage and there is a fagin" (292). The Fagin individual fuels the tensions between various ethnic groups, pitting them against one another. Guarding their own interests, they hardly ever coexist in harmony. Their interests frequently clash. Henry concludes: "It's the uneasy coalition of our colors" (260). Usually it is not a matter of accident that these groups find themselves in close proximity to each other. They are posed in their particular locations by the invisible cartographer. The presence or absence on the map depends on who is the cartographer. Neil Smith and Cindi Katz speak about an "absent" cartographer (70). The cartographer may be absent from the map, but he draws it, posing people in particular locations. Similarly, whites are absent from the neighborhoods inhabited by minorities. They are also invisible in the conflicts that flash between various marginalized groups. Yet they are the ones who keep all these groups incarcerated in their particular locations, preventing them from living or doing business in other areas.

"Uneasy Coalition of Our Colors" and the Black-Korean American Conflict

Discussing interracial and interethnic relations, Chang-rae Lee devotes most place in the novel to the conflict between Korean Americans and African Americans. A myriad of factors is at stake in the dispute between both groups: the socio-political situation, identity politics, cultural differences, misinformation. All these issues are vital for the full understanding of the conflict. Ultimately, however, whites are responsible for fomenting the tensions. Kwang reflects on the instigating role of whiteness and on different positionings of Korean Americans and African Americans by saying: "It's a race war everyone can live with. Blacks and Koreans somehow seem meant for trouble in America. It was long coming. In some ways we never had a chance" (181). As long as African Americans and Korean Americans battle it out among each other away from the white turf, "it's a race war anyone can live with."

Korean Americans and African Americans come into immediate contact with each other mostly during customer-merchant relations in black neighborhoods, since a large portion of Korean American grocery stores is located in black districts. Korean Americans began to enter those districts as traders in the 1970s and took over after Jewish merchants who were moving out at the time. It is not without significance that at a certain point of *Native Speaker* one of the white merchants calls Korean American storeowners "Oriental Jews" (53). Korean Americans indeed came to play a similar role in minority districts as Jews used to play — namely the role of a "middleman minority." I borrow the term "the middleman minority" from Pyong Gap Min and Andrew Kolodny. According to Min and Kolodny, the middleman minority has the following characteristics:

(1) a concentration in small business
(2) a focus on providing services to minority customers
(3) a dependence on U.S. corporations for supply of merchandise
(4) a strong ethnic cohesion
(5) a subjection to stereotyping (Min and Kolodny 132)[3]

Invisibility in African American and Asian American Literature

Middleman minorities are usually hated by both sides of the racial spectrum of a given society. The middleman merchant is an intermediary passing on corporate products to minorities. Korean Americans opened their businesses in minority neighborhoods because of low-rent and because they would not have survived competition in white neighborhoods. Whites found minority neighborhoods unattractive because they feared violence and the prospect of robbery. Most Korean American merchants opened their stores in black districts in the 1980s, at a time when the state was withdrawing capital from those areas, leaving them impoverished.

The Reagan policy of the 1980s led to further degradation and impoverishment of those already underprivileged areas. Trying to deprive minorities of the gains won during the civil rights era, Reagan proclaimed the United States a color-blind country, where everyone supposedly had equal opportunities (Omi and Winant, *Racial Formation* 2). He declared a virtual war on affirmative action. In the color blind state there was no need for affirmative action. The withdrawal of capital from inner-city areas consisted of:

- migration of business to the margins of the city
- cutting back of the funds for various community organizations
- the cessation of federal programs extended to impoverished areas (Park 63).

Korean Americans and African Americans find themselves in a state of mutual dependence. Watching his father argue with a female black customer, Henry compares their relationship to an unfortunate cohabitation doomed to continue because Korean Americans cannot open their stores elsewhere due to high renting costs, while African Americans have no other stores in the area, where they could purchase equally fresh produce (186). Now these are Korean Americans doing business with Afro-Americans and Latinos. Before these were Jewish Americans trading with African Americans. When one minority integrates into the mainstream society, another takes over, representing whites in the districts which they shun. Most children of Korean American immigrants do not follow in their parents' footsteps but enter different professions. Henry's father sends Henry to college and gives him a white middle-class education. The question arises which group will take over after Korean Americans.

Different historical, social and economic experience of both groups

Four: Multicultural Invisibilities

contributes to the tensions in their relations. Korean American immigrants who came to the United States after the 1965 changes in American immigration policy were mostly highly educated white-collar workers (Kwang Chung Kim and Shin Kim 28). The language barrier and discrimination made it impossible for them to find white-collar employment. They were able to open small businesses because of the support of their own communities and thanks to the Korean American financial system called "kye."[4] Because of their relative cultural homogeneity, Korean Americans are a much more cohesive group than Afro-Americans (Min 143). Henry's father seems to be unaware of the impediments that Afro-Americans grapple with. John Kwang, on the other hand, has a much better understanding of their position. In one of his speeches he tries to familiarize Korean Americans with the complicated situation of African Americans living in inner-city areas. Special emphasis in his speech falls on the fact that African Americans are at a disadvantage while applying for loans and unlike Korean Americans, they cannot boast an equally supportive, well-organized community because it has been ruptured by all the struggles which they had to endure (153).

As I demonstrated in Chapter Two, African Americans in inner city ghettos are cut off from the resources of the American economy. Events unfolding in *Native Speaker* take place thirty years after those described in *The Spook Who Sat by the Door*. Still, the situation of black Americans inhabiting urban ghettos has not changed diametrically. Nancy Denton and Douglass Massey report that the level of segregation in the United States remains at approximately the same level (225). In New York — the setting of *Native Speaker*— segregation in 1970 was 81 percent, in 1980 82 percent, while in 1990 82.2 percent (225). In the above cited passage Kwang tries to acquaint Korean Americans with the adversities haunting African Americans. A great number of Korean American immigrants are unaware of the scope of persecution and discrimination that Afro-Americans suffered and still suffer in the United States.

Insufficient information is one of the causes behind the antagonism between Korean Americans and African Americans. Both groups believe that one feels superior to the other. Edward T. Chang argues that Korean American perception of the American reality and racial situation in the United States is incomplete. Since they spend most of the day at work, they have a partial vision of the American world ("Jewish and Korean Merchants" 12). Nor do they have sufficient understanding of the civil rights campaign. Most of them do not seem to realize that it paved the way for their immigration to the United States.[5] Henry's father is no more knowledgeable on the issue. Engrossed in his arduous life of an immigrant, he displays no sympathy for black people marching in the streets at the time. Civil rights demonstrations provoke his greatest hostility. According to him, only hard work can bring about concrete changes. Walking with banners will not change anything. It will not relieve him from IRS officials, venal city inspectors and street criminals (196). His hostility towards African Americans is, to a great extent, fuelled by a near death encounter with black robbers who broke into his store. Unlike many white people, Henry's father does not assume a holistic approach towards all black people. He does not mind hiring black Haitians or Puerto Ricans who are also new to the country. His assumption is that since they are newcomers, they will not try to cheat him and will work harder, because their situation is much more uncertain than that of long-time citizens. Korean Americans often harbor stereotypes of African Americans already before coming to the United States (Abelman 149). Most of those stereotypes come from the American media.[6]

Korean American storeowners and Afro-American customers may have haggled with each other already at the time of the civil rights debate, but as I emphasized in Chapter Three, Asian American activists were part of the civil rights movement.[7] Black Power was an inspiration for them. While Henry's father looks down on civil rights demonstrators, John Kwang watches from the sidewalk in amazement and in the end joins the demonstration. As a young man, a fresh immigrant into the United States, he sees black people marching in the streets as a true embodiment of power. Their exhilaration and positive energy inevitably spread to him (195). Enchanted as Kwang is with the fervor of Black Power, he does not fully identify with black demonstrators' ideals. His tentative approach is hardly surprising if we take into account that Afro-Americans and Asian Americans were exposed to different forms of discrimination. Unlike African Americans, Korean Americans were not subjected to segregation in the South. Reminiscing further on Black Power demonstrations, John Kwang remembers his visit to the Southern United States, where, unlike African Americans, he did not need to use separate public facilities (195). The fact that Asian Americans were free of segregation in public places does not

Four: Multicultural Invisibilities

mean that segregation did not and does not affect them at all. Although Henry's father moves into an upper class neighborhood, he would not be able to live anywhere he chose, for example in one of the estates of the Sound. His presence would be unpalatable to rich people of the area, among them film stars, financiers, and "rich old Italians" (346). Still, most Korean American storeowners do not live in the neighborhoods in which they trade. Therefore black people accuse them of draining their communities and taking their resources somewhere else.

African Americans envy Korean Americans their purported financial success, whereas Korean Americans begrudge the place that Afro-Americans hold in the racial debate of the country. There is hardly any place for Asian Americans in politics — either as elected officials or as major players within political parties. As mentioned earlier, the stigma of alienness keeps haunting Asian Americans, at least in certain walks of life. They are still not perceived American enough to be entrusted with the affairs of the country.[8] Although the events of the novel unfold in the 1990s, Asian Americans still feel left out of the picture:

> It is still black and white world.... The landscape is changing. Soon there will be more brown and yellow than black and white. And yet the politics, especially the minority politics, remain cast in terms that barely acknowledge us. It's an old syntax [Lee 196].

Asian American exclusion from racial politics of the country is seen during every election campaign. In 2000 during the Gore-Bradley debate over racial problems there were only black people in the audience. In 2004 Asian Americans were never mentioned either.[9] No politician seems to jockey for their votes. Still, the political syntax is not exactly black and white. While politicians do not canvass Asian American votes, they do try to attract Hispanic voters. Both Al Gore and George Bush tried to appeal to Latinos in 2000. As suggested in Chapter Three, during the presidential campaign in 2004, George Bush proposed legislation that would turn "illegal aliens" into "legal aliens." The move was designed to entice the growing Mexican American population. There are no overt attempts to win Asian American voters.[10] Certain politicians assume that they are already fully integrated into American society. Influenced to a degree by white rhetoric, some African Americans are prone to such reasoning as well.

Black people are not happy about the presence of Korean Americans in their neighborhoods, because they believe that they sap their economic resources. Many of them would like to see African Americans in the place of Korean Americans. However, because of the reasons mentioned earlier African Americans usually cannot open their own stores. Rather than blame white politics for cutting them off from the rest of the economy, some black people vent their hostility against the most visible target. Still, others perceive Korean Americans as white people's accomplices. The stories of Korean American financial success are usually exaggerated (Chang, "Jewish and Korean Merchants" 10). Henry's father accumulates a sizeable fortune, but most other storeowners earn just enough to support themselves. Just as Korean Americans are often ill informed about the situation of African Americans in the American society, black people usually do not have sufficient information either. The lack of closer contacts is a source of misinformation as well. African Americans usually are not aware that Korean Americans, like them, have limited possibilities. Nor are they aware that for many of those merchants running a store is not a dream career option, considering their high educational background.

Cultural differences play a role in the conflict too. Some Afro-Americans are not aware of those differences. That is why they read hostility into the behavior of Korean American merchants, when in fact there is no hostility. African Americans expect a smile, "How do you do?," "Have a nice day," etc. They are not aware that in Korea it is not customary to smile at a stranger or establish eye contact with them (Heon Cheol Lee 119).

African Americans also strongly resent the fact that they are presented as deficient, while Asian Americans are portrayed as a model of successful assimilation into society. Once again white people come into the picture since they propagated the myth of model minority. The model minority myth emerged in the context of civil rights and affirmative action debate. White people did not become appreciative of Asian Americans because they suddenly discovered their long overlooked qualities, but because they needed the model minority myth to silence the voices of black people. Keith Osajima observes that the model minority myth helped to uphold the American dream (167). The authors of the myth maintained that the success of Asian Americans proved that the American society was open to all minorities. Thanks to the model minority myth white people could sign away their own responsibility for African American misfortunes and pin all the blame on African Americans themselves. Model minority arti-

Four: Multicultural Invisibilities

cles revolved around Asian American educational achievements, the integrity of their families, their cultural superiority, and traditional Asian values. Comparing the hardships as well as achievements of Asian Americans and African Americans, the authors of model minority articles concluded that Afro-Americans did not possess attributes which would predispose them to succeed in the American society.

Most of the model minority articles pretend to draw a historical and a sociological analysis, yet their enquiry carries major flaws. For instance, the author of "Success Story of One Minority in the U.S." contrasts the tribulations suffered by Chinese Americans in the past with those experienced by Afro-Americans in the 1960s: "What you find, back of this remarkable group of Americans, is a story of adversity and prejudice that would shock those now complaining about the hardships endured by today's Negroes" (*U.S. News and World Report* Dec 20, 1966, p.6). The assumption is that the "hardships" suffered by Chinese Americans by far surpass the privations of African Americans in the 1960s. Why does the author compare the oppression of both groups in two different historical periods? Chinese Americans were not a "model minority" when they were exposed to all those adversities. Why not mention the past tribulations of African Americans and their impact on African American mentality and history? And finally why detract from the hardships of African Americans in the 1960s?

The author of the above cited article draws explicit and implicit comparisons between Harlem and New York's as well as San Francisco's Chinatown, presumably a model minority community. Chinatown is presented as a haven of law and order: " 'Chinatown streets are safer than most other parts of the city' despite the fact that it is one of the most densely populated neighborhoods in the United States" (7). Even though the author admits high density of population, he asserts that "a sizeable number" of Chinese Americans who could move out to other districts choose to stay "not because of fears of discrimination on the outside, but because they prefer their own people and culture" (8). The truth is that those who could move out — professionals, merchant businessmen, white-collar workers — usually did move out (de Bary Nee 9).

Already in these early articles on model minority we can see white attempts to pit one minority against another. White authors do not want to create an impression that the model minority is entirely their invention so they cite Asian American voices to corroborate their claims. Ironically, one of the interviewees in the 1971 Newsweek article refuses to cooperate and says bluntly: "The whites use us by saying to the others, 'Why can't you be like the Japanese? The chicanos and the blacks turn against us" ("Success Story: Outwhiting the Whites" *Newsweek* 26, June 21, 1971, p. 27). The author hastens to assure us that such cases of rebelliousness can be encountered mainly among third-generation Japanese Americans — the Sansei. He gives the last word in his article to the Japanese American man who is afraid of the black people in his neighborhood: "If a black family moved in next door, I wouldn't like it. I've just moved in here and it would drive property values down.... If they want to get ahead, they have to work — just like the Nisei did" (27). The underlying message to black people is that they should not look to the outside world for help, but pull themselves up by their bootstraps, as the conservative general tells Dan Freeman in *The Spook Who Sat by the Door*: "Pull yourself up by the bootstraps like the immigrants. These demonstrations and sit-ins stir up needless emotion" (63).

Asian Americans were also praised for their patriarchal family. Implicitly Afro-American failure to succeed arose from the disintegration of their families. Similar arguments were raised by the U.S. Assistant Secretary of Labor — sociologist Patrick Moynihan, already mentioned in Chapter Two. He also placed emphasis on the lack of the father in African American families and the disastrous consequences for the sound development of black children. White psychologist Erik Erikson comes to similar conclusions in the chapter of his book *Identity, Youth and Crisis*. The emphasis on strong family among Asian Americans is part of a larger corollary of the discourse on the cultural superiority of Asian Americans. Proponents of the model minority myth argued that Asian Americans cherished the values which allowed them to succeed in the United States. "Success Story: Outwhiting the Whites" cited traditional Japanese values: group obligation, duty, reserve, restraint, patience, perseverance (27). Articles devoted to Chinese Americans related their success to the Confucian ethics. The assumption is that all these cultural traits are not so much unlike those espoused by white Anglo Saxon protestants. The caption under the photograph of Japanese American scouts asks whether they are "wasps at heart" (*Newsweek* 26, June 21, 1971). Model minority articles draw a distinction between culture in the sense of treasured values and culture as artistic

Four: Multicultural Invisibilities

achievements. We may remember Wittman's question "What do we have in the way of a culture? Where is our jazz?" (Kingston 27). He might be partly infected by white rhetoric that emphasized Asian American ethics and effaced their artistic achievements.

Native Speaker highlights the inconsistencies of the model minority discourse. Elements of the discourse come among others in Henry's conversation with his white father in law Stew. Stew utters the stereotypes embedded in the model minority rhetoric. Like the authors of earlier mentioned articles, he places stress on hard work, self-reliance, ambition and self-restraint of Asian Americans. According to Stew, these qualities give Asian Americans an undeniable advantage over whites, who usually want to have everything at the cost of minimal effort on their part (121). For Stew, Henry's father is a perfect example of modesty, superb efficiency and self-reliance. There is still a note of resentment and envy in Stew's apotheosis of "Oriental" culture. The model minority myth had its reverse side — yellow peril — Asians and Asian Americans as a threat to the "Western" world. Seeing American culture as spoiled, he is considerably comforted by the fact that Japan follows in America's footsteps (121). The fact that Stew is happy about Japan's alleged fall from prominence shows that he sees the second biggest economy as a potential threat, a rival to be reckoned with. The tensions in the relations between the United States and Eastern economic powers become visible in their trade relations. American politicians are quick to blame their economic problems on the economic policies of Asian countries. Major issues of contention are: the proportion of Asian export to import and the value of Asian currency in relation to the dollar. During the Clinton presidency Treasury Secretary Robert Rubin put a lot of pressure on the Japanese to lower the value of Yen. Clinton's administration was also locked in the dispute with China over the alleged distribution of pirate cassettes by the Chinese. The end of President George W. Bush's first term in office also saw an increase in the frictions between the United States and China over trade relations as well. The American Treasury Secretary John Snow pressed China to revalue its currency and decrease the surplus of their exports over imports.

Native Speaker not only presents the white model minority rhetoric, but also shows the Asian American response to the discourse. Lee observes that Asian Americans are, to a certain extent, complicit in its perpetuation. Kwang argues that they should sometimes resist the discourse and expose its loopholes, but for most of the time they stay quiet because it is difficult to resist when other people "construct" and "model" them positively (193). The words "construct" and "model" underscore the constructedness of the discourse. Kwang is all too aware that it is a social construct. Henry notes that his parents corroborate the discourse, afraid to show their human side and betray any cracks in their armor of perfection. In their self-consciousness and estrangement from the American land, they become as self-effacing as possible, afraid that they may disconcert their WASP or Jewish neighbors. In Henry's portrayal, they behave as if everything with them was always fine, fitting to some extent into the stereotype of Korean Americans who work virtually round-the-clock, wear immaculate clothes, always have money in their bank accounts and take to arms against African Americans, while at the same time passively watching the flames consume their stores and offices (52–53). Henry jabs irony at the discourse, pointing to its fissures and discrepancies. His statement "as if everything with us were always all right" is one of the blind spots of the model minority rhetoric. The architects of the model minority myth see only the surface of Asian American performance, never looking beneath. Immigrants feel a lot of pressure to perform, to prove themselves. Being new to the country and treading on uncertain ground, immigrants often put on a happy face even if they are anything but happy. The model minority myth and outwhiting the whites stories account for one more kind of Asian American invisibility. Perfectly assimilated, thus no longer salient, visibly different from the rest of society. The myth also helped whites to assuage their fears of racial difference.

Just as Henry is suspicious of the model minority myth, he also has his doubts about "from rags to riches stories." It is true that upon arrival to the United States many Korean Americans adopt an immigrant mentality. However, the myth of an American immigrant is no less overdrawn than the model minority myth. The official version of the myth presents every successful immigrant as a hard-working, self-sufficient newcomer overcoming single-handedly all obstacles. Henry conjectures that even his down-to-earth father would give the official version of the myth, forgetting to mention that he received his first injection of money from a Korean money club (49–50). Hence the stories of immigrant self-reliance are partly compromised. Henry's father achieves success, but many Korean American grocers earn just enough to support themselves. At a certain point

Four: Multicultural Invisibilities

Henry speaks about the myth of an immigrant in a wry, almost sarcastic way, as if wondering whether the success is worth the sacrifices they suffer:

> These were the inalienable rights of the immigrant ... you worked from before the sunrise to the dead of night. You were never unkind in your dealings, but then you were not generous. Your family was your life, though you rarely saw them. You kept close handsome sums of cash in small denominations. You were steadily cornering the market in self-pride. You drove a Chevy and then a Caddy and then a Benz. You never missed a mortgage payment or a day of church. You prayed furiously until you wept. You considered the only *unseen forces* to be those of capitalism and the love of Jesus Christ [47, emphasis added].

Henry as well as other immigrants know all too well that there are more "unseen forces" than "those of capitalism" and "the love of Jesus Christ." The socio-economic situation of people living in the United States is not of its own making, but a meticulous design drawn by those at the helm.

"Unseen forces" also become visible in the conflict between African Americans and Korean Americans. White people, who are usually physically absent from direct clashes between both minorities, most often have a hand in stirring up the disputes. Henry finds the white media partly responsible for fomenting the tensions between Korean Americans and African Americans. The mainstream and especially the white media tailor the image of Korean Americans to their own needs, portraying them either as a model minority or as ruthless misers. Covering the events, the white media remain to a great extent invisible, creating an impression that it is simply the conflict between Korean Americans and African Americans. Henry complains about the media brutalization of Korean American grocers during the unrest following the death of "Saranda Harlans" (193). The events alluded to by Henry occurred on March 18, 1991. The obvious reference is to Latasha Harlins, who was shot by a Korean American female grocer Soon Ja Du[11] after punching her three times on the face, having refused to return the bottle of orange juice which she allegedly stole.

While after the Latasha Harlins incident Korean American grocers were vilified, during the Rodney King rebellion[12] they were presented as a model minority protecting its property. David Palumbo-Liu maintains that the white media elevated Korean Americans to the status of "surrogate whites" locked in the battle for their property ("Los Angeles" 369). Such a portrayal of Korean Americans creates an impression of equal access to property, notwithstanding anyone's race and ethnicity. According to Palumbo-Liu, white viewers identified with property owners (374). On that particular occasion some whites may have indeed sympathized with Korean American store owners. However, on numerous other occasions they resented and still resent Asian American property ownership. It is only in 1948 that Japanese Americans gained the right to own and lease the land (Takaki 399). In 1913 California passed an alien land law barring Asian Americans from land purchase and land lease for a period longer than three years (Chan 195). The law was supposed to exclude Asian Americans from property ownership and prevent them from setting roots in the state. It was repealed only in 1956 (Chan 197). In 1989 Los Angeles City Councilman Nate Holden proposed legislation which would prohibit non–American citizens from purchasing property in Los Angeles (Chang, "New Urban Crisis" 47). The rhetoric generated by the white apparatus of power smoothed over the fact that Afro-Americans were no less attached to property if they had any. This attachment becomes particularly conspicuous in *Devil in a Blue Dress* by Walter Mosley, cited already in Chapter Two. The protagonist — Easy Rawlins — derives enormous satisfaction out of being a "homeowner," "a man of property," "landowner": "That house meant more to me than any woman I ever knew. I loved her and I was jealous of her and if the bank sent the county marshal to take her from me I might have come at him with a rifle rather than to give her up" (11). The importance of property for African Americans is also visible in Hisaye Yamamoto's story "Fire in Fontana,"[13] when a black family refuses to leave their house located in a predominantly white neighborhood. As a result they fall victim to arson. The first person narrator — a Japanese American journalist sympathizes with the African American family. Still, her sympathy is not deep enough to rally more support for the black family. She ends up wondering whether she could have done more. The narrator wraps up the story with the TV coverage of Watts riots in 1965. She mulls over her position as a viewer of the unfolding events, "sitting safely in a house which was located on a street where panic would be the order of the day if a Black family should happen to move in" (373). She derives considerable comfort from the fact that she is on the other side, just watching from the safe distance of her middle-class neighborhood, rather than participating in the revolt. The act of spectatorship marks her elevation to the status equivalent to that of middle-class whites.

Four: Multicultural Invisibilities

The role of the media in the Black–Korean American conflict is not unlike the role of the police in the conflict. Sasha Torres notes that most of the Rodney King rebellion coverage was shot from helicopters, which merged "the view afforded by its [television's] cameras with the perspective of the police that regularly patrol South Central in similar helicopters" (51). The police were hardly present in the conflict zone, since most of its forces protected white property, leaving Korean Americans to their own resources. During the picket in front of Kwang's house there is not enough police either. As in the case of ghetto revolts in the 1960s, the police represent the interests of white people.

As a middle-man minority, Korean Americans find themselves literally and figuratively between white Americans and African Americans. Whites use Korean Americans as scapegoats. Henry Park says that his merchant father is a bulwark, meaning that he is a buffer for whites, who incite the tensions but when the unrest takes place, they stay on the sidelines and make someone else take the heat. Occupying a buffer zone, Korean Americans shelter whites from the anger of other marginalized groups — African Americans and Latinos.[14] Those who create and perpetuate the system of oppression are out of sight and the gun range of people whom they keep stuck at the very bottom. As I have been arguing throughout this study, oppressors can sometimes be equally invisible as the oppressed. Nowhere is it more visible than in the conflict between Korean Americans and African Americans. Conspiring to keep the forces of oppression unseen, they do their best to prevent the invisible on the other side from claiming visibility. As it is the case in *The Spook*, whites begin to see people whom they make invisible only when they threaten to venture outside the area designated for them. It is then that those who are responsible for the creation of the ghetto are forced to see what they pretend not to see. It is also then that those who remain blissfully oblivious are shaken into awareness.

White forces are the main culprit in the Black–Korean American conflict, but racial identity politics is not without significance either. Black nationalist leaders often stoked the tensions between Korean American storeowners and African American customers. Among them were such figures as Sonny Carson, the head of the December 12 Movement, Coltrane Chimurenga, Amowale Clay, Ernest Foster (Heon-Cheol Lee 97). Emphasizing the significance of economic autonomy in black communities, they were usually responsible for organizing the boycotts of Korean American stores.[15] Outspoken as all those leaders are during the conflict situations, they hardly ever take any concrete measures to boost the level of life in their own communities. Has any of them made any effort to secure loans for their people? How many jobs have they obtained for people in all-black businesses run by the lower middle class or in any other businesses? It is true that the sheer numbers of African Americans do not allow for the kind of organization that Korean Americans have. Yet it is also true that triggering the boycotts, black leaders serve primarily their own interests, trying to rally potential voters. As I pointed out in Chapter Two, many of those leaders have a stake in the perpetuation of the ghetto, because they can count on the greatest numbers of votes from those constituencies. They are not very much unlike *Invisible Man* Brothers, for whom people are just names on the ballots. Chasing out of Korean American grocers will not lead to a major redistribution of economic resources. Nor will it efface black ghettos from the map drawn by white cartographers. Manning Marable argues that all these leaders would be much more accountable before their own communities if they forged multiracial and multiethnic alliances (325). Then the focus would be no longer to such an extent on racial difference but on class difference. Playing up the racial difference of Korean American storeowners, they can shift the emphasis from their own class privilege onto Asian Americanness of Korean American grocers. Income differences between them and people in the ghetto become much less visible. Like whites, they use Korean Americans as scapegoats. Underprivileged African Americans are frequently unaware of the long history of oppression that Korean Americas have. Hedging their own interests, black leaders keep them in the dark.

The leaders prodding African Americans to the boycotts claim to speak for all African Americans, completely obliterating the internal heterogeneity within African American community. Heon Cheol Lee calls this racialization and ethnicization of blackness (103). New black immigrants may not necessarily identify with mainland African Americans. Their interests are often different. Lee points to the frictions between African Americans and Caribbean Americans. We could observe a similar situation in *Tripmaster Monkey*, when Asian American nationalists tried to include everyone under the banner of Asian America.

Marginalized racial and ethnic groups — in this case Afro-Americans and Korean Americans — bicker and haggle with each other, failing to identify the real enemy and unite against those who create and perpetuate the system of oppression. The marginalized groups also need to see that they share common interests. Their own oppression often blinds them to the oppression of others. Assuming the role of a mediator, John Kwang sensitizes Korean Americans and African Americans to their similarities, arguing that these similarities will always preponderate over differences (153). Korean Americans and African Americans have much more in common than their past histories of oppression.[16] Both Korean Americans and African Americans lack access to really big capital. They do not control banks or large corporations. Marable observes that: "While African Americans, Latinos, and Asian Americans scramble over which group should control the mom and pop grocery store in their neighborhood, almost no one questions the racist redlining policies of large banks which restrict access to capital to nearly all people of color" (329). Attempts to expose white oppression must be accompanied by transformations within the marginalized groups themselves. Those groups also need to be more inclusive.

Beyond Conventional Identity Politics Towards a Politics of Translation

Constructing his narrative, Henry is "writing a new book of the land" (279). His new book of the land includes people who speak pidgin English, Spanish, Mandarin and languages he has never seen (278). Unlike Dan Freeman or Wittman Ah Sing, Henry Park moves beyond traditional identity politics, striving for the visibility of marginalized people from various ethnic backgrounds. He speaks for all minorities "on lower frequencies," not just one group. Unlike a traditional Korean American ggeh, John Kwang's ggeh brings together individuals across racial and ethnic divides. Henry observes that his father would never enter a ggeh that affiliated people of non–Korean American descent. He would not trust people of non–Korean origin and he would see no motivation for cooperating with Hispanics, Hindu Americans or Vietnamese Americans (280). Henry's job as a campaign volunteer is to write down the names of all contributors. That is what he does in his autobiography. He also writes their names and later spells them out, translating their experience to the reader. People for whom he speaks occupy opposite subject positions in relation to each other and in relation to the white mainstream. Their interests are often at odds. A former spy, Henry in the end literally becomes a good middleman, negotiating between all these diverse positionalities in pursuit of some common ground.

He rejects conventional identity politics in favor of transformational identity politics, which enables the building of broader coalitions and alliances between various oppressed groups. While supporters of conventional identity politics overly concentrate on their own difference, proponents of transformational identity politics seek similarities between themselves and other marginalized people. They do not pursue universalism or sameness, but at the same time they realize that divisions between identities are not set in stone, because all identities are fluid. Cherishing their particular experience, they are still aware of what they have in common with other people. Analouise Keating notes that transformational identity politics allows the oppressed to "unite across differences" (36). If recognized as a social construct, difference in itself does not have to block potential alliances. Keating encourages us to recognize the other in ourselves and ourselves in the other (40). Peter McLaren speaks about differences in relation and relational differences, which bears striking resemblance to Susan Stanford Friedman's discourse of relationality (McLaren 53). No differences exist in a vacuum, but against the background of other differences and without them people who treasure their own uniqueness would have nothing to treasure. Judith Butler speaks about a "language between languages" that needs to be found (178). The problem of in-betweenness comes back time and again in *Native Speaker*. As I pointed out earlier, both Henry and Kwang position themselves in between, trying to strike a middle ground between often conflicting standpoints. According to Butler, translation is successful only if it allows "foreign vocabulary into its lexicon" (168). Just as Kwang's ggeh unites people speaking languages which may be unknown to many of its members, Henry's narrative includes native speakers of various languages. In order to receive help, associates of Kwang's ggeh must speak to Henry in person. They often bring an interpreter or a phrasebook to translate their needs. Drawing upon what he has learnt from them and from many others like them, Henry — as an already self-conscious narrator — in turn translates their experience to the broader audience.

The distinction between Henry — the spy and Henry — the self-conscious narrator is crucial. Henry — the spy gives those people's names to the enemy. It is true that when he does it, he has already made up his mind to quit his dishonorable profession and he does not know that by passing on the list, he will bring doom on the people whose names are inscribed there. Still, you do not pass on something sacred into uncertain hands. He comes to understand this when it is already too late. Only then does it occur to him that he should have predicted that Dennis would turn the list to some evil end (336). It is strange that while reflecting on the whole matter, Henry should call the list a "throwaway," since earlier he speaks of it almost as if it were sacred scrolls. Even earlier, however, there are signs that he might abuse the power which he has over the associates of Kwang's ggeh. Professing his deep attachment for all members of the list, Henry still defines his relationship to them in terms of "possession" (279). The fact that he claims to "possess" all these people and their families anticipates his future betrayal (279). Well-intentioned as Henry may be, uttering these words, the statement sounds ominous and it foreshadows the abuse of power that Henry has over those people's lives. He tries to explain his actions by citing his Confucian upbringing that tells an employee to preserve unquestioning loyalty towards an employer. Apart form being simply afraid of his boss — Dennis Hoagland — he sees himself tied to him by an obligation that he does not choose to breach until his contract expires. He fulfils an obligation towards his people only in his autobiography.

Unlike Wittman, Henry — as a self-conscious narrator — strongly identifies with immigrants, seeing them as his antecedents. *Native Speaker* is, to a great extent, an attempt at the recovery of diaspora, not the diaspora of one ethnic group, but a multiethnic diaspora. Lee acknowledges people who constantly revitalize the nation, giving full sense to the principles upon which it was built. Writing the narrative, Henry returns his debt to those who came before. Their story is his story:

> The story is mine. How I come by plane, come by boat. Come climbing over a fence. When I get here, I work. I work for the day I will finally work for myself. I work so hard that one day I end up forgetting the person I am. I forget my wife, my son. Now, too, I have lost my old mother tongue. And I forget the ancestral graves I have left on a hillside of a faraway land, the loneliest stones that each year go unblessed [279].

In this passage Henry speaks first of all for the generation of his parents and for all other newcomers. They are the ones who paved the way for him, waging immigrant battles. The excerpt tracks the fate of an immigrant into the new land and back into the fading memory of the old land. Regretting loosening community ties between Korean Americans, Henry's father comes to the conclusion that in the United States it is difficult to remain faithful to one's ethnic origin (51). As immigrants settle into the new reality and some of them move to better-off neighborhoods, the bonds between them weaken. At the beginning the uncertainty and novelty of their situation keeps many of them together. Wittman observes that "f.o.b.'s" run in a clan. Henry forgets Korean as he becomes a native speaker of English. The last part of the passage in which Henry speaks about the "ancestral graves" corresponds to the passage in David Mura's *Where the Body Meets Memory*, in which the narrator's aunt looks in vain for the grave of her father, who returned to Japan, having spent World War II in an internment camp. Mura declares "I speak against their extinction" (266). Like Mura, Henry speaks against their extinction, forging a link between newcomers and already settled immigrants. The motif of searching for one's roots returns again in the Korean songs chanted by John Kwang. One of the songs tells the story of a young man who leaves his ancestral village and comes back only after years to see his parents dead. It is not without significance that Chang-rae Lee dedicates *Native Speaker* to his mother and father.

Henry looks for immigrants in the streets, listening for their accents, studying their faces and trying to uncover what is beneath. In the figures of immigrants he discovers his dead parents, his father's housekeeper Ahjuhma and himself as a small boy overwhelmed by an immigrant reality. For most passers-by, immigrants are enigmas, nonentities to be passed without recognition. Most New Yorkers remain indifferent to their daily struggles. Henry, on the other hand, cannot walk by indifferently. Their weariness, exhaustion and their sorrows are all too visible to him. He feels the need to "write them out," "to undo the cipherlike faces" (170–171). Writing out their faces in his narrative, he makes them visible to those for whom they are invisible for most of the time. Henry's autobiography is a reversal of his earlier spy reports. As a spy he also writes out the faces of immigrants on whom he was supposed to spy. His spy reports were very much in line with old time ethnographies of the 1930s, the ethnographies envisioned by people like Bronisław Malinowski: cold, dispassionate, detached, presumably objective and strictly to the point. Henry's boss

Four: Multicultural Invisibilities

Dennis Hoagland expects him to be a "clean writer," "of the most reasonable eye" (203). Having swapped ethnographic science for the art of fiction, Henry now renders his people visible in a different way, no longer exposing them but trying to make them really seen.

Henry's narrative captures the poetry of immigrants' daily life. Wandering the streets of Flushing, he soaks the scene. New York and especially Flushing is "the city of words" (344). The language they speak is not so much unlike Judith Butler's "language in between": "We live here. In the street the shouting is in a language we hardly know. The strangest chorale" (344). Their language exerts a deep emotional impact on him, evoking memories of his childhood: "they speak to me ... not simply in new accents or notes but in the ancient untold music of a newcomer's heart, sonorous with longing and hope" (304). The music of a newcomer's heart is untold because language can hardly give the full extent of their experience. It may also be untold since they often have problems with expressing their thoughts in the language of their new country. Some of them do not communicate strictly in words, but "tender the native language with body and tongue" (334), for example Henry's father switches to the "language of fruit stand and cash register" (280). As a boy Henry feels hostility towards people who cannot speak standard English. Their attempts at the English language make him want to shout insults in response (337). Back then he believes that their stilted English marks them as foreigners, bringing disrepute on all immigrants. Now he would long to hear those people again. Their language no longer seems to be a deviation from the norm. Twisting the sounds of English, they do not distort it, but enrich it, leaving their imprint. Rather than merely imitate others, they contribute their own interpretation.

Henry listens for immigrants' voices in the streets, but most people hardly ever care to hear them, let alone listen to what they have to say. Realizing that immigrants feel vulnerable as newcomers, the mainstream pays little attention to their concerns or misgivings. Uncertain of their standing in the country and afraid of the backlash against them, immigrants often fear to voice their sorrows. Often they lack the words. For the rest of society immigrants are first of all a cheap labor force amplifying the American economy: "countless unheard nobodies, each offering to the marketplace their gross of kimchee, lichee, plantain, black bean, soy milk, coconut milk, ginger, grouper, ahi, yellow curry, cuchifrito, jalapeno, their everything" (83). They are unheard and unseen. Remembering the days of his childhood when he helped his father in the store, Henry says that he was invisible to customers (53). He does not threaten them if he speaks Korean, because then they are not afraid of his penetration into the mainstream. Once immigrants are inassimilable, other Americans can keep their culture pure, free of "alien" intrusions. Back then Henry does not make any overt attempts to make himself visible. To spite his father, who wants him to speak "some Shakespeare" to impress the customers, he grunts the best Korean he can. Only by venturing upon the narrative enterprise does he aim at transcending his own invisibility and the invisibility of his people. And he does not achieve it by speaking Korean or Shakespeare but by choosing the language in between.

There is no embellishment in Henry's narrative. The immigrant reality presents itself in stark colors. Henry consistently demotes the myth of the United States as the gold mountain, contending that it is primarily a white fantasy. Immigrants who are to arrive in the country expect to encounter harsh reality rather than the land of milk and honey. They are prepared for violence, rape and extremely crowded living conditions (335). Similarly, Henry portrays an immigrant journey in a very down-to-earth way. In Henry's description, the journey to the United States gains the semblance of the Middle Passage. Like slave narratives, *Native Speaker* draws our attention to what happens in the holds of the ships. For many immigrants it is not so much a journey of hope, but a journey of exile, of the last resort.

The anti-immigrant rhetoric leveled among others at Asian Americans is another side of the model minority myth. Suspicions of yellow peril lurk under all these positive stereotypes about Asian Americans. People who stage a demonstration in front of Kwang's house are mostly white steel workers accusing Kwang's potential voters of stealing their jobs. Almost one hundred years after Du Bois spoke about "compensatory wages of whiteness" and fifty years after Ellison noticed the same phenomenon in *Invisible Man*, the thesis still holds. People of color remain an easy target for white underprivileged groups. Just as Afro-Americans vent their anger on Korean Americans, the white working class rallies against Asian American immigrant workers, rather than blame the government for its faulty policies.[17] Another example of Asian American and immigrant invisibility comes when a group of illegal Chinese American immigrants is caught aboard a cargo ship. We can see them while they are interviewed

Four: Multicultural Invisibilities

by reporters. Unlike Henry, the media do not tell their story. They are "interviewing for a position" (327). Only a Chinese American interpreter "imparts a formality and respect to their statements" (327). Henry's dispassionate, reportorial tone employed in the passage renders the attitude of the media. He lets the reader see what the viewer can see. The INS inspector speaks about illegal immigrants associated with Kwang's ggeh as if they were objects, not people. They are seen as unwanted intruders who sneak into the country (329). Commenting on the tightening of American immigration policies, Kwang says "there is a closing going ... a narrowing of who can rightfully live here and be counted" (274). The closing has been coming and going throughout American history. Depending on what suited the American economy, gates were opened or closed.

Henry wonders whether non–Asian Americans perceive John Kwang as an American or as a foreigner. Unlike other Korean Americans, Kwang has much more far-reaching ambitions, going beyond the sphere of his family and private success. He does not speak quietly and a little, but delivers speeches in front of large gatherings of people. For Henry, Kwang is an embodiment of a Korean American who has made it in the American society, exuding confidence and shifting at will between various registers of language. Kwang can speak English "like a Puritan," but he does not shy away from speaking it "like a Chinaman," or "like every boat person in between" (304). That is also how Henry imagines the United States. He would like it to be a country where one can comfortably switch between their old heritage and a new one without compromising their Americanness or incurring anyone's indignation. Some do indeed see Kwang as an American, while others look at him as a foreigner. At least he is defined this way by the lady who shows Henry around Kwang's former house. At the end of his visit Henry asks: "Who lived here?" and the answer is "Foreigners. They went back to their country" (347).

The invisibility of American minorities is only one type of invisibility present in *Native Speaker*. As I emphasized at the very beginning, oppressors can be invisible as well. They are invisible because they conspire to render forces of oppression invisible. Apart from being figuratively invisible, they can also be literally invisible. As a spy, Henry is invisible to his victims, yet the people for whom he spies are not entirely visible to him either. He is left wondering who might want to spy on Kwang. Henry would not let himself be deluded into thinking that it is just a "wealthy voyeur" (295), instead visualizing the client who can see reality "with the soberest eyes" (295). This sober-eyed client pursues a broader agenda than simply quench his voyeuristic xenophobia. Unlike workers in front of Kwang's house, the people spying on Kwang are invisible and thus much more menacing. Their racism is aimed at eliminating those who dare to challenge the existing power dynamics and stake their claim to visibility in a broader sense. People like Kwang threaten to tilt the status quo. Henry is very well aware that the purpose of the investigation is not so much to eliminate Kwang himself, but to keep Asian Americans and other minorities in their place. Whiteness in *Native Speaker* is invisible and all too visible at the same time. It is invisible, because Henry can never see people who want to eliminate Kwang. Still, structures of oppression are hyper-visible to him and they become visible to the reader as well.

Native Speaker not only makes whiteness visible by exposing the system of oppression, but also by underscoring its internal heterogeneity. Lee distinguishes between different ethnicities within whiteness, those who are closest to the centre and those who hover on the fringes. As Ruth Frankenberg observes in "Whiteness and Americanness," "there are two kinds of whites, just as there are two kinds of Americans: those who are truly or only white" (68). Lee claims that Polish Americans and Greek Americans belong to the margins of whiteness. Not all phenotypically white groups were white straight away. Once elevated to the status of whiteness, they passed on their subsidiary status to other ethnic groups. Their social boost was usually accompanied by a relocation to another neighborhood. Buildings were mute witnesses of those changes, watching old owners move out and new inhabitants move in. The churches that now belong to the Vietnamese Americans, in the past belonged to Korean Americans and still earlier to German American (346). Vietnamese Americans are probably not the last believers worshipping in those churches. It is only a matter of time before they welcome followers of some other ethnicity.

Henry does not merely reflect on other people's invisibility, but on his own as well. As a second generation Korean American, he is a focal point for contradictory subject positions. In childhood he is very much like other newcomers plagued by fear and uncertainty. At school African American, Puerto Rican and white children call him names and make slant eyes at him. He portrays himself as a "confused school boy" (304). To boost his confidence Henry invents an alter ego, an "invisible brother," a model of athleticism popular with girls (205). All along Henry's father keeps reminding him not to tell anyone what his trouble is. As a result, he withdraws into himself, sheltering his feelings from the eyes of strangers. In the end silence becomes for him a protective shield against any injury that may always come from the outside world.

Autobiography marks the climax of his silence breaking. Henry says that speaking out can be problematic for immigrants and descendants of immigrants like himself because they were often brought up in the culture revering silence and reticence, whereas "the notions of where [they] come from and who [they] are need a maximal approach" (182). In his autobiography he breaks his silence and assumes a maximal approach. Apart from being an inversion of his spy reports, it is also an elaboration on personal narratives which he writes before each assignment as a spy. Prior to each case Henry and other fellow-spies write their own "legend," an autobiography that is partly fictitious, partly based on appropriation of their every-day identities (22). They never become totally someone else, for example during his assignment with Kwang, Henry impersonates an unemployed novelist who writes a detective novel on the side. As Henry tells us, "a certain borrowing is always required." Especially "when lines between identities were thin, there was no point in inventing an altogether new story" (181). To a certain extent their alter identities entail mimicry of their old selves and their new selves. Their alter identities become an overlap of their new and old selves. Drawing upon Homi Bhabha's definition of mimicry, Parama Roy defines mimicry as an "imperfect doubling" (195). Part of the spy's everyday self is inevitably doubled, finding its way into their newly assumed identity. We can remember from Dan Freeman's reflections on the identity of a spy that the spy is undone when he or she loses a distinction between his or her everyday self and his or her impersonated self. This takes place at least in some degree during Henry's assignment to spy on Doctor Luzan, when he stops living out his "chosen narrative" and starts to speak openly about himself and his family (22). Rather than play the role of a patient, Henry really becomes a patient and opens up before the doctor, breaching his father's advice and for the first time trying to tell someone what his trouble is. Although he divulges before Luzan his real-life confidences, he still does not reveal everything as it really is, but rather repeats with a difference. Inconsistencies multiply in his confessions before Luzan. Henry changes his stories almost weekly. All his unfulfilled longings become part of the tales which he tells Luzan. He presents some events not as they really happened but as they might have happened or as he wanted them to happen.

Henry's adventure with Luzan is a prelude to a fully-fledged autobiographical enterprise. The second step of his silence breaking comes during the conversation with Jack, when he announces to him that he is going to quit. Having told Jack what he thinks about the American system and the role that immigrants play in it, Henry says: "This is my mind finally speaking" (288). He never tells his story in its entirety only until he does it in his autobiography. Shedding the cover of a spy and revealing everything in the narrative, he becomes visible not only to the reader but also to himself. Through his autobiography he achieves visibility for his people and for himself. Unlike Henry's spy autobiographies, his real-life autobiography helps him to resolve all inconsistencies and piece together a comprehensive picture of his life. In his venture with Luzan he completely loses himself (22). Now he is fully in control and his narrative is no longer running away from him.

Henry draws inspiration from his invisibility. The autobiography is his response to the society which to a certain extent made him and people like him. Earlier he never cared to answer or retort in any way. His own experience of invisibility belongs not only to Henry and other Asian Americans or other immigrants, but to the people who thrust the condition of invisibility upon them. Like the Invisible Man, Henry has "set out to throw [his] anger in the world's face" (Ellison 437): "This is your own history ... the song of our hearts at once furious and sad. For only you could grant me these lyrical modes" (320). Fury and sadness add up to their invisibility. Still, it is also a well-spring for "those lyrical modes." Henry seems to reflect not only on his racial invisibility, but also on his invisibility as a spy. The above cited passage is to a certain degree an accusation against society which conditioned him to be a spy: "This is your history." As he makes it evident throughout the narrative, it is not so much a history of peaceful cooperation, but of mutual exploitation. The statement "We are your most dutiful brethren" (320) seems to be a further reflection on the model minority myth and its double edge implications. It carries an implicit threat.

Any autobiographical enterprise entails its risks. The Invisible Man says: "having tried to put it down, I have disarmed myself in the process"

(438). Unlike the Invisible Man, Henry is much less reflective and tentative about the success of his endeavor. Yet autobiographical writing has been the subject of much controversy and speculation in Asian American community, much greater controversy than it ever caused in African American literary circles.[18] Frank Chin dismisses autobiography as a confessional and hence a Christian form of writing. Lashing out against Maxine Hong Kingston and Amy Tan, he contends that "The autobiography is not a Chinese form" (*Big Aiiieeeee* 11).[19] Chin seems to forget that the people whom he criticizes are not Chinese, but Chinese Americans and their writing is a reflection of their Chinese American, not Chinese experience. Why should they be expected to write the way the Chinese wrote years ago rather than express themselves through literary forms of the country in which they live? On numerous occasions Chin himself underlines that people of Chinese ancestry in the United States are not Chinese, but Chinese Americans. Why does he change his stance when it comes to their writing?

Considering Chin's arguments, we could ask whether by writing autobiography, Henry gives away his people, just the way he does as a spy. A similar dilemma arises before the narrator of "No Name Woman"—the first chapter of Kingston's *The Woman Warrior*.[20] Maxine has doubts about the ethnographic venture she sets upon in her book. Will other members of the community read her text as "telling on them" or as an attempt to make them more visible? What will be the outcome of Henry's autobiography and Lee's novel? Do they not risk the perpetuation of the stereotype of an Asian American as an invisible enemy, a "gook," an unseen Vietcong fighter who may leap up any moment and attack you? Such a reading would be ironic if we take into account that Henry spies for whites, not against them. Still, will the readers see Lee's novel and Henry's autobiography as an incisive analysis of power relations in the American society or will they read something else into it? As I emphasized at the very beginning, *Native Speaker* is not a restatement of some earlier Asian American autobiographies, in which their authors brag about living out the American dream. It is their antithesis. Writing the narrative, Henry exposes much more than himself. First of all he exposes the system of oppression. If in the case of other first-person Asian American narratives, the distinction between fiction and non-fiction was often blurred, with Lee's novel the situation is clear. The first person narrator is for Lee only a device, which helps him to launch an extensive critique of power relations in the United States.

Mimicking for the Mainstream

As a spy Henry mimics his everyday self as much as he mimics the white stereotype of Asian Americans. The assumption is that by remaining a quiet Asian man, he can befriend his victims and put to sleep their vigilance. His "amenable Asian face"(89) arouses no suspicion in the people on whom he spies. Henry's boss advises him: "Just stay in the background. Be unapparent and flat. Speak enough so that they can hear your voice and come to trust it, but no more, and no one will think twice about who you are" (44). Denis's spies are supposed to reenact the roles which they play in real life: "stay in the background." As citizens of the United States they are also expected to stay in the background, dutifully do their job and be hardly seen, let alone heard. Adopting or rather preserving their unpretentious posture, they are to win over the trust of people on whom they spy and become their confidantes.

Native Speaker undermines Dan Freeman's statement: "The nigger is the only natural agent in the U.S." (109). Immigrants are no less predisposed to be spies than African Americans. According to Henry, being a newcomer is like being a spy. Newcomers need to be constantly on the watch not to make a false move. Like spies, they find themselves in an unfamiliar territory, surrounded by strangers, people whom they are expected to reassure and convince of their reliability. Once new to the culture, they often watch and listen more than speak and act. Unlike spies, however, they frequently encounter open hostility of the host society. Because of their watchfulness and uncertain position in a new environment they develop acute powers of perception. The animosity of the host country further enhances their perceptiveness, sensitizing them to the nuances that usually pass unnoticed by the rest of society. Invisibility gives them the gift of second-sight: "You can keep nothing safe from our eyes and ears" (320). Koreans call their second-sight "nunch'i" (Lee O-Young cited in Engles 12). The above citation gains the semblance of a threat. Just as they can decipher the people they spy on, they can also read the people for whom they spy and potentially turn against them.

Four: Multicultural Invisibilities

Immigrants and especially immigrants from the same ethnic group are visible and invisible to each other at the same time. Their cultural bonds and similar positioning in the American society accounts for their mutual visibility. They understand each other without any translation of their experience. That is why Henry derives so much satisfaction from his acquaintance with John Kwang, to whom he does not need to explain anything because he has a fair understanding of Henry's background and of the struggles that his family had to go through (182). Ironically, immigrants' visibility to each other can contribute to their mutual invisibility. Since they know each other so well, they also see mutual vulnerabilities. Henry's father exploits other newcomers, paying them next to nothing, because he realizes that they cannot procure any other employment. Henry's father is convinced that since he was exploited and learned business this way, other immigrants should follow his path. Because of such a reasoning and conditions which they face in a new environment, immigrants perpetuate a vicious circle of exploitation. Repelled as young Henry is by his father's practices, he follows in his footsteps. Henry's father exploits with an eye for profit. Henry derives considerably more than a sizeable salary from his spying. What counts most is the psychological compensation. His job gives him an illusion of being several people at once. It allows him to "reside in his one place and take half-steps out" (127). It also offers Henry an illusory feeling of melting away, of assimilation. He is wondering: "Is this my assimilation so many years in the making?" (202). Henry's job makes him feel that he belongs to the American culture (127). The culture is set up in such a way that immigrants find themselves being exploited by whites or exploiting for them. Henry's spying costs his victims much more than just a living.

Unlike his father, Henry as a self-conscious narrator, reflects on the cycle of oppression that immigrants are drawn into: "My ugly immigrant's truth, as was his, is that I exploited my own, and those others who can be exploited" (319). Mulling over his betrayals of other marginalized people, Henry grapples with remorse, longing for their forgiveness. Although it is apparent to Henry that the policies of the implicitly racist society push many immigrants onto the path of exploitation, he does not try to pin all the blame on the dominant system. His spy colleague Jack, on the other hand, portrays immigrants as a family of people who have no choices (293). Henry's father would also probably see Henry's betrayals in terms of a battle for survival (319). Henry rejects such a line of argumentation and emphasizes that immigrants cannot sign away all responsibility. They cannot be reduced to passive objects, but need to be seen as active subjects that can take their own choices, limited as they are.

Throughout this study I have been trying to problematize the term mimicry. In this section I use it to describe Henry's invisibility as a spy and immigrants' exploitation of their own people. Since Homi Bhabha used the term mimicry in 1987, it has been employed both in reference to white impersonation or portrayal of colonized people and to illustrate oppressed people's response to that oppression either through embodiment of stereotypes attributed to them or through impersonation of their oppressors. Usually, however, mimicry when used to illustrate the tactics of the oppressed carried an element of subversion. Their underlying motive was undermining of the oppressive power. How does mimicry come into the picture when the oppressed mimic white oppression and exploit their own people? There is certainly no subversion here, but rather perpetuation of the existing power relations. Still, if we interpret mimicry as a repetition with a difference (Bhabha 88), then the term can be applied here. Immigrant imitation of white oppression is never fully complete, because ultimately they do not speak from the position of power. They may be above the people whom they exploit, but they themselves still have someone above them as well. With Henry the situation is even more complicated. Unlike Korean American grocery store owners, he does not exploit indirectly for the white apparatus of power. His exploitation takes a much more direct form.

We can distinguish one more type of Korean American and immigrant mimicry of whiteness in *Native Speaker*. By moving into rich upper-class neighborhoods, by seemingly living out the dream of an immigrant who first drives a Chevy, later a Caddy and then a Benz (47), they in a sense also mimic the mainstream, just the way the black middle class does it in *The Spook*. The anxiety which Henry's father feels while living in the rich neighborhood is a good illustration of Bhabha's definition of mimicry as "almost the same but not quite" (89). His integration into Ardsley is hardly complete. Whenever Henry's father appears in public, it is only because of Henry. The tragic death of Henry's son Mitt further supports an outsider status of Henry's family in Ardsley. Conscious of their illusory integration, Henry comments tersely on Connecticut Korean Americans who do not contribute to Kwang's ggeh: "They think they've escaped" (278). Like Dan Freeman, Henry believes that people of color can never fully escape.

Chang-rae Lee goes further than any of the authors examined here in his critique of interracial tensions and power relations in the United States. Speaking from the perspective of the 1990s, when certain problems can no longer be overlooked, Lee can boast the hindsight of all the years that separate him from his predecessors. He also draws upon a long tradition of invisibility writing. To a certain extent, however, he is presented with a much more demanding task. How to convince the readers of the persisting invisibility of minorities amid aggressive rhetoric accentuating the American commitment to equality and diversity? Lee's study of racial invisibility is deeply anchored in the critique of American multiculturalism and whiteness. *Native Speaker* brings together the voices of various, often competing communities. Their voices do not compose a harmonious chorus but are torn by multiple dissonances. Lee makes those dissonances audible and visible. In the American setting the musicians are sometimes much more visible than the conductor who intentionally sends false signals to stir up discordance. Lee does not spare him the spotlight, making sure that he will get a fair share of booing for a spoiled concerto. At the same time Lee makes it clear that power does not rest solely with the white conductor, but reverberates among the oppressed as well. Oppression runs in multiple directions. It is by no means an exclusive prerogative of white people. Individuals subjected to exploitation often inflict it upon others as well. Lee does not limit himself to critiquing existing power relations, but proposes his own agenda. In his vision of a multicultural society minorities forge alliances and cooperate with each other in their struggle against those who want to keep them in their place.

Conclusion

> I hear something about the Chinese — something odd, improbable. I will ask my father. He will know whether it is true, say that the Chinese eat with sticks. ... He shrugs. He pretends not to understand. Or he scowls and says, "Chinese just like everybody else." ...
> "Is it true the Chinese write backwards?"
> "Chinese just like evvybody else."
> "Is it true they eat dog?"
> "Chinese just like evvybody else."
> "Are they really all Communists?"
> "Chinese just like evvybody else."
> "What is Chinese water torture? What is footbinding? What is a mandarin?"
> "Chinese just like evvybody else."
> He was not like evvybody else.
>   (Sigrid Nunez, *A Feather on the Breath of God* 5, 6)

> "[T]he points of human difference, great as they, upon first sight, seem, are as nothing compared with the points of human agreement" (Frederick Douglass cited in Prashad, 78).

I have chosen to open the last section of this project with these particular epigraphs because the tension between the sameness and difference underlies any invisibility and any striving for visibility. The "points of human agreement" intersect with particular histories and particular socio-historical experiences created by distinct power relations. What matters much more than putative sameness or difference of the invisible is the manipulation of this sameness and difference by the white apparatus of power. An overriding assumption is: If the same, then presumably already enfranchised. If different, then different only culturally rather than because of socio-economic standing. If too different, then dismissed out of hand. Analyzing African American and Asian American invisibility in the cho-

Conclusion

sen texts, I have emphasized the specific power dynamics that prevent African Americans and Asian Americans from competing on equal footing with the rest of society. I have also emphasized power differentials inside and between both communities. African Americans and Asian Americans are invisible in a different way and various strata of the two communities also experience their invisibility differently. Outside pressure, interference and discrimination intensify inner divisions and animosities. African American and Asian American invisibility to broader American society works its way inside both communities, spawning multiple internal invisibilities. The authors of the four texts analyzed here have their characters transcend invisibility and take upon themselves the task of representing their people in striving for visibility.

Since this is a diachronic study and I have been emphasizing all along the importance of visibility, let me wrap up by analyzing what kind of visibility would await the Invisible Man, Dan Freeman, Wittman Ah Sing and Henry Park in the present-day United States. The visibility they would be offered in today's American reality is not the visibility they are hoping to achieve for themselves and their people. None of them is striving for the visibility which boils down to flaunting difference precisely for the purpose of keeping it "checked and balanced," to use Ellison's phrase ("Introduction" xiii).[1] As I stressed in Chapter Four, minorities are granted spurious visibility by the state that boasts its embrace of diverse cultures. This kind of visibility approximates what Foucault called "visibility which exists to serve a rigorous, meticulous power" (*Power/Knowledge* 152). That is still visibility which strikingly resembles Dan Freeman's visibility when he is paraded inside his glass CIA office, while scores of other African Americans are incarcerated behind the invisible yet extremely tangible plate glass that Du Bois speaks about in his metaphor. Minorities theoretically have the right to keep their cultural distinctness and at the same time claim all the benefits of the American citizenship. In practice they still languish on the perimeter of an ostensibly multicultural American state.

African Americans, unlike Asian Americans, are present today in the mass media as sports stars, fashion models, actors, sometimes television anchors or politicians. Michelle Wallace — the author of *Invisibility Blues*[2] — would no longer need to complain about the lack of spotlight on an Ethiopian runner who won a major city marathon in the United States. There is no shortage of black athletes in the media today. However, the picture emerging from the media coverage still frequently reflects popular stereotypes of African Americans as gamblers, runners, lovers, criminals and laggards. The visibility granted to people of color is highly selective and it often leads to further misrepresentation rather than clarification.

Audre Lorde distinguishes three ways to handle difference: ignore, copy, or destroy it (Lorde cited in Keating 27). All three are alive and well today. Ignorance of difference assumes various shapes. You can ignore difference by pretending that it does not exist and everyone is the same. Proponents of universalism and liberal multiculturalists play up equal human potential, gliding over a host of issues which prevent people from tapping that potential. The white apparatus of power is very well aware that people deemed the same are really different in their socio-economic status, but ignoring the difference is an easier way out for them. Žižek's term "racism with a distance" very appropriately describes such an approach to racial difference (Žižek cited in Prashad 61). The second way to handle difference — "copy" — is just as popular nowadays. The white mainstream often fetishizes and appropriates racial difference. White artists appropriating styles practiced by people of color are the best example. Hair styles and fashion trends also frequently result from cross-racial appropriation. The third way of approaching difference — "destroy it" — enjoys popularity among declared racists and among conservative multiculturalists who accept the presence of people unlike them on condition that they adopt their cultural standards. Obviously, different does not mean only non-white. White is just as different for people of color as they are different for whites. This becomes visible in Olaudah Equiano's slave narrative[3] during the first encounter of captive slaves with white people. They find whites ugly. If today whiteness is in any way desired by people of color, it is not because there is anything special about whiteness in itself, but because it instantly connotes all the privileges that go together with it.[4] As I have been emphasizing throughout this study, whiteness is no less a racial category than any other racial category.

There is one more way to approach difference, which Lorde does not mention. One can also study difference. Dan Freeman would no longer need to descend to the bowels of East Lansing library in search of information on the history and culture of his people. He could easily find such books in libraries. He could also study the history and culture of his

Conclusion

people at departments existing at a number of American universities. I take issue with individuals who claim that the existence of such departments is a pure exercise in rhetoric. Apart from enabling people of color and whites to analyze the socio-cultural experience of minorities, they help to build bridges across communities.

Let us take a close look at how each protagonist would be visible/invisible today. In the Epilogue to *Invisible Man*, the Invisible Man says "I've sometimes been overcome with a passion to return into the 'heart of darkness' across the Mason-Dixon line" (437). If he returned nowadays, he would be spared the pain and humiliation that he suffered in the 1930s and that haunted the Southerners well into the 1960s. This does not mean, however, that color-lines have disappeared in the South or in the rest of the American society altogether. Jim Crow days may be gone but segregation persists in the United States in more than one way. Until 2000 some high schools in the South organized separate proms for black and white students. Also until 2000 the conservative Bob Jones University in South Carolina banned interracial dating among the students. The days of sharecropping may be gone from the South but African Americans living there still wrestle with material deprivation. Most Southern rural blacks compose a low-skill labor-force employed in low-wage industries (Harris and Zimmerman 3). 28 percent of African American men nationwide are employed as operators, fabricators and laborers. 36 percent of African American women nationwide work in technical, sales and administrative support jobs ("US Census Press Releases" 1). Manufacturing industries which began to open their plants in the rural South in the 1960s have mostly relocated to Southern urban centers and to other countries, which leaves rural African Americans with very limited job opportunities. African Americans in the rural South find themselves caught in a vicious circle of poverty since the earliest years of their childhood. Born into disfranchised families, they are disadvantaged in all areas that are vital for their further development: education, healthcare, social opportunities, housing quality and the type of residential neighborhood they inhabit (Harris and Zimmerman 3). Their childhood and family situation most often bear on the rest of their lives, significantly reducing their chances of success in adult life. The Invisible Man tells us that the smell of cooking cabbage reminds him "the leaner years of his childhood" (Ellison 225). For many African American children in the South their childhood remains lean. The South has the highest rate of poor children in the United States: 18.9 percent. African American children are twice as likely to be poor as white children. Children in impoverished families often inherit from their parents a sense of hopelessness that has disastrous effects on their aspirations[5] (Harris, Zimmerman 2, 3).[6]

An average index of residential segregation in the South is 67, while in the North it is about 77 (Denton, Massey 223). Living in the basement of a white-owned building, the Invisible Man breaks segregation ordinances. With legal ordinances gone, white people found other ways to keep blacks at a distance. Real estate agents and developers are still at the forefront of the segregation crusade. As stated earlier, consecutive Republican administrations kept withdrawing federal funding from inner city areas. There are no housing projects constructed or funded by federal authorities, which stopped constructing and funding such projects in the 1970s, when it became evident that they could no longer renege on the Fair Housing Act and would need to place the projects outside the ghetto. It will not be much of an overstatement if we say that African Americans in Northern inner city ghettos live in the "heart of darkness," different than the one that the Invisible Man finds in the South of the 1930s, but nonetheless the "heart of darkness." Recent media talk about the gentrification of Harlem is a good story rather than any substantial turn of events for people living there, let alone a trend in other ghettos.

The conditions in inner cities would prove Dan Freeman right in his prediction that "there will always be two countries here: one white, rich, fat and smug; the other black, poor, lean and striving" (Greenlee 128). His people are still largely striving on their own, unassisted by those who could make a difference. The poverty rate of African Americans in 2004 was almost twice the national rate — 24.4 percent of black people living below the poverty line. In 2003 it was 24.1 ("Poverty spreads" 2). President George W. Bush's policies are largely a continuation of the course pursued by his Republican predecessors — Reagan and Bush Senior. Both of the previous Republican administrations saw a rise in the rate of extreme poverty among African Americans. At the most critical moments the percentage of African Americans living below the poverty level reached 35.6 in 1982 and 35.7 in 1983. It significantly declined during Clinton's years in office. At the outset of Clinton's presidency in 1993 it was 33.1 percent, at its end in 2000 — 22.1 percent, which does not change the fact that it

Conclusion

still was more than twice the rate of extreme poverty for whites. Those numbers began to climb once again since the inception of the Bush Junior administration in 2001: from 22.7 percent in 2001 to 24.4 percent in 2004 ("Persons Below Poverty Level" 1, 2). An income gap between the most affluent and the most underprivileged keeps widening, just as it was the case during the previous two Republican administrations. Incomes of the first sharply rise, while incomes of the latter steeply decline. The disenchantment of people inhabiting inner city ghettos today provides a fertile ground for riots similar to those which took place in the 1960s. What in Freeman's days could still be called the black lower class has turned into the black underclass. Naomi Cassirer finds a correspondence between large concentrations of black population and their propensity to discrimination. The higher concentration of African Americans increases white people's fear of possible competition from black population (Cassirer 1).

The deepening degradation of inner cities widens the cleavage between the black middle class and the ghetto. While the black ghetto is firmly shut out of the sight and mind of the American society, the black middle class is often showed off, very much in the way Freeman is showed off by the CIA. More and more often one can see commercials featuring young black men in an executive guise, their black skin providing a good contrast for their white shirts. One of such black middle class commercials shows a young couple debating the color of their new car: "We're going over it each time. Blue, red...." Such a portrayal creates an illusion of equal access to the American dream. It takes one racial profiling incident to shatter the dream and give a renewed validity to Freeman's words "There's no way I can spin a middle-class cocoon thick enough for them not to penetrate any time they choose" (52). Most of the racial profiling incidents go unreported. Usually they come to light only when someone famous[7] is singled out or when the black community begins to simmer following a particularly drastic case.[8] The showing off of black individuals and black portions of society that presumably made it goes hand in hand with the continuing stereotyping of other African Americans. A black man running at night, particularly in a white district, is still likely to be taken for a criminal. Black women filling the pages of tabloid magazines are most often textualized as exotic and promiscuous.

Dan Freeman espouses black nationalism. What is the fate of the nationalist movement today? It definitely does not enjoy the popularity it used to enjoy in the 1960s and 1970s. However, it is still part of the African American political agenda. In 1995 the Nation of Islam managed to mobilize one million black men marching on Washington. Despite this onetime manifestation of activism, an active support for overtly nationalist or militant organizations is rather diluted. Although the Nation of Islam is not the only nationalist organization, it is definitely one of the most known and controversial. The movement and its leader Louis Farrhakan arouse general suspicion in the broader American public. Especially Farrhakan's anti–Semitism provokes a lot of commotion. Considering that Freeman's nationalism is free of religious zeal and prejudices against other minorities or oppressed people, it is doubtful whether he would identify with Farrhakan's organization. There are also such nationalist organizations as Sonny Carson's December 12 Movement, the Brotherhood Crusade in Los Angeles, the African Nationalist Pioneer Movement in Harlem, all of them active in the boycott of Korean American grocery stores of which I spoke in Chapter Four. Of course, one cannot forget about Molefi Kete Asante's Afrocentric movement. Even though the Black Power movement of the 1960s is gone, its impact on the consciousness of black people is indelible. Undoing the stereotyping of blackness, it has inculcated African Americans with self-esteem and pride in their heritage. The influence of Black Power is hyper-visible in the arts, especially in music, by no means only black. As William Van Deburg notes, Black Power is not dead. It has simply taken a life of its own (*New Day in Babylon* 308).

To what extent would Wittman Ah Sing find Asian Americans visible nowadays? The activism and commitment of people like him led to the creation of Asian American studies departments both on the West and the East Coast. A conference in Asian American studies is held annually in the United States and more conferences in the field take place both on American soil and abroad. Asian American panels are a permanent feature of various American studies and ethnic studies conferences. Courses in Asian American literature and Asian American studies are taught not only in the United States, but also abroad. Today Asian American studies are firmly a part of American studies, although they do not always attract as much interest as African American studies, especially in Europe. Asian American studies may belong to the academic world, but Asian American students point to unofficial quotas designed to limit their numbers at Californian universities.[9] In "Affirmative Action: Choosing Sides" Norimitsu

Conclusion

Onishi argues that Asian American students see certain affinities between university quotas and immigration quotas placed in the past on Asian population that wanted to enter the country (Onishi 27).

Wittman's real life counterpart — Frank Chin — complained about the problems which he and his fellow-editors of *Aiiieeeee* faced back in the early 1970s when they were trying to publish the first anthology of Asian American literature. They would not encounter such difficulties today, after at least thirty anthologies in the field appeared.[10] This does not mean, however, that Asian American authors do not face various unwritten constraints. The broader reading public continues to expect a certain amount of "otherness" and "ethnic authenticity" from minority writers. Wittman might still have a good reason to rage mad over statements like "Say something Chinese," "Do something Chinese" etc. (Kingston 325). Asian Americans remain to a great extent invisible to the rest of the American population.

Most stereotypes pertaining to Asian Americans in the 1960s hold today. Some of them may have lost their intensity, but they refuse to go away completely. Many Asian Americans keep complaining about sometimes being mistaken for foreigners who need to declare their national origin. Even today it is not uncommon for them to hear "Where do you come from?" For many Americans the word "American" remains synonymous with "white." Non-white is automatically labeled as exotic, culturally different, suspicious. All these features are often inscribed upon long-time citizens of the United States. Stereotypes swirling around Asian Americans are no less contradictory than they used to be: often an alien, but when convenient a model minority citizen assimilated to the point of being culturally indistinguishable from "wasps." A model minority myth preserves its double edge associations of an Asian American as an exemplary citizen and at the same time a treacherous, undercover, invisible enemy. All these success stories about Asian Americans carry a note of envy. They are still frequently seen as sly cheats who sneaked into the United States to usurp the right to the American dream. The popular belief is that no matter how hard you work, they will always outperform you. The media and the film industry are all too eager to present them as spies who pose a danger to national security. Asian American spies, real or presumed, always receive more attention from the media than their white counterparts.

Conclusion

Wittman dreams about making Chinese Americans culturally visible and winning for them a place in popular culture equal to that of African American jazz and blues musicians. They have not achieved such visibility, but as I argued in Chapter Three, Wittman's expectations of his people in this matter are hardly realistic. African Americans and Asian Americans have different socio-historical experience. Therefore it is difficult to expect that they will enjoy the same cultural visibility. On the other hand, as successive generations of Asian Americans mature, there may be less pressure on them from their parents to enter medical and legal professions. More and more Asian Americans may graduate in humanities and it is hard to predict what the future holds. What happens to Wittman's dream of reviving Asian American theatre? Perhaps it does not enjoy the popularity Wittman envisions for it, but there are ninety Asian American theatre companies and theatre houses today.[11] Every now and then an Asian American play attracts popular attention. However, these are usually plays that would arouse Wittman's strong criticism. They stir up controversy in the Asian American community. A major line of critique is that they reinscribe stereotypes of Asian Americans instead of dismantling them.[12] A number of Asian American critics argue that the audience shows interest in such productions because they pander to its racist preconceptions of Asian American population.

Even if Asian Americans are not entirely visible to the rest of society, they definitely enjoy greater visibility than they used to and it is through efforts and commitment of actively involved members of the community.[13] What matters most is that they have become more visible to themselves and to each other. Because of self-searching and the pursuit of visibility in various sections of the Asian American community, Asian American studies can boast greater heterogeneity than they did. Together with the waning influence of cultural nationalists, previously overlooked Asian Americans gained more visibility to other members of their own community. Today there is more room for non-normativity within the very realm of Asian American studies. People ostracized by Wittman Ah Sing have been acknowledged as legitimate members of the community. Immigrants and members of the Asian diaspora receive more attention nowadays than they did in the past. They are no longer invisible in a double way to such an extent as they used to be. We also need to take into account that for some Asian Americans, immigrants may be easier to accept once they have spent around forty years in the country. Many Asian American scholars are themselves immigrants or descendants of immigrants. If in the past Asian American immigrants constituted a minority, now they compose the majority within the Asian American community. Still, the greater visibility of immigrants within Asian American studies usually does not bring substantial changes in the material situation of these people.

Despite attempts to muzzle the voices of Asian American women who refused to embrace the nationalist vision of Asian American community, they have remained outspoken and continue to express themselves in a multitude of ways. Some of the anthologies of Asian American women's writing are: *Making Waves: An Anthology of Writings by and about Asian American Women* by Diane Yen-Mei Wong, *Making More Waves: New Writing by Asian American Women* (1997) by Elaine H. Kim, *Asian/Pacific Islander American Women: A Historical Anthology* (2003) by Shirley Hune, *The Forbidden Stitch: An Asian American Women's Anthology* (1989) by Shirley Geok-Lin Lim, *Unbroken Thread: An Anthology of Plays by Asian American Women* (1993) by Roberta Uno, *Kin: New Fiction by Black and Asian Women* (2004) by Karen McCarthy. Homosexuality is no longer swept under the carpet in the community either.[14] Most Asian American scholars and writers understand that striving for visibility should not happen at the sacrifice of internal diversity. All this unfolds in a diametrically changed socio-cultural climate within the broader society. Pioneers of Asian American studies in the 1960s and 1970s were faced with altogether different circumstances.

Acceptance of difference and commitment to diversity within Asian American studies alone will not make Asian Americans more visible unless it is accompanied by an equal commitment to heterogeneity in the rest of society. One of the sentences in Lee's *Native Speaker* reads "It is still a black and white world" (195). As I pointed out in the Introduction, the world is no longer exactly black and white. The growing population of Latinos makes some American politicians see more colors than black and white. However, electoral appeals to Latinos do not cause any radical improvement in the situation of the people concerned. It all usually boils down to rhetoric. Most influential leaders of color are still black. Asian Americans remain effaced from the political map of the country. Double-edge stereotyping is once again visible in electoral politics. Some

Conclusion

see Asian Americans as too alien to be part of the American politics, while others play up their alleged financial success, arguing that they have already integrated and therefore no special efforts need to be made to win them over.

Immigrants take a central place among the invisible in *Native Speaker*. How do they fare nowadays outside the Asian American community? The United States' policy towards immigrants follows mostly the same old line. On the one hand, they are treated as cheap labor and therefore accepted. On the other hand, they are perceived as an alien intrusion defiling the purity of the American state.[15] Strengthening of the borders goes hand in hand with the discourse of the United States as a safe harbor that welcomes "tired, ... poor ... huddled masses yearning to breathe free" (Lazarus 1). All these contradictions are well encapsulated in the already mentioned 2004 legislative proposal turning "illegal aliens" into "legal aliens" on condition that they could prove that they had an employer.[16] The very phrase a "legal alien" is an oxymoron. How can you be a "legal" "alien"? The term "alien" leaves no room for legality. Either you are wanted or not. Why does one of the most conservative administrations that sees in terms of black and white suddenly allow for the existence of the twilight zone? The "legal alien" proposal illustrates a usership mentality hidden behind the discourse of American exceptionalism.

Native Speaker shows more commitment to interracial and interethnic diversity than any other text discussed here. Lee emphasizes the need for diversity within a broader socio-political landscape, not just Asian America. Writing a "new book of the land," Henry Park imagines people from different ethnic and racial backgrounds working together. To fulfill the dream of a truly multicultural state, one needs to go beyond the confines of one's ethnic and racial group. John Kwang's coalition reaches outside the Korean American and Asian American community. The coalition in the end collapses because of external forces. Kwang's failure in no way decreases the need for such coalitions.[17] Throughout this project I have been highlighting the potential stemming from transformational identity politics. Only by joining forces, can minorities create leverage strong enough to win substantial gains for themselves and each other. Particular socio-historical experiences and particular histories of oppression do not change the fact that they share common interests and have a stake in working together to accomplish their goals. Despite various interracial projects

Conclusion

there is no large influential multiethnic, multiracial coalition or pressure group today. The creation of such a coalition is crucial for the achievement of visibility by African Americans, Asian Americans and other marginalized racial and ethnic groups in the United States.

The action of *Native Speaker* concludes about one year before the outbreak of the Rodney King rebellion. The verdict in the Rodney King trial merely provided a fuse for the outpouring of long-brewing anger of African Americans from inner cities. That anger kept accumulating during all the years of neglect suffered by inner cities at the time of the Reagan and Bush Senior administrations. The end of George W. Bush's first administration and the beginning of its second term does not augur anything good for racial relations in the United States and for the most underprivileged members of racial minorities. It may just as well set the stage for future rebellions of the oppressed.

George W. Bush's first term in office saw a further withdrawal of capital from inner cities, a total collapse of welfare programs[18] and tax cuts for the most affluent sectors of the United States' population. An approach of the administration to inner city schools illustrates its attitudes to the whole districts. If a given school does not perform, then it is totally abandoned. Only schools that show results can count on subsidies of the government.[19] Such a reasoning locks the underprivileged further in a vicious circle of poverty. In past policies towards the ghetto the effects were addressed, not the causes. Now we have come to the situation when neither the effects nor the causes are touched. Democrats do not fare much better in their stand on the ghetto and their policies to the most disadvantaged people of color. In the presidential campaign of 2004 President Bush put stress on "ownership society," courting big entrepreneurs and all those who enjoy the privilege of "ownership" in a big sense of the word. The Democratic candidate — John Kerry — claimed to represent "the middle America." Both left a large spectrum of the population unaccounted for. One solicited the votes of those who boast extensive property ownership. The other canvassed the votes of those who own considerably less, but still count themselves among property owners. Omi and Winant's 1993 claim that both Republicans and Democrats bargain for the votes from the suburbs still holds. Both shudder from "group-specific" measures that would lead to concrete remedies ("The L.A. Race Riot and U.S. Politics" 110). Whiteness keeps hedging its bets, cautiously

Conclusion

guarding access to property. At the same time there is not enough pressure from African American leaders to ensure visibility and accountability to people stranded in inner cities. As I argued in Chapter Two, the leaders also have a stake in segregation, for a large concentration of African American population in one place helps to secure greater support of the population that is more likely to vote along racial lines.

Henry Park's dream of a country where one is "unafraid to speak like a Puritan, like a Chinaman and like every boat person in between" is a long way off especially with the amplified suspicion of difference, following the September 11 attacks in 2001 (Chang-rae Lee 304). John Kwang's statement "the public may begin viewing anything outside mainstream experience and culture too threatening and dangerous" gains more currency in the post–September 11 climate. Proponents of corporate multiculturalism and opponents of any form of difference won extra ammunition. Some of them used the attacks to further stigmatize any non-normative experience. In the immediate aftermath of the attacks, calls for racial profiling were made on major Sunday news programs, including the CNN Late Edition. An argument in favor was that none of the hijackers was a white Anglo-Saxon Protestant. Not enough attention was devoted to the fact that, ironically, immediately before the attacks, each of the hijackers successfully minimized their difference by emulating white Anglo-Saxon Protestants in their dress, haircut etc. None of them looked like a Moslem fundamentalist.

Difference fatigue is even more conspicuous in the United States foreign policy under President Bush. The rhetoric of the clash of civilizations and "either you are with us or against us" resembles Kipling's line so much abhorred by Wittman Ah Sing: "East is east and west is west and the twain shall never meet." The flipside of Kipling's "twain" is "East meets West." One of the most recent appropriations of "East meets West" is "East meets Wal-Mart" publicized by the media. The apparent cleavage between the East and West does not preclude economic expansion into the East. In the face of the falling dollar, there is once again pressure on China to revalue its currency and reduce the discrepancy between exported and imported goods. Expansion into the East happens both on the economic and the military front. Military interventions take place under the pretext of spreading democracy. Some analysts see in President Bush's policies attempts to resuscitate the dream of the American century. Penetration into

Conclusion

foreign lands coincides with growing hermetism at home — fortifying of the borders with legislation like the Patriot Act, which includes fingerprinting of foreigners at the borders.

Despite all these moves, white authorities still do their best to efface their power and to make oppression inflicted on people of color invisible. The American media controlled largely by conservatives help them in this task. Those who are most invisible never make it to the domain of public visibility. They never appear on TV screens or on the pages of national and international newspapers and magazines. Keeping these people invisible, the white apparatus of power plots to make structures of oppression invisible, erasing the effects of its policies and dispelling any suspicion that there may be a link between these policies and the disenfranchisement of the most invisible citizens.

As I have been emphasizing throughout this study, oppressors can be equally invisible as the oppressed. Today they are more invisible than they used to be. Gone are the white clad figures burning the crosses.[20] Respectable looking men observing the rules of political correctness arouse hardly any suspicion in a casual viewer. In most cases only people immediately touched by oppression can see through its modern guise. They see it because they feel it on their own backs. The "invisible yet horribly tangible plate glass" of which Du Bois spoke one hundred years ago is more invisible to the broader public than it used to be, but it is just as tangible and visible to people incarcerated behind it. Chitra Divakaruni captures this mixture of tangibility and invisibility in her poem "Yuba City School." A young Sikh student who has long hair in accordance with the customs of his people is constantly harassed by other students:

> In the playground ... invisible hands snatch at his uncut hair,
> unseen feet trip him from behind,
> and when he turns,
> ghost laughter
> all around his bleeding knees [Divakaruni in Hongo 79–80].

Oppression is all too palpable to him even if he does not always literally see his oppressors. Unlike the oppressors in Yuba City school, those who draft and execute racist policies usually keep out of immediate contact with the oppressed.

Ellison, Greenlee, Kingston and Lee ensure visibility both for the oppressed and oppressors. The exposure of white oppression is a necessary prerequisite to undermining it. However, a substantial redistribution of power will be possible only if people of color meet cooperation on the other side of the color line. None of the authors under scrutiny here treats whiteness as a monolith, slotting all whites into one category. All of them manage to avoid the trap of essentialism. Still, they are painfully aware that there are not enough white Americans who would like to see major changes in power relations. Those willing to make a difference usually do not have enough power themselves to successfully challenge the status quo. Never stopping to think of their own privilege, most white people are not aware to what extent they are invested in their own privilege and to what extent they help to perpetuate it. Those who are aware and those who could change power dynamics do not show the least intention. The white apparatus of power never gave up even the tiniest portion of its power without pressure. Therefore it is so important for various minorities to combine forces in their striving for visibility. Ellison, Greenlee, Kingston and Lee do not limit themselves to critiquing whiteness. They look inside their own communities, making it clear that transformations are needed not only outside, but also among their own rank and file. Greater visibility of people of color to each other will make it easier for them to contend for visibility in the society at large.

CHAPTER NOTES

Introduction

1. I first encountered the term "relationality" in Susan Stanford Friedman's essay "Beyond White and Other: Relationality and Narratives of Race in Feminist Discourse" published in 1995. Other authors who underscore the importance of location also use such terms as "relationality," "relational differences," "differences in relation." Neil Smith and Cindi Katz speak of the "relationality of social location" and "relationality of geographical location" (77).

2. The terms "second-sight" and "double consciousness" originally appear in the 1897 article "Strivings of the Negro People" published in the *Atlantic* magazine. The essay was republished in 1903 in *The Souls of Black Folk*.

3. Critics provide us with diverse interpretations of the veil. Donald B. Gibson claims that Du Bois "inverts the meaning of the folk notion of being born with a veil" (xv). Traditionally, being born with a caul portends luck, whereas here it becomes an ominous sign. The fate of blacks is sealed from birth and the veil signifies blindness rather than clairvoyance. Thomas C. Holt refutes this theory, suggesting that alienation can become "the source of second sight" (306), a springboard for action. If blacks were not endowed with second sight, whites would manage to keep them in the dark. Second sight enables African Americans to penetrate into the world of whites. According to Holt, Du Bois's later writings imply that "African Americans accept, even embrace, the contradiction and paradox arising from dual identities and consciousness. Because they live in two worlds at once, African Americans possess the power to see where others are blind" (306). In the light of such interpretation the second sight gains the semblance of a visionary quality. Stephen H. Browne sides with Holt's positive reading of double-consciousness. Picking up on his observations about African Americans' existence in two realities at once, Browne argues that alienation and "twoness" are a prerequisite for privileged insight (83).

4. Some African American writers made more overt references to Native Americans and encounters between both groups. Alice Walker raises the subject in her novel *Meridian*. The protagonist's father studies the maps of the land on which he lives with his family only to conclude that in the past it belonged to Native Americans. Himself a descendant of slaves, he still sees African Americans as partly complicit in the colonization of Native American territories. In *Beloved* Toni Morrison speaks of runaway slaves who strike a friendship with a Native American tribe. Some of them choose to stay with the tribe for good. One of the chief characters in the novel — Paul D. — walks North. His journey North bears some reminiscence to *China Men* Ah Goong's journey West. Ralph Ellison alludes briefly to the relations between African Americans and Native Americans in an interview conducted by Ishmael Reed: "Historically, we were trying to escape from slavery in a scene consisting of geographical space. First, to the North and then to the West, going to the Nation (meaning the Indian Nation and later the Oklahoma Territory), just as Huckleberry Finn decided to do, and as Bessie Smith states in one of her blues. Of course, some of us escaped South and joined the Seminoles and fought with them against the United States. Geography forms the scene in which we and our forefathers acted and continue to act out the drama of Afro-American freedom" (Ishmael Reed's Interview with Ellison 155).

Notes — Introduction

Ellison's statement corresponds to Foucault's statement cited by me in Chapter Two: "A whole history remains to be written of spaces — which would at the same time be the history of powers" (*Power/Knowledge* 149).

5. This in no way detracts from the uniqueness of Ellison's text. He had every right to focus exclusively on his people, but some of Ellison's African American contemporaries paid a little more attention to the disenfranchisement of other marginalized racial groups. In *If He Hollers Let Him Go* Chester Himes condemns the Japanese American World War II internment in relocation camps. In *I Know Why the Caged Bird Sings* Maya Angelou wonders why African Americans did not launch any large-scale protest against the internment. The internment also attracted the attention of the African American press. Many of the African American journalists displayed sympathy for the plight of the internees. (For a detailed account see Reginald Kearney's *Afro-American Views of the Japanese*). In one of the interviews Ellison brags that his father fought in Cuba, in the Philippines and in China against the "Boxer Rebellion" (Hersey's Interview with Ellison 288). It is interesting that he fails to emphasize the colonial nature of those enterprises. Gary Okihiro points out that many of the African American soldiers fighting in the Philippines between 1899–1902 identified with the Filipinos rather than with white American soldiers. Some chose to stay in the Philippines (57). Originally, Ellison planned a novel reaching beyond the borders of the United States and unfolding during World War II, not the 1930s (Ellison's Introduction IX). Ellison himself spent World War II in the United States marine merchant service. He intended to place his protagonist — a black soldier — in the German camp for prisoners of war. At stake then, according to Ellison, would be the relation of his black protagonist to white fellow-prisoners of war and German captors, also white. He would be confronted with "native and foreign racisms" (Introduction IX).

6. I elaborate on "signifying," relating it to Henry Louis Gates in Chapter One.

7. In Charles Chesnutt's "The Passing of Grandison," the son of a slave owner — Master Dick — is a trickster too.

8. I thank Professor Werner Sollors for referring me to William James's fragment on invisibility and Richard Wright's appropriation of this fragment.

9. In his autobiography *Dusk of Dawn* Du Bois claims that in the town of Great Barrington "the racial angle was more clearly defined against the Irish:" "in the ordinary social affairs of the village — the Sunday school with its picnics and festivals; the temporary skating rink in the town hall; the coasting in crowds on all the hills — in all these, I took part with no thought of discrimination on the part of my fellows, for that I would have been first to notice" (563). The town directed its hostility against Irish Americans, rather than African Americans because Irish Americans by far outnumbered them, thus posing a greater challenge to the status quo. There are more striking differences between Du Bois's and Sin Far's experience. Du Bois had the privilege of first class education, graduating from Fisk and Harvard. Sin Far, on the other hand, was withdrawn from school in her teens. As adults both were activists. Still, they considerably differed in their activism. While Du Bois co-founded and belonged to numerous African American organizations, Sin Far had a more hands-on approach, coming directly in touch with people whom she represented as a journalist and a writer. She worked as a volunteer in Chinatown and Chinatown missions (Ferens 186). Du Bois spoke for lower class African Americans from a safe distance of his consecutive posts either as a professor at Atlanta University, a newspaper editor or as a leader of such organizations as the Niagara Movement (founded on July 2 1905), National Negro Committee (founded in 1909 and in 1910 reorganized into the National Association for the Advancement of Colored People) (Nathan Huggins 1291). He hardly ever came into immediate contact with people at the very bottom, people whom he represented for most of his life. An example of a closer contact comes when a poor black man — Sam Hose — was accused of murder and subsequently lynched in 1899. Du Bois unsuccessfully lobbied for a fair trial (Huggins 1287). Both Du Bois and Sin Far were people of mixed racial heritage. Sin Far had a British born father and a Chinese mother, whereas Du Bois had a "brown mother" and a "light mulatto father" (*Dusk of Dawn* 561). In her adult life Sin Far was treated as a white person unless she announced herself otherwise, which she often did. If not for his high public status, Du Bois could easily have passed for white as well.

10. The exclusion of Chinese Americans from photographs at Promontory Summit also

features prominently in Frank Chin's novel *Donald Duk*.

11. Similar charges were also made against African American workers. Conflicts between white and black workers flared at various points of American history. Rather than blame the system and white employers, white workers often sought the source of their disfranchisement in the presence of black labor. White employers sometimes used black workers as a bargain card against the demands of white labor force. In his book *Genesis of the Black Working Class in the American South, 1863–82*, Gerald Jaynes reports, for example, the practice of replacing white workers in the middle of a strike (268). Fearing competition from African Americans, white workers often targeted their black counterparts, for instance in 1858, 1859 whites attacked black caulkers in Baltimore shipyards. In 1865 they successfully lobbied for their complete exclusion. You can find more examples of hostility against African American workers in David Roediger's *Wages of Whiteness* and in the above mentioned book. I return to "compensatory wages of whiteness" while discussing the attitudes of white paint factory workers to the Invisible Man.

12. The narrator of *Obasan*—Naomi—utters these words when she compares herself and many other Japanese Canadians with her activist Aunt Emily. Naomi's narrative is an attempt at capturing part of that activist spirit and chipping away at the invisibility of her people.

Chapter One

1. Initially, the immature Invisible Man keeps stifling his second-sight. All along he is aware of its existence, but for a good while he shies away from it, fearing to see things as they are. He realizes that part of himself is detached and can see everything. This part of his personality tells him to brood over his grandfather's words. Yet he is afraid to recognize it as an essential part of himself, preventing it from springing to the surface and flourishing (253, 254). The Invisible Man dreads to acknowledge the power of second sight. The voice of his grandfather symbolizes the Invisible Man's dormant self-consciousness. The grandfather's voice haunts him throughout the novel, but he keeps silencing it. He tries to efface the recalcitrant part of his personality, the part that questions instead of blindly obeying and accepting things at face value. The Invisible Man's suppression of second-sight goes hand in hand with his suppression of internal division and multiplicity. Only after accepting internal discord and beginning to perceive himself as a multiple subject, does the Invisible Man embrace second sight and come to see it as an asset, not a drawback. His second sight allows him to "look around the corners" (383). It is not until he gives up the pursuit of uniformity that he can achieve the full measure of individuality and humanity (435). The final recognition of all facets of his experience allows the Invisible Man to achieve the feeling of coherence. He can never be dispossessed of his experiences even if he is dispossessed of everything else (383).

2. In his double-consciousness formula Du Bois argues: "the Negro is ... *born with a veil*, and *gifted with second-sight* in this American world,—a world which yields him no true self-consciousness, but only lets him *see himself through the revelation of the other world*. It is a peculiar sensation, this double-consciousness, this sense of always *looking at one's self through the eyes of others*, of measuring one's soul by the tape of the world that looks on in contempt and pity. One ever feels his twoness,—an American, a Negro, two souls, two thoughts, two unreconciled strivings in one dark body, whose dogged strength alone keeps it from being torn asunder" (Du Bois, *The Souls of Black Folk* 5, my emphasis). As mentioned in the Introduction, while the "veil" signifies blindness, "second-sight" stands for the clairvoyance of black people. Second-sight allows African Americans to see where others are blind. Du Bois acknowledges the existence of second-sight, but overall he concentrates in *The Souls of Black Folk* on black people's distorted perception, rather than their illumination. Most researchers dealing with the double consciousness formula dwell on the blurred vision of African Americans, virtually overlooking the problem of the white world's blindness.

3. Proponents of polygenesis maintained that white people were created in a different way than people of color. Monogenesis assumed common origin. Some of these pseudoscientific theories sought substantiation in the Bible. According to the theory already mentioned in the Introduction, black people were descended from Ham cursed by God and

Notes — Chapter One

therefore condemned to constant toil and servitude to Shem and Japheth. Pseudo-scientific statements propagated in Arthur de Gobineau's *Essay on the Inequality of Races* (published between 1853–1855) kept surfacing for the next hundred years. De Gobineau distinguished between higher and lower races. According to de Gobineau, superior races composed higher cultures. The matches between higher and lower races led to the degradation of superior races (Omi, Winant 59). Proponents of eugenics argued that interracial relationships were a transgression against nature and lead to biological throwbacks. A legal ban on interracial relationships was held in some states until the 1980s of the 20th century. Mississippi was the last state to repeal the ban in 1987 (Tennessee in 1978, Virginia 1967, Wyoming 1965, Nebraska 1963) (Sollors 410). Social Darwinism — especially popular at the end of the 19th and the beginning of the 20th century treated all racial and class inequalities as "natural." Social privilege was attributed to inherent qualities like industriousness, moderation, self-restraint, frugality. Major representatives of social Darwinism in Britain were Herbert Spencer and Walter Bagehot, in the United States William Graham Sumner. The American law treated race as a biological concept. It was especially visible in the theory of hypodescent, the term coined by anthropologist Marvin Harris (Cheryl Harris 1738–1739). The theory of hypodescent made a person with black and white ancestors automatically black legally. Hence people of biracial origin found themselves deprived of privileges reserved for white citizens. Even if a person was phenotypically white, they were classified as black. Very remote black ancestry sufficed to make someone black. The theory of hypodesecent did not apply to Native Americans. The legal situation of people with Native American descent was and is precisely opposite to that of people with black ancestry. Very remote Native American ancestry is no longer enough to define oneself as a Native American before the law. Once again financial issues are at stake. Anyone who proves one-eighth of Native American descent is entitled to financial benefits from the state (Piper 427).

4. Anthropologist Franz Boas separated the concept of race from culture, emphasizing the plurality of cultures and refuting the notion of one dominating culture (Ferens 121, 152). Horace Meyer Kallen coined the term "cultural pluralism" (Omi, Winant 15). The 1920s research conducted by the Chicago School of Sociology and supervised by Robert E. Park promoted the concept of race as a social category, not a biological one (Omi, Winant 15).

5. In "Swing Low, Sweet Cadillac," the chapter of *Possessive Investment in Whiteness*, George Lipsitz refers to the fragment of Chester Himes' 1971 *Autobiography*, in which Himes recalls the purchase of a family car at the end of World War I — the first in the county of rural Mississippi. An envy of their white neighbors was such that Himes' father lost his job at Alcorn A&M University (Lipsitz 163). Local whites forced the Himeses to leave the state. Speaking of the incident from the perspective of the 1970s, Himes notices that "white people just the same today ... if a black man owns a big and expensive car, they will hate him for that" (Himes cited in Lipsitz 163). Car ownership was a significant ego-booster for African Americans, usually inscribed as objects of property, not its subjects. Himes' statement still holds if we consider all cases of racial profiling against African Americans driving expensive cars. A frequent suspicion on the part of the police is that they must have been stolen. Just as car ownership is empowering to African Americans, racial profiling provides psychological compensations to many white policemen who resent black ownership.

6. As I go on to argue in Chapter Two, some black people had a stake in the perpetuation of the ghetto. Black real estate developers like Chicago's Jesse Binga and New York's Philip A. Payton made small fortunes on creating black settlements (Denton, Massey 40).

7. I use the term "immigrants" in reference to African Americans from the South with caution. That is how some of them referred to themselves, but obviously they were "immigrants" in a different way than European immigrants. Denton and Massey emphasize among others that immigrants from Europe experienced a higher degree of upward mobility and found it easier to integrate into more ethnically heterogeneous sections of Northern cities (27).

8. Ardent proponents of segregation banded themselves in neighborhood associations, which were to execute restrictive covenants. In 1924 the National Association of Real Estate Brokers decided that real estate agents should refrain from striking deals with people of any race or nationality whose presence

Notes — Chapter Two

might lower property values (Denton, Massey 37).

9. Ellison's mother was an avid activist opposing among others segregation. Like the Invisible Man, Ellison's mother breaks anti-segregation laws, but she does it openly. Ellison reminisces: "When I was in college, my mother broke a segregated-housing ordinance in Oklahoma City, and they were throwing her in jail, and the NAACP would get her out and they would come back and throw her in jail again. This went on until my brother beat up one of the white inspectors, then she decided that it was about time to get out of that situation before he got himself shot" (Hersey's Interview with Ellison 288).

10. Ellison reflects on the problem of African American infighting in an interview conducted by Ishmael Reed. He blames it partly on segregation of African Americans from the rest of society: "we grow up in our own segregated neighborhoods and have our initial contacts and contentions with our own people" (131). He also notices reverse power dynamics at play: "people who didn't dare to lift a finger against a white man would give other Blacks hell" (131). Overall, he emphasizes the importance of uniting black efforts on "bigger and more important targets for intellectual assault out there in the broader society" (131).

11. Ellison claims that in his fiction he wants to answer the following questions: "Who am I, what am I, how did I come to be" (Ellison cited in Schaub 152)

12. Ellison himself is emphatic about the fact that as a young man he also walked with shoes with holes to save money for some of the literary classics: "During the late 1940s when I was walking around with holes in my shoes, I was spending twenty-five dollars a volume for Malraux's *The Psychology of Art*" (Ishmael Reed's Interview with Ellison 149).

13. He reads and blows his music underground. There is also an indication that every now and then he comes in touch with other people, limited as his contacts are at the time.

14. Search for home is a recurring motif in African American literature. The recurrence of the theme indicates that the United States is not black people's homeland, but rather a foster land. Searching for home is especially pervasive in spirituals. In the last chapter of *The Souls* Du Bois quotes spirituals in which the word "home" plays a crucial role: "Swing, swing low chariot to carry me home" (209),

"I want to go home" (210), "But the lord shall bear my spirit home" (212), "My mother took her flight home" (209). The Invisible Man is seized with the feeling of displacement whenever he can see the Star Spangled Banner hoisted: "there was always that sense in me of being apart when the flag went by ... my star was not yet there" (298). Searching for home together with self-searching comes up in Ellison's short story "Flying Home" (1944), in which the protagonist — Todd, one of the first black pilots — crashes in rural Alabama, where he is confronted by the Jim Crow reality. An encounter with a black folktale teller — Jefferson — helps him out of a cumbersome situation and allows him to find his racial consciousness.

15. I elaborate on the special relationship that African Americans have with the night in Chapter Two.

16. In an interview conducted by Reed, Ellison claims that he called Bledsoe this way because he bled his people (157).

Chapter Two

1. Sam Greenlee was born in 1930 in Chicago. He is a poet and novelist. In the preface to *The Spook Who Sat by the Door*, his first published novel, Greenlee says: "I am a black American and I write; not necessarily in that order of importance." The order of importance may not be accidental nonetheless, if we take into account that black consciousness comes to the foreground in all of his written works: *The Spook Who Sat by the Door* (1969), *The Blues for an African Princess* (1971), *Ammunition and Other Raps* (1975), the second novel *Baghdad Blues* (1976), and a collection of all his poems *Be-Bop Man/Be-Bop Woman* (1995). Back in the 1960s and 1970s Greenlee was a member of the black cultural nationalist movement, cooperating with such artists and activists like Nikki Giovanni and Sonia Sanchez. In the 1970s he was also a film producer. Greenlee received B.S. in political science from the University of Wisconsin in 1952. He studied at the University of Chicago between 1954 and 1957 and at the University of Thessalonikki for one year (1963–1964). Greenlee professes fluency in Greek, Indonesian, Malay and much more limited knowledge of Arabic, French and Italian, the languages which he mustered while working as a

Notes — Chapter Two

United States Foreign Service officer in Iraq, Pakistan, Indonesia and Greece. The United States Information Agency awarded Greenlee a Meritorious Service Award. He quit the job in 1965 to pursue his writing in Greece until 1968. Remembering this stage of his life, Greenlee says: "I gave up a very comfortable existence. I wasn't making a whole lot of money, but I was living very well. I had a lot of status and prestige, but that wasn't what I wanted to do, so I sat down on a Greek island and I starved for three years 'cause that's what I wanted to do" (*Black World* 46). Sam Greenlee currently lives in South Side Chicago. He still writes and participates in poetry readings. The credo accompanying Greenlee for most of his life seems to be encapsulated in his statement dating back to 1971: "if you can content yourself with just making a living and making a living at doing something you believe in, then you stick to the real Black thing" ("Black World Interview" 46).

2. The text which I analyze in Chapter Four — *Native Speaker* by Chang-rae Lee — shows that other minorities are just as predisposed to become spies.

3. Having said that, it is important to remember that the night can be as much a foe as it is an ally to African Americans. Any black person spotted by a white policeman at night is instantly suspected of a criminal intent. Freeman says: "Any nigger running at night has got to have done something wrong" (198). Easy Rawlins from Walter Mosley's *Devil in a Blue Dress* feels very uncomfortable when he finds himself in the white neighborhood at night: "I wasn't used to going into white communities, like Santa Monica ... I never loitered anywhere except among my own people, in my own neighborhood" (51) ... "I left the station at a fast walk but I wanted to run. It was fifteen blocks from John's speak and I had to keep telling myself to slow down. I knew that a patrol car would arrest any sprinting Negro they encountered. The streets were especially dark and empty. Central avenue was like a giant black alley and I felt like a small rat, hugging the corners and looking out for cats" (76). In Greenlee's poem "Cats" black people are compared to cats (*Blues for an African Princess*). Here the police are the cats that pose a threat to the protagonist.

4. In an attempt to wrench African Americans out of materialist white culture, Maulana Karenga founded "back to black" organization Us. The movement adopted kawaida as its ideology. Seven key values which governed the lives of Us followers were compressed in Nguzo Saba. Karenga found white Christmas too materialistic; therefore, he replaced it with Kwanzaa connected to harvest festivals of Africans (Van Deburg 275).

5. Sojourner Truth, an African American slave for forty years, was a speaker for the rights of women of color. One of her most famous speeches came on May 9, 1967. It was an address to the First Annual Meeting of the American Equal Rights Association, New York City.

6. Denmark Vesey, born in Africa, purchased his freedom from the captain of a slave ship in 1800. In 1822 he was trying to launch a slave rebellion in Charleston, South Carolina. Upon the discovery of the plot, Vesey and thirty-four other black men were executed.

7. It is worth mentioning that Nikki Giovanni wrote a poem introduction to Greenlee's volume of poetry *Blues for an African Princess*. One of his poems is dedicated to Sister Nikki. Giovanni won the title "the Princess of Black Poetry" when she was still in her twenties (Geourgoudaki 159). However, taking into account that Greenlee dedicates his poems to various African American women of the 1960s, we should not assume that the Princess from the title of his volume is one woman, but rather diverse African American women.

8. Some of the greatest hits by James Brown — a soul and blues performer — are "Say It Aloud — I'm Black and Proud," "Soul Pride," "Soul Power," "Let Yourself Go."

9. Aretha Franklin was a soul, blues performer and a chaired university professor (Van Deburg 78). Some of her hits are "A Natural Woman," "Son of A Preacher Man."

10. Leaders of SNCC (the Student Nonviolent Coordinating Committee) make similar observations in their "Position Paper on Black Power": "The myth that the Negro is somehow incapable of liberating himself, is lazy, etc., came out of the American experience. In the books that children read, whites are always 'good' (good symbols are white), blacks are 'evil' or seen as savages in movies, their language is referred to as a 'dialect,' and black people in this country are supposedly descended from savages" (in Van Deburg 120). Freeman criticizes color imagery employed in most of the films. A good female character usually has blond hair, while a bad one is most

Notes — Chapter Two

often dark haired. The same pertains to male characters.

11. It still needs to be emphasized that they stressed their African origins to the varying degree. Although most nationalists referred in one way or another to their African past, they usually devoted little place to the issue in their programs or declarations. Pan Africanists and Afrocentrists, on the other hand, made it a cornerstone of their philosophy. Afrocentricity is first of all the model of education promoted by Molefi Kete Asante and his followers. Asante argues that African American students should find themselves in the centre (Asante in Van Deburg 290). The Eurocentric model of education places them on the margins, making them objects rather than subjects of educational experience. While Eurocentrists adopt a linear view of identity, Afrocentrists endorse a circular view (Marable 322). Critics of Afrocentricity point out that if it indeed acquaints African American students with their history and culture, it does very little to change existing power relations. Still, others notice that it does not really help African American students to map out their place in the American context, because it shifts the focus from the United States to Africa. Hence it fails to prepare them for the challenges they will need to confront in America. Some representatives of petite black bourgeoisie tried to usurp Afrocentricity as its own ideology, leading to the vulgarization of the original model. Manning Marable observes that Afrocentricity enabled them to claim their racial pride, accept their privileged position and at the same time disregard historical realities (324).

12. Malcolm X co-founded OAAU in 1964 after splitting with Elijah Muhammed and the Nation of Islam — the organization through which he became converted to Islam and in which he had been a minister since 1952 to 1964. He was assassinated one year later in 1965.

13. Founded in 1960, SNCC (the Student Nonviolent Coordinating Committee) included at first both black and white members. It organized civil rights demonstrations and sit-ins, freedom rides and voting rights campaigns throughout the South. In 1966 white members were excluded from the organization. Stokely Carmichael and Rap Brown initiated the expulsion, maintaining that the presence of white students inhibited their progress. They drafted their new program — Position Paper on Black Power. The word Black Power was used for the first time by Carmichael during the June 1966 march through Mississippi (McCarthey 128). Martin Luther King strongly opposed the use of the term, claiming that it will detract their sympathizers and empower their opponents, rather than black people. Still, he understood the desperation and disenchantment of people who rallied behind Black Power. In the Position Paper on Black Power, published in New York Times in August 1966 black nationalist leaders substituted black power for their previous catchword: freedom. The phrase Black Power was originally used in Richard Wright's book *Black Power* (published in 1954). In the book Wright registers his journey through Africa.

14. CORE (Congress of Racial Equality) was set up during World War II in Chicago. It became popular in the 1960s thanks to its involvement in freedom rides in the South. It also launched various community initiatives. In summer 1968 CORE expelled white members from its ranks, two years after SNCC took a similar step (Van Deburg 175). Roy Innis rejected the notion of "black capitalism." According to him, African Americans had to create a new system that will "fit" their needs. Innis envisioned a major restructuring in urban areas, seeing a conflict of interests between ghettos and larger urban units in which they were located. Innis was quick to point out that institutions that are supposed to provide service to African Americans take their money and later do not serve them ("A New Social Contract" in Van Deburg 179).

15. The discrepancy between the United States' noble ideas abroad and their policy towards African Americans at home has attracted attention of many other black people. Richard Wright, for example, observes in the Introduction to Drake's and Cayton's *Black Metropolis:* "How easy it is to leave Chicago and fight and die for democracy in Spain! How soothing it is to prefer to civilize the heathen in Japan when slave conditions exist in Florida" (XXI). The term "heathen" strikes a chord of the missionary discourse employed by white missionaries who converted the Japanese (Ferens, *Japanese Romances and Chinatown Missions*). It is unlikely that Wright himself thought of the Japanese as "heathens." As Reginald Kearney notices in *African American Views of the Japanese*, most African American intellectuals admired the Japanese for their achievements, seeing them as a slap on the face of white supremacists (XXV).

Notes — Chapter Two

16. Around twenty years after Freeman utters these words, some representatives of the white apparatus of power came to compare the fight against inner city gangs to the war in Vietnam and members of these gangs to Viet Cong fighters. In 1988 the chief of the Los Angeles District Attorney's Hardcore Drug Unit said of the situation in Southcentral Los Angeles: "This is Vietnam here" (cited in Mike Davis 268). Mayor James Van Horn of Artesia called gang members "Viet Cong abroad in our society" (Mike Davis 268), classifying militant African Americans as internal enemies and inner city ghettos as alien territories within a native land.

17. I cite Giovanni's statement with caution, since it is in many ways dangerous to make comparisons between racial oppression and gender oppression. Drawing such parallels, we may risk obliterating the differences between the two. Still, in the context of my discussion of animosities between African Americans and various other oppressed groups, I find her statement relevant. It also needs to be mentioned at this point that Giovanni herself might be accused of anti–Semitism in an earlier cited poem "The True Import of Present Dialogue: Black vs. Negro," asking her people if they can take the life of a person of Hebrew origin (Giovanni 19–20).

18. Nikki Giovanni's poem introduction to Greenlee's volume of poetry *Blues for an African Princess* playfully reflects on the fact that Greenlee celebrates in his poetry African American women although he sees some of them as rivals. "African Princesses" also featured in other writings by African American nationalists of the period, for example Eldridge Cleaver's *Soul on Ice* and George Jackson's memoirs. Usually they were highly idealized and sexualized.

19. In the foreword to *The Spook* Sam Greenlee identifies himself as "a second generation immigrant from the deep south."

20. The reference to a runner strikes a chord of Johnson's speech in which he says: "You do not take a person who for years had been hobbled by chains and liberate him, bring him up to the starting line of a race and then say, 'You are free to compete with all the others,' and still justly believe that you have been completely fair" (Johnson cited in R. Lee 150). Robert Lee claims that Johnson's administration has been sending mixed signals all along, because the President's statement does not square well with Moynihan's report which remains silent on institutional racism (150). The same can be observed in the response of the Johnson's administration to the riots. In August 1965 Johnson drew a parallel between Watts rioters and Ku Klux Klan members (Gale 21). In July 1966 Vice President Hubert Humphrey reflected on the abominable living conditions in the ghettos and admitted that he himself might be planning a revolt if he lived in such conditions. Humphrey proposed the replacement of urban slums and construction of new communities (Gale 43). A few days later after Humphrey's speech Johnson strongly condemned outbreaks of violence in Chicago and Cleveland.

21. In an already mentioned Introduction Richard Wright also uses the term "jungle" in reference to the ghetto: "this forgotten jungle of black life that lies just across the street ... from white Americans" (XXXI). Freeman makes similar reflections on the proximity of ghetto slums from government buildings in the city of Washington (Greenlee 33).

22. Denton and Massey speak about specific mentality of the ghetto. Children at school encounter a lot of pressure from their peers not to do well at school (Denton and Massey 168). Since African Americans are discriminated in search for jobs, many black people see no point in obtaining education. One of the members of the Cobra gang in *The Spook*—gifted Willie Du Bois—wonders why he needs education if he will still end up on an unemployment benefit (Greenlee 127). To protest the conditions in which they live in the ghetto, a lot of African Americans embrace a different set of values—in opposition to the rest of society. This perpetuates the vicious circle in which they are locked. By revolting against the values espoused by the rest of society, they further decrease the chances of ever getting out of the ghetto. In an act of desperation, some go as far as to claim that they do not care to change their situation.

23. In a 1971 interview for *Black World* Greenlee says "This is a racist country in an institutional sense" (45).

24. The police and politicians play out the drug issue one way or another, depending on what suits them at a particular moment. On the one hand, drugs are a convenient mechanism of pacification. On the other hand, they furnish an excuse to launch police raids into urban ghettos. Under the pretext of fighting drugs, the Chief of Los Angeles Police Department, Daryl Gates, spearheaded the

Notes — Chapter Two

creation of "drug-enforcement zones," the territories barricaded and sealed off from the rest of society (Mike Davis 277). Kenneth Clark's "invisible walls of the ghetto" suddenly became all too visible, further amplifying the abject status of the areas hidden behind them and adding to the air of the taboo hovering over those places. The visible walls ensured even greater invisibility for inhabitants of the sealed districts. Drug-enforcement zones were open only to their residents. The Pico Union neighborhood in Los Angeles is an example of such a drug-enforcement zone.

25. Robert Taylor was the black head of the Civic Housing Authority. He was unsuccessfully trying to obtain consent for the public housing project from the Chicago City Council.

26. I use the term lower class rather than underclass, because the action of the novel unfolds in the 1960s, while the black underclass began to emerge in the ghetto in the 1970s (Denton 61).

27. Greenlee himself might have been spiritually together with people who staged Watts, Newark and Detroit, but physically he was outside the United States — doing his writing in Greece.

28. That fear rises to the point of mental asphyxiation in Chester Himes' *Lonely Crusade*.

29. The frictions between the black middle class and the lower class of African Americans did not emerge in the 1960s, but reach far back into the past. In *The Autobiography of an Ex-Colored Man* (published in 1912) James Weldon Johnson speaks about the same tensions at the end of the 19th century. The narrator of the first person simulated autobiography reflects on the hermeticity of upper echelons of the African American community and its isolation not only from lower classes of black people, but also from well-to-do African Americans who do not have appropriate reputation: "they have formed society — society as discriminating as the actual conditions will allow it to be.... These social circles are connected throughout the country and a person in good standing in one city is readily accepted in another. One who is on the outside will often find it a difficult matter to get in. I know of one case personally in which money to the extent of thirty or forty thousand dollars and a fine house, not backed up by a good reputation, after several years of repeated effort, failed to gain entry for the possessor" (38). A representative of this "society" whom the Ex-Colored Man encounters expresses his revulsion with the lowest class of African American community. The source of revulsion lies mostly in the fact that, according to him, it is the most visible group of black people and the rest of society is quick to associate all African Americans with it: "You see those lazy, loafing, good-for-nothing darkies, they're not worth digging graves for; yet they are the ones that create impressions of the race for the casual observer. It's because they are always in evidence on the street corners, while the rest of us are hard at work, and you know a dozen loafing darkies make a bigger crowd than fifty white men of the same class" (73). The doctor approaches black people in question as outsiders, not as members of the same race. It is interesting that he uses the word "darkies" in reference to them, while he speaks of the lowest class of white people "white men." The picture presented by the black doctor is hardly comprehensive. He does not take into account that many of his black colleagues who "are hard at work" have work, because they were born into the families that gave them the skills and connections which enabled them to be "hard at work," whereas the "loafing darkies" often have nothing but institutional racism on their side.

30. Apart from Homi Bhabha's essays, Huggan refers among others to such works as *Mimesis and Alterity: A Particular History of the Senses*; *Shamanism, Colonialism and the Wild Man* by Taussig and to *Aesthetic Theory* by Adorno.

31. One might wonder whether the distinction is not at some points artificial since as Huggan himself admits, both indeed overlap. Defining mimicry as "imitation," Huggan seems to follow into Bahabha's footsteps. Bhabha sees mimicry as imitation, rather than representation. I am dubious whether mimicry is merely imitation. It also includes elements of representation. Freeman's mimicry at least does.

32. In a 1971 *Black World* interview Sam Greenlee says "[luxury] tempts me. I don't have anything against luxury" (73).

33. The earlier mentioned Ex-Colored Man says after passing into the white race: "I have sold my birthright for a mess of pottage" (100).

34. Billie Holliday's song employs the metaphor of children's independence from their parents. Freeman cites the lyrics of the

song several times in the novel, stressing the need for African American autonomy.

Chapter Three

1. I thank Doctor Dominika Ferens for encouraging me to devote more place in my project to this aspect of the novel — namely to Wittman's real life performance of his ethnic identity and also for referring me to Judith Butler's text *Gender Trouble. Feminism and the Subversion of Identity.*
2. Only in one scene of *The Spook* do Freeman and his friends engage in a mock semi theatrical performance when they come up with an impromptu improvisation of racial stereotyping in films produced by white people.
3. This chapter is to illustrate Asian American invisibility and contrast it with African American invisibility. However, I by no means treat all Asian Americans holistically, as a homogenous group. Wittman Ah Sing is a Chinese American and so is Maxine Hong Kingston. Therefore at many points I will refer specifically to Chinese American invisibility, especially that according to Wittman, Chinese Americans are more invisible than other ethnic groups among Asian Americans. When certain implications can be drawn about the invisibility of all Asian Americans, I will speak about Asian American invisibility. When only Chinese American invisibility is at stake, I will make it clear.
4. Perception is inscribed in the very etymology of the term "theatre." "Theatre" has the same root as "theoria," which in Greek meant "to behold," "to look attentively" (Jay 23).
5. Some of the African American plays of the period are for example Amiri Baraka's "The Eighth Ditch," *Dutchman, The Baptism, Slave Ship, The Slave, The Toilet.*
6. Robert G. Lee distinguishes between the word "alien" and "foreigner" (3). According to Lee, "foreign" is distant, while "alien" is close at hand, but in general perception aliens do not belong to the place of their residence. Lee compares foreigners to tourists and aliens to immigrants. Tourists are usually identified as foreigners, whereas immigrants as aliens. While the word "foreign" is rather neutral, "alien" often brings up negative connotations. However, it is worth emphasizing that the coloring of "alien" also depends on the context and on who bears the label, or consciously assumes it. Some people, especially the privileged, associate "alien" with positive alienation from the values of conventional society. White Sting may proudly declare in one of his songs the status of an illegal alien but no third world immigrant is likely to brag about being an "alien." The word "alien" keeps evolving, assuming various shades of meaning. It almost began to appear in the collocation "legal alien." In January 2004 President Bush proposed legislation that would transform "illegal aliens" into "legal aliens." The condition was that they had an employer. They would still have no citizenship, but they would no longer stay in the United Sates illegally. Proponents of the legislation claimed that "illegal aliens" would "earn their right to legality through their work." President Bush most probably came up with the initiative in the hope of securing the votes of Hispanic Americans, since they were most likely to benefit from the legislative change. The President himself claimed that he wanted to help the American economy. He argued that the employers apparently needed those workers if they kept hiring them. The proposal was announced one week before the American Summit, during which President Bush met Mexican President Vicente Fox. Proposed legislation encountered fierce opposition from a number of Republicans, who maintained that it would reward illegal immigration. Reacting to this opposition, President Bush replaced the "legal alien legislation" with a guest worker program, which boils down to the same thing under a different name. The opposition from the far right wing of the Republican Party did not subside, but gained in strength. In 2006 some Republicans proposed intensifying the battle against illegal immigration by turning all illegal aliens into felons. Congressman Steven King went as far as to claim that anyone who supported the guest worker program "was branded with scarlet letter A, A for amnesty for illegal immigrants."
7. In 1619 a Dutch slave ship arrived in Jamestown, Virginia, beginning the era of slavery in the future United States (*African American History* 1).
8. Asians were never enslaved in the United States, but they were exploited as slaves by the Dutch and Portuguese in Asia and Africa. The Dutch and Portuguese also used Asian slaves aboard Portuguese ships sailing in the Indian

Notes — Chapter Three

Ocean (Okihiro, *Margins and Mainstreams* 38). After the abolition of slavery in the British Empire slave owners began to replace African slaves with coolie workers from Asia. They toiled in slave-like conditions for very meager gratification of thirteen cents a day. Their predecessors — apprenticed workers (former slaves who in the period of transition were forced to work for their previous owners) received twice as much (Okihiro 38).

9. Kingston describes the brutalities perpetrated against Chinese Americans in *China Men*, in the chapter devoted to her grandfather. After the railroad is completed, expulsions begin: "[he] eluded bandits who would hold him up for his railroad pay and shoot him for practice as they shot Injuns and jackrabbits ... the demons [white people] killed for fun and hate. They tied pigtails to horses and dragged chinamen." (144). Running away from persecution, her grandfather is forced to become invisible. He is a master of hiding and disappearing. Thus he sleeps in hidden places, hides in grass, enters the towns only by night. No sooner does he appear in one place than he needs to leave it and head for another. Ironically, Ah Goong also hides against the shaking ground at the sound of the train "in case a demon with a shotgun was hunting from it" (144). All along he travels on foot. Sucheng Chan points out that Chinese Americans who built the railroad were not allowed to ride it free of charge back to California (32). Invisibility as a protective device returns in Kingston's fiction in *The Fifth Book of Peace*. Draft resisters and AWOL-s wish for invisibility to evade authorities. Invisibility is a "favorite power" for the soldier who hides in Tana and Wittman's house (231). It also becomes a "favorite power" for Wittman and Tana's child — Mario/Ehukai. It is worth mentioning at this point that Wittman himself wore the costume of the Invisible Man when he was a child (*Tripmaster Monkey* 191). Time and again Kingston returns to the theme of invisibility. She brings up the persona of the Invisible Man once again in *The Fifth Book of Peace* when Wittman visits a hospital ward full of soldiers bandaged from top to toe "like the Invisible Man" (233). At this point the narrator probably refers to H.G. Wells's Invisible Man, who in one of the scenes wraps a bandage around himself to give some material shape to his formless, invisible body.

10. In *China Men* Maxine Hong Kingston also emphasizes the change in the labor situation of the United States, following the collapse of slavery, which triggered the influx of the Chinese to the United States: "Also there were not enough working men to do all the labor of building a new country. Some of the banging came from the war to decide whether or not black people would continue to work for nothing." (125).

11. Wittman plays a pun on the word "wetback" when he says that his back "is turning wet whenever he is asked for a green card" (332).

12. In *The Woman Warrior* the first person narrator Maxine reminisces on her participation in the movement of the 1960s. She says: "I marched to change the world" (56). Openly sympathizing with Afro-Americans, she stands up to the boss who arranges the banquet in the restaurant boycotted by CORE and the NAACP (58). As a result she ends up being fired.

13. Orientalism is also the title of Edward Said's book published in 1970. Said acquaints us with the textualization of the Orient. He discusses various modes of representation of the East by colonizers and by whites in general. I am going to elaborate on it in the further part of the paragraph.

14. The accentuation of the conflict between the East and West attracted just as much criticism from Wittman's real-life counterpart Frank Chin, who claims in *Aiiieeeee* that the alleged conflict is a white invention (XXI).

15. If Asian Americans are seen as inscrutable, Afro-Americans were frequently perceived as impenetrable. Like Asian American autobiographers, Afro-American first person narrators were supposed to raise the veil and introduce outsiders into the black world. The publishers of James Weldon Johnson's *The Autobiography of an Ex-Colored Man* (1912) announce: "In these pages it is as though a veil had been drawn aside: the reader is given a view of the inner life of the Negro in America, is initiated into the 'freemasonry,' as it were, of the race" (VII). Nowadays Afro-Americans are no longer perceived as impenetrable to such an extent as in the past. What accounts for it is their greater presence in society — especially the mass media. The stereotype still sticks to Asian Americans, but it has lost part of its intensity as well.

16. In "Questions of Multiculturalism" Gayatri Spivak criticizes whites who comfortably slip into their own position without questioning it in any way. She imagines a putative

white male who claims that he "can't speak" on people of other races because he is "only a bourgeoisie white male." Spivak responds to such a claim by saying: "Why not develop a certain degree of rage against history that has written such an abject script for you that you are silenced? ... if you make it your task not only to learn what is going on there through language, through specific programs of study, but also at the same time through a *historical* critique of your position as the investigating person, then you will see that you have earned the right to criticize" (62).

17. As already mentioned in the Introduction to this study, Richard Wright speaks about the split consciousness of white people in his Introduction to *Black Metropolis*. Ever since Du Bois used the term "double consciousness" in reference to African Americans, it has been attributed to Afro-Americans and other people of color. Wright, on the other hand, ascribes split consciousness to white people. White people's split consciousness is a clash between their self-assumed air of righteousness and their attitudes to African Americans: "when the Negro problem is raised, white men, for a reason which as yet they do not fully understand, feel guilt, panic, anxiety, tension; they feel the essential loneliness of their position which is built upon greed, exploitation, and a general denial of humanity; they feel the naked untenability of their *split consciousness*, their *two-faced* moral theories spun to justify their right to dominate" (XXV). It is crucial to emphasize that both states are different. If African Americans' double consciousness is underlain by separation from the world of privilege, white people's split consciousness is triggered by the fear that their privilege may be lost or significantly compromised.

18. The Chinese communities in the United States were composed almost exclusively of men. Chinatowns made bachelor societies (Kwong 14). Chinese women were not allowed to join their husbands until 1942 when the sentiment towards China swung. The 1870 Act and 1875 Page Law were passed by Congress to ban the immigration of Chinese women for the purpose of prostitution (Chan 54). Hing argues that such legislation almost equated all Chinese women with prostitutes (Hing 45).

19. In *China Men* Kingston mentions the massacres of Chinese Americans in Los Angeles, Denver and Rock Springs (146). She also speaks about the drivings out of Tacoma, Seattle, Oregon City, Albania and Marysville.

20. Charles Waddell Chesnutt describes the riots against African Americans in his novel *The Marrow of Tradition*. Walter White depicts Atlanta racial riots of 1906 in his memoirs. At the time of the riots he was a boy of thirteen. His account can also be tracked on the website: http://historymatters.gmu.edu/d/104. Another African American writer—James Weldon Johnson—almost lost his life in the Atlanta riots of 1906.

21. It does not mean, however, that there were no plans to repatriate African Americans back to Africa. The most notable example is the colonization movement, vibrant before the Civil War. The idea of repatriation received certain support from both African Americans and white people. Some whites supported repatriation because they saw African Americans as a drag on the whole nation, while others envisioned repatriation as a potential solution to the problem of slavery. Abraham Lincoln and Thomas Jefferson belonged to the latter (McCarthey 16). In 1816 American Colonization Society was established. By 1830 the society managed to send back to Africa 1, 420 black people. They settled in Liberia, a West African colony set up in 1922. Liberia gained independence in 1948. Monrovia, named after President Monroe, became the capital of Liberia. In 1832 the Abolitionists began to dispute the rectitude of the whole venture (McCarthey 15). Repatriation ideas gave way to the growing support for abolition. Still, the Society survived in its diluted form until 1910. The idea of repatriation gained support among such black people as: Paul Cuffe, Bishop James T. Holly, Martin Delaney, Alexander Crummel and Bishop M. Turner (McCarthey 16). Especially Bishop Turner extended his wholehearted support to emigration. Another organization promoting repatriation was the Chief Sam movement active in Oklahoma. Between 1897 and 1914 African Americans from Oklahoma were especially sympathetic towards repatriation because of the worsening economic situation in the state. Ashanti Chief Alfred C. Sam tried to settle disenchanted African Americans on the Gold Coast (Ghana). Unfortunately his expedition failed (McCarthey 18). In the 1920s Marcus Garvey was one of the chief supporters of the Back to Africa Movement.

22. It is worth noting that immediately after the abolition and their naturalization

Notes — Chapter Three

Afro-Americans did no take to creating jazz either, but first tried more established artistic forms. While Walt Whitman wrote *The Song of Myself*, Frederick Douglass wrote *Narrative of the Life of Frederick Douglass: An American Slave*. It is by no means my intention to detract from the greatness of Douglass's text, but there is no denying that both texts ranked quite differently on the scale of innovation. If we take a look at Walt Whitman's photograph and Frederick Douglass's photograph, we will see a striking difference as well. Walt Whitman — wearing a cowboy hat, in a hardly conventional pose contrasts sharply with immaculately dressed Frederick Douglass posing for a portrait photograph. In a later period — in the 1920s — not all Afro-Americans were willing to experiment with new artistic forms either, for example James Weldon Johnson wrote his fiction in a traditional, highly elevated syntax. His poetry was also written in a classic Victorian verse.

23. Wittman rejects the label "yellow," because for him it is too evocative of gold and the stereotype of "tight-fisted Chang" (326).

24. The use of Chinaman by Chinese Americans is an example of reappropriation. In a similar way it is not uncommon to hear African Americans call each other "nigger," although both words have a different history and carry a different intensity. Helene A. Shugart sees the practice of appropriation as an act of resignification. In the process of appropriation "the original meaning ... is destroyed" (211). Shugart gives examples of appropriation practices among other oppressed groups, for example homosexuals referring to themselves as "dykes" or "faggots." She nonetheless warns that appropriation carries its own risks. David Eng draws our attention to Maxine Hong Kingston's appropriation of the term Chinaman in her book *China Men* (69). Eng notices that Kingston pluralizes the term and inserts a space, capitalizing both nouns. It is also worth noting that in this way she accentuates their masculinity and makes them more visible, underlining that they were a collectivity present in the Unite States. By separating "Men" from "China," she very effectively illustrates their position if we take into account that they were indeed separated from China.

25. The experiment and the Siamese brothers episode reflect the popular belief in dual personality of Asian Americans. Frank Chin and his fellow *Aiiieeeee* editors tried to undermine the notion of dual personality. Chin emphasizes that Asian Americans have a uniquely Asian American sensibility, rather than one or the other: "We have been encouraged to believe that we have no cultural integrity as Chinese — or Japanese-Americans, that we are either Asian (Chinese or Japanese) or American (white) or measurably both. This myth of being either/or and the equally goofy concept of the *dual personality* haunted our lobes while our rejection by both Asia and white America proved we were neither one nor the other" (VIII, my emphasis). Throughout the preface to *Aiiieeeee*, the first Asian American anthology published in 1974, Chin, Chang, Inada and Wong hyphenate the term Asian American, Chinese American, Japanese American and Filipino American. Kingston, on the other hand, speaks strongly against hyphenation. Kingston's views on the issue parallel those of Wittman. She also believes that the hyphen dilutes their Americanness. Like Wittman, Kingston argues that Chinese Americans should not present themselves to the world by the names that they use in their own community: "We ought to leave out the hyphen in 'Chinese American,' because the hyphen gives the word on either side equal weight, as if linking two nouns. It looks as if Chinese-American has double citizenship, which is impossible in today's world. Without the hyphen, 'Chinese' is an adjective and 'American' a noun; a Chinese American is a type of American" (60). Kingston underlines that she has never talked about the hyphen issue to anyone, giving an impression that she is the first to raise the problem. Since then the problem of hyphenation has been hotly debated in Chinese American community. No other racial or ethnic group in the United States has devoted so much time and attention to the issue. With all the focus on hybridity and fluidity within Asian American community, it is no longer so obvious whether to hyphenate or not.

26. I mention only some of those articles. For an extensive study of other model minority articles that appeared in the American press see Keith Osajima's article "Asian Americans as the Model Minority: An Analysis of the Popular Press Image in the 1960s and 1980s."

27. I am going to elaborate on the model minority myth in Chapter Four, when I analyse invisibility in *Native Speaker*.

28. A popular jingle goes: "Ching Chong Chinaman/sitting on a fence/trying to make

Notes — Chapter Three

a dollar out of fifty cents." Lawson Inada incorporates it into his self-ironic poem "Chinks" (*Aiiieeeee* xliv).

29. Graham Huggan sees this disruptive play on stereotypes as "mischievous imitation" (95). Bahabha defines mimicry as repetition. Still, it is not just mere repetition, but repetition with a difference: "mimicry must continuously produce its slippage, its excess, its difference" (86).

30. In the passage cited below Mark Twain muses over Chinese American propensity towards imitation: "They do not need to be taught a thing twice, as a general thing. They are imitative. If a Chinaman were to see his master break up a center table ... and kindle a fire with it, that Chinaman would be likely to resort to the furniture for fuel forever afterward" (Twain cited in Moy 144). Mark Twain and Bret Harte wrote together a play *Ah Sin*, which included a Chinese American character Ah Sin played by white actor C.T. Parsloe (Moy 39). Ah Sin was an embodiment of white stereotypes about Chinese Americans: quick to make a profit, good at gambling and cheating. He also presents the threat of miscegenation, because he wants to marry an Irish American girl and take her to China. His desire to go back to China makes him only a temporary presence in the United States. Such were the hopes of whites.

31. The intertextuality of Wittman's play matches the intertextuality of *Tripmaster Monkey* which is no less rooted in Anglo American culture than it is in Chinese American heritage. Kingston alludes among others to *Faerie Queen*, *The Maltese Falcon*, *Vertigo*, the Beat poets, *The Wasteland*, *The Misfits*, *The Lady from Shanghai*, *Seven Brothers for Seven Sisters*, *West Side Story*. Wittman himself is very enthusiastic about the Beat poetry and American films.

32. Jade Snow Wong (1922–2006) is best known for her autobiography *Fifth Chinese Daughter* (1950) ("San Francisco Chronicle Obituary" B7). In the book she describes her childhood in a traditional San Francisco Chinatown family and her youth. The book, hugely popular among readers, was translated into several foreign languages. It also invited attacks from Asian American cultural nationalists who charged her with bowing to the demands of white publishers and doing the "snow job" [white job] (Preface to *Aiiieeeee* 15). In 1953 the United States State Department sent Wong on a promotional tour of Asia, during which she spoke about her own life in the United States. The sequel to *The Fifth Chinese Daughter — No Chinese Stranger* — was published in 1975. Wong was also an accomplished ceramist.

33. Edith Eaton (Sui Sin Far) (1865–1914) was a Chinese American short story writer, journalist, poet and activist. Eaton's short stories published over the years in American newspapers and magazines were collected in the volume *Mrs. Spring Fragrance* published in 1912. In 1909 Eaton published her autobiographical essay "Leaves from the Mental Portfolio of an Eurasian" in the *Independent*, in 1911 "The Persecution and Oppression of Me" also in the *Independent* (Ferens 186). Throughout her life Edith Eaton was deeply involved in charity work in Chinatowns. I am citing excerpts of her writing in the Introduction. Winnifred Eaton (Onoto Watanna) (1875–1954) was an author of novels, many of them romances, short stories, poems. Her novels include among others: *Marion*, *A Japanese Nightingale*, *The Diary of Delia*, *Me: A Book of Remembrance*. She also worked for the film industry both as a screenwriter and between 1928–1931 as a chief story editor for the New York branch of the Universal Studios (Ferens 186–187). Unlike her sister Edith, Winnifred Eaton publicly claimed a Japanese American identity for a good part of her life, hiding her Chinese descent. For a thorough study of Edith and Winnifred Eaton's works see Dominika Ferens' book *Edith and Winnifred Eaton. Chinatown Missions and Japanese Romances*.

34. Patricia Chu notices that unlike Kingston and Wittman, Chin originally wanted to reject Chinese culture altogether (171). Indeed in his first Asian American anthology *Aiiieeeee* he makes no references to Chinese myths at all. Only responding to Kingston's work in his 1985 essay "This is not Autobiography" he invokes the "authentic" versions of Chinese myths.

35. I use the word mimicry in this case with caution. In Bhabha's formulation mimicry is repetition with a difference. Usually this difference is supposed to be the source of disruption. We can certainly trace some difference in Wittman's imitation of the centre. However, we cannot say that it is in any way disruptive.

36. At some points Kingston overtly parodies Wittman and his real life equivalent — Frank Chin, for instance when she "tweak[s]"

Notes — Chapter Three

Wittman's one ear, and "kiss[es] his other" (340), which is illustrative of her attitude to Wittman and Asian American nationalists. On many issues she agrees with them. Still, she makes it clear that on many others they are at odds.

37. President Kennedy proposed an immigration reform that was enacted several years after his death — in 1965. In a letter to Lyndon B. Johnson, President of the Senate and John Mc Cormack, Speaker of the House, Kennedy calls for the abolishing of the "national origin system of selecting immigrants," because it discriminates among applicants for admission into the United States on the basis of accident of birth" (Kennedy 1). Kennedy put stress in the proposed legislation on the skills of prospective immigrants and their family ties to people already living in the United States. Proponents of the reform did not expect that it would lead to the large influx of Asian population (Hing 39). They anticipated more immigrants from southern and eastern Europe, from countries like Greece and Italy. In his already mentioned letter Kennedy draws our attention to the fact that Greek and Italian immigrants have to wait eighteen months or longer before their relatives can join them in the United States.

38. A lot of attention has been devoted to the attitudes of Chinese Americans born in the United States to fresh immigrants, but very little to fresh immigrants' impressions of several generation Americans. During an earlier described tunnel encounter between Wittman and the f.o.b. we have no access to the f.o.b.'s thoughts either. We find out only what Wittman thinks about the f.o.b. In his article "A Case of Mutual Exclusion" Marlon K. Hom looks at the other side of equation, pointing out that fresh immigrants were no less hostile to Chinese Americans born in the United States. For most newcomers whiteness was a marker of Americanness. They did not see them as fully American, but Americanized. They also identified Americanization with certain negative behaviors, which they attributed to Asian Americans born in the United States. This hostility shows in Wittman's encounter with the president of the Chinese American Family Association. Kingston also speaks about Chinatown elders looking down on the young generation of college educated Chinese Americans, whom they see as jook tsi ting, in other words too Americanized (11).

39. Neil Gotanda observes that the changes in the U.S. racial policies and specifically in the United States immigration and naturalization laws were frequently influenced by the American foreign policy. The progress in American civil rights was often driven by the discordance between American domestic policy and foreign policy. The ideals of equality uttered in the international arena did not tone in with the minority politics at home. That was the case in 1965, when the United States engagement in South East Asia did not play well with its national origin quotas on immigrants from Asia, including refugees from the Vietnam war. The Cold War provided the background for the unfolding civil rights campaign. Gotanda draws similar parallels in reference to earlier changes in the immigration and naturalization policies. The 1943 Magnuson Act, which abolished exclusion laws was to a great extent an attempt to counter anti American Japanese propaganda (141). The 1952 McCarran Walter Act, which gave Asian Americans the right to citizenship was passed during the war in Korea.

40. In the rest of the passage Wittman mulls over the Chinese ideogram "I." In *The Woman Warrior* young Maxine compares Chinese ideogram standing for "I" to the English "I": "The Chinese 'I' has seven strokes, intricacies. How could the American 'I,' assuredly wearing a hat like the Chinese, have only three strokes, the middle so straight? Was it out of politeness that this writer left strokes the way a Chinese has to write her own name small and crooked? No, it was not politeness; 'I' is a capital" (193).

41. On many occasions the third person narrator chimes in and makes up for Wittman's failures. That is how Kingston describes the narrator in an interview with Marilyn Chin: "And she is actually pushing Wittman Ah Sing, telling him to shut up ... as I was writing along, I saw that she has a personality. First of all, the omniscient narrator is a woman. And, second, she has a memory that goes back to China. She has a memory that sees a little bit into the future.... And she is also sometimes very tough on Wittman, and she captures him. Remember, in the *Monkey* story, as Kuan Yin takes a rock and throws it on top of the monkey for 500 years? I felt that as narrator I took a rock and threw it on top of the protagonist and captured him. And kept him in place. So I was beginning to see that my narrator is Kuan Yin, and she is very merciful ... nobody is going to get killed or

hurt. She keeps giving people wonderful opportunities" (*Conversations* 88). She moderates Wittman's statements, providing a counterbalance to his ideology. At some points she literally tells him to shut up (*Tripmaster Monkey* 282). Time and again she prods him to action and comments on his choices. In the further part of the interview Kingston says that she did not want Wittman to end up as a reader, as Madam Bovary or Don Quixote (89). Hsiao-hung Chang notices that the combination of a female narrator and a male protagonist helps to negotiate the tension between heroism and feminism, to "break the impasse" halting Asian American studies (30). Chang calls it "narrative transvestism."

42. In the fragment preceding this particular scene the narrator of *The Woman Warrior* says: "From the fairy tales, I've learned exactly who the enemy are. I easily recognize them — business-suited in their modern American executive guise, each boss two feet taller than I am and impossible to meet eye to eye" (57). She revolts against sexism and racism and can easily recognize its modern guise. In her works she tears off its robes and exposes it.

Chapter Four

1. For example autobiographies by Leong Gor Yun (1936), Pardee Lowe (*Father and Glorious Descendant,* published in 1943) and Calvin Lee. This is not to say, however, that all Asian American autobiographers make such claims. I will return to autobiographical controversy in Asian American Literature towards the end of the chapter.

2. It was for example the case when Chinese Americans made contributions to the Democratic party in 1997 and after Vice President Gore visited the Buddhist temple. Robert Lee argues that a host of other issues is overlooked whenever allegations of illegal contributions are made (1). People who point a blaming finger at Chinese American contributors and their recipients usually are not alerted by contributions of big entrepreneurs or multinational corporations. In a similar vein, we can also assume that no one would be alerted if an elected official visited a temple of some western religious denomination.

3. Min and Kolodny emphasize that their middleman minority theory differs from that offered by Edna Bonacich. Bonacich defined middleman minorities for example Jewish Americans, Japanese, Chinese and Korean Americans as sojourners who set up small businesses to speed up their return home. Bonacich's theory was challenged among others by Walter Zenner, Robert Cherry and Eugene Wong. All of them dispute Bonacich's characterization of middle- man minorities as sojourners. Cherry and Wong point out that her theory inadvertently contributes to stereotyping of middleman minorities as "inassimilable and alien" (Cherry and Wong cited in Min and Kolodny 133). They also counter Bonacich's argument that Jewish Americans and Chinese Americans entered small businesses by choice. Rampant discrimination forced them to choose those professions. In reality sojourners usually prefer other employment over self-employment.

4. Kye is a credit association, in which each member contributes a specified amount of money weekly or monthly. A pool goes each week or month to a different member of the association. Usually you can be a recipient only once (Lee 50; Heon Cheol Lee 128). "Ggeh" is a money club that operates under the system.

5. Another matter is that Korean Americans nowadays show a greater degree of racial consciousness than they did in the past. One of the grocers interviewed by Kyeyoung Park in the first half of the 1990s says: "I try to understand them better. Thanks to their civil rights movement, we Koreans ... are able to live now in America" (68). This particular grocer seems to have a more comprehensive view of the situation. Still, towards the end of the interview, when he speaks about the American welfare system and its effect on African Americans, his analysis becomes somewhat reductive and ill-informed. Efforts are made to boost the level of consciousness among Korean Americans and Asian Americans. Mediation efforts were undertaken among others by African-Korean American Christian Alliance founded in 1991 (Okihiro 63), the Community Mediation Project of the Korean American Community Services and the Korean American Merchant Association of Chicago (Choi and Shin Kim 180), Black-Korean Alliance founded in 1986 and disbanded in 1992 (Chang, "New Urban Crisis" 55).

6. Some of the stereotypes also come from contacts with black soldiers serving in Korea (Abelman 150).

7. Another matter is that those activists

Notes — Chapter Four

usually were not immigrants, since the latter usually showed little involvement in political affairs of the United States. As I stress in Chapter Three, the interests of long-time Asian Americans and fresh immigrants often clashed. Being new to the country, immigrants had more down-to-earth concerns, concentrating first of all on breadwinning.

8. During President George W. Bush's first term in office there were two Asian American secretaries — Norman Y. Mineta, Secretary of Transportation and Elaine Chao, Secretary of Labour — both very much token figures that toe the line in the Bush administration. Mineta was hailed by whites as an example of successful assimilation, a model minority paradigm already in the 1970s. One of the model minority articles — "Success Story: Outwhiting the Whites" features Mineta, back then Mayor of San Jose (Newsweek, June 21, 1971). The picture of Mineta's Anglo-American style, nuclear family cooking in the garden is placed side by side with Mine Okubo's sketch of life in the World War II internment camp for Japanese Americans. The implied message is obvious: how Japanese Americans progressed from the outcasts of the United States to the "model minority" of the country. At the beginning of President Bush's second term in office both Chao and Mineta are still part of the administration. Still, there are speculations about Chao's potential departure from the post. A new addition to George W. Bush's parade of token figures is Alberto Gonzales, the first Latino Attorney General, chosen at the beginning of President Bush's second term in office to replace John Ashcroft.

9. Nor are they mentioned by the media that also devote most of their time to African American and Asian American minority voters. Having said that, it needs to be acknowledged that during 2004 election campaign, a CNN reporter Richard Quest came up with a several minute report that reflected on the neglect suffered by Asian American voters. Focusing in his report on Asian Americans in Seattle, he emphasized that in comparison with African Americans and Latinos, Asian Americans languished in oblivion. He also noticed quite astutely that it would be much more difficult to appeal to Asian American population due to its ethnic heterogeneity. It seems, however, that it is rather an assumption of full integration by Asian Americans that keeps politicians from making any overt attempts to win them over. On the other side of the equation there is an air of foreignness clinging to all Asian Americans across the board, not just immigrants. Politicians do not appeal to Asian American voters, because many of them still see them as aliens.

10. There are enough Asian Americans in the United States to make a difference, especially if we take into account that the electorate in the last two elections (in 2000 and 2004) has been fairly evenly divided and both Democrats as well as Republicans were emphasizing that every vote counted. There are 13.5 million Asian Americans in the United States. It is important to stress that two-thirds of Asian Americans are working-age adults (eighteen to sixty-four year olds), the highest proportion of any race or ethnic group — 66 percent (Bernstein, "US Census Press Releases" 1). Hence they have a high percentage of population that can vote and that is immediately affected by federal policies.

11. The sentencing of Soon Ja Du came about six months later. The judge fined her $500, gave her a probationary sentence and declared that she should perform 400 hours of community service (Park 60). The black community reacted to the incident and the sentencing with the boycotts of Korean American stores. For an incisive interpretation of the events see Kwang Chung Kim's *Koreans in the Hood* and Nancy Abelman's *Blue Dreams*.

12. Rodney King rebellion in South Central Los Angeles was sparked by the acquittal of four white policemen on April 29, 1992 by a predominantly white jury in Simi Valley, California with black population of only two percent (Baker 43). Everything began on March 3 1991, when afore mentioned four white policemen brutally beat a twenty-five year old man Rodney King, who initially was trying to evade a police chase before eventually stopping the car only to find himself beaten by "guardians" of law and order. King and his two black companions were by far outnumbered by the police officers — twenty-one of them at the site. For a detailed analysis of the incident and the Los Angeles urban uprising that followed, see Robert-Gooding Williams *Reading Rodney King. Reading Urban Uprising,* Haki Madhubuti's *Why L.A. Happened* and *Los Angeles Struggles Towards a Multiethnic Community* by Russell Leong and Edward T. Chang.

13. I was encouraged to read Hisaye Yamamoto's "Fire in Fontana" by Grace Hong's essay "'Something Forgotten Which Should

Have Been Remembered': Private Property and Cross-Racial Solidarity in the Work of Hisaye Yamamoto." Hong looks at the story against the background of property laws and property relations in the United States between the 1910s and 1940s. For an alternative reading of "Fire in Fontana" see James Kyung-Jin Lee's book *Urban Triage*.

14. Although I focus on the conflict between Korean Americans and African Americans, it is important to remember that Latinos are part of the conflict as well. For an analysis of the interaction between Latinos and Asian Americans, see Leland T. Saito's essay "Asian Americans and Latinos in San Gabriel Valley, California: Ethnic Political Cooperation and Redistricting 1990–92" in *Los Angeles Struggles Toward Multiethnic Community* edited by Russell Leong and Edward T. Chang.

15. The longest boycott began in January 1990 and lasted till May 1991 (eighteen months in the Church Avenue and Fulton Street) (Cheol Lee 194).

16. Kwang speaks of the occupation of Korea by Japan.

17. 1989 Secretary of Labor—Elizabeth Dole's statement cited below illustrates how people in power play out immigrant labor to their own advantage: "As baby boomers move toward retirement and the birth rate stays low, employers are drawing a larger proportion of entry-level workers from populations where the human resource investment has been historically inadequate—women, minorities, and immigrants ... obviously, the United States faces a serious human resource development challenge" (Dole cited in Palumbo-Liu's *Ethnic Canon* 7). Whenever the U.S. faces such a crisis, people normally overlooked are called upon to buttress the American economy.

18. To the most famous texts on the controversy surrounding Asian American autobiography and the debate between Kingston and Chin belong: "The Woman Warrior vs. Chinaman Pacific" by King-Kok Cheung, "Autobiography as a Guided Chinatown Tour?" by Cynthia Sau-lin Wong, "This is not Autobiography" by Frank Chin, the introductions to *Aiiieeeee* and *Big Aiiieeeee*.

19. Henry also notes that his Korean American father would be sickened by his display in front of Luzan (182).

20. "No Name Woman" originally appeared separately as a short story in the January 1975 issue of *Viva*. Kingston returns to the issue in *The Fifth Book of Peace*. The narrator cites her mother, who chastises her for "telling on" her people: "The Han people, the Tan'g people hate you for writing books. You endanger them. You tell immigration secrets, and ruin families.... You tell on them. You point them out" (55). A moment of self-reflection follows: "So they read me, they hate me. They think I hate them, and snitch on them. I cause the suffering that I write about. I make money off of Chinese people's hard lives. I sell them out. I exploit them" (55). Maxine inverts this self-deprecation in the next lines, arguing that she told old immigration secrets and tricks, which everyone knew and which went out of use with the changing modes and routes of immigration. She also rebuts the claim that Chinese Americans hate her, pointing out that those who hate her do not read her books: "I'm sure that people who hate me haven't read me. They are nonreaders" (56). Does she mean that they literally do not read her books or that they cannot unravel various layers of meaning in her works?

Conclusion

1. In his Introduction to *Invisible Man* Ellison attributes the phrase to his unnamed friends.

2. Wallace looks in her 1990 book at the portrayal of African Americans in popular culture.

3. The full title of Equiano's text is *The Interesting Narrative of the Life of Olaudah Equiano, or Gustavus Vassa, the African, Written by Himself* (published in 1789). The emphasis put on the fact that the narrative was "written by himself" is very significant, because sometimes slave narratives were written through amanuenses. The fact that there were no intermediaries in this case is to increase the veracity of Equiano's text.

4. In her article "Whiteness as Property" Cheryl Harris quotes the study reported by Andrew Hacker in his book *Two Nations*. A group of white students was asked to say how much money they would like to be paid for the change of their skin color from white to black. The majority asked for $50 million or $1 million for each year of being black (Harris 175).

5. Toni Cade Bambara shows a group of such children (inhabitants of Harlem) in her short story "The Lesson." A Harlem teacher—

Ms. Moore tries to instill them with fighting spirit and prevent them from simply resigning themselves to the life in poverty.

6. Harris and Zimmerman's data covers southern Appalachia, the Black Belt and the Delta areas of the South (1). The Black Belt extends from East Texas, Louisiana, Arkansas to Mississippi, West Tennessee, Alabama, Georgia, North Florida, North and South Carolina and Virginia. 83 percent of the nonmetropolitan African Americans and 46 percent of all African American population live in the Black Belt (2).

7. Like for example Diana Ross singled out at the airport in 1999.

8. The black community rose in protest following the fatal shooting of Amadou Diallo, an immigrant from Guinea, in the Bronx on February 4, 1999. Four white police officers in plain clothes shot unarmed Diallo forty-one times, having allegedly mistaken him for a suspect they were looking for. Members of the African American community who protested the killing were asking how you could have shot someone forty-one times by mistake. Prosecution forensic pathologist Dr. Joseph Cohen stated that three wounds indicated that officers were still shooting Diallo when he was falling or already down ("Medical Examiner" 1). The shooting triggered daily protests and rallies in front of Diallo's Bronx building, police Manhattan headquarters and the State Supreme Court in Bronx. 1200 protesters were arrested, among them former mayor of New York David Dinkins, actress Susan Sarandon and the Reverends Al Sharpton and Jesse Jackson. On April 15 thousands of protesters marched across the Brooklyn Bridge to challenge not only Diallo's shooting, but also police brutality all over the United States. Mayor Rudy Giulianni condemned the protests and proclaimed his unwavering support for the New York Police Department, an attitude which brought about a steep decline in his popularity ratings. Bronx Supreme Court Justice Patricia Williams was the first judge in the case. She refused to dismiss the case. The trial was relocated from Bronx to predominantly white Albany, which sparked fierce protests from the black community ("Diallo Chronology" 1, 2). All four policemen were acquitted. Peaceful demonstrations followed the acquittal. Diallo's family won financial compensation in a civil suit.

9. One of the most famous cases came back in 1986 when Yat-Pang Au, the son of Vietnamese immigrants was rejected by the University of California at Berkeley. The case received a lot of publicity in the media but UCB refused to admit racial discrimination against Au (Takagi 255). In her article "Admissions and Race in Higher Education" Dana Takagi contrasts Au's case with Allan Bakke's case in 1978. Bakke was a white man in his thirties rejected by University of California at Davis. Bakke argued that he was dropped because sixteen admission slots were reserved for minority students (Takagi 233). The Supreme Court ordered that Bakke be admitted, but it did not condemn positive discrimination towards minorities. Unlike Bakke, Au did not challenge his rejection legally. Takagi cautions against drawing parallels between both cases. In "Affirmative Action: Choosing Sides" Norimitsu Onishi draws our attention to the fact that another contentious issue among Asian Americans at Californian universities is affirmative action for African Americans. The Regents at some of those universities recommended a ban on affirmative action (30). Themselves often battling unofficial quotas, Asian American students have conflicting feelings on affirmative action. Some African Americans complain that even if their grade point average is exceptional, their Asian American colleagues still see them as beneficiaries of affirmative action rather than people who were admitted to an elite university because of their outstanding academic performance (Onishi 30).

10. These anthologies are among others: Jessica Hagedorn's *Charlie Chan Is Dead* (1993), *Charlie Chan Is Dead 2: At Home in the World* (2004), *Asian American Literature: An Anthology* (1999) by Shirley Geok-lin Lim, *The Nuyorasian Anthology: Asian American Writings About New York City* (1999) by Bino A. Realuyo, *Asian American Literature: A Brief Introduction and Anthology* (1997) by Shawn Wong, *Chinese American Poetry: An Anthology* by L. Ling-Chi Wang and Henry Yiheng Zhao, *Growing Up Asian American: An Anthology* by Maria Hong, *Asian American Heritage: An Anthology of Prose and Poetry* by David Hsin-Fu Wand, *Quiet Fire: A Historical Anthology of Asian American Poetry 1892-1970* by Julian Chang, *Premonitions: The Kaya Anthology of New Asian North American Poetry* (1995) by Walter K. Lew, *Collected Voices: An Anthology of Asian North American Periodical Writing* (1997) by Terry Watada, *Asian American Drama: 9 Plays from the*

Multiethnic Landscape (1997) by Brian Nelson, *Breaking Silence: An Anthology of Contemporary Asian American Poets* by Joseph Bruchac, *Asian American Poetry: The Next Generation* (2004) by Victoria M. Chang and Marilyn Chin, *American Dragons: Twenty Five Asian American Voices* (1995), *Becoming Asian American: Second-Generation Chinese and Korean American Identities* (2003) by Nazil Kibria. As already mentioned, the first Asian American anthology *Aiiieeeee* was published by Chan, Chin, Inada and Wong in 1974. They published *The Big Aiiieeeee* in 1991.

11. Some of them are Angel Island Theatre Company in Chicago, Arizona Asian Theatre in Phoenix, ARTH South Asian American theatre group in Washington, D.C., Asian American Repertory Theatre in Stockton and San Diego, Asian Misbehavin' in Philadelphia, Asian Pacific Performing Artists Alliance in Las Vegas, Asian Story Theatre in San Diego, CATS in Nevada City, California, Contemporary Asian Theatre Scene in Santa Clara, Deep Yellow in Long Beach, California, i was born with two tongues in Chicago, Mellow Yellow Theatre in New York, ReAct in Seattle, Sudden Enlightenment Korean American Theatre in New York. For an extensive list of Asian American theatre companies links visit the site: http://www.aatrevue.com/Directory.html. Some of the earlier Asian American theatre companies are: East West Players (founded in Los Angeles in 1965 among others by Japanese American actor, director Mako Iwamatsu), the Asian Exclusion Act which emerged under the guidance of the poet and playwright Garret Hongo from the merger of Asian Multimedia Centre (set up in 1973) and the Theatrical Ensemble of Asians (TEA established at the University of Washington in 1974). In 1980 the Asian Exclusion Act changed its name to Northwest Asian America Theatre (NWAAT) located in Seattle (Shimakawa 59–60). We cannot forget about the Asian American Theatre Company of San Francisco (AATC) founded in 1973 and Theatre Mu established in Minneapolis in 1992 (Shimakawa 64).

12. One of such plays is David Henry Hwang's *M. Butterfly* (1988).

13. Some Asian American activist organizations are: Chinese Progressive Association (CPA) Workers' Centre in Boston, Asian Immigrant Women Advocates (AIWA) in Oakland, and Korean Immigrant Worker Advocates (KIWA) in Los Angeles, all of them affiliating low-income immigrants (Omatsu 52). To other Asian American activist organizations belong: Asian Law Caucus promoting and advancing the legal and civic rights of the Asian and Pacific Islander communities, Boston located Asian American Civic Association whose goal is to help Asian immigrants and refugees in their transition to the United States, Asian American Coalition, Asian American Exchange, Asian American Politics, Asian Americans for Community Outreach, Chinese for Affirmative Action, Chinatown Service Centre. You can view the list of Asian American organizations on the website: http://chineseculture.about.com/cs/organizations/index.htm.

14. Some of the anthologies on the homosexual experience among Asian Americans are: *The Very Inside: An Anthology of Writing by Asian and Pacific Islander Lesbian and Bisexual Women* (1994) by Sharon Lim-Hing, *A Lotus of Another Color: The Unfolding of the South Asian Gay and Lesbian Experience* (1993) by Rakesh Ratti, *Piece of My Heart: A Lesbian of Color Anthology* (1993) by Makeda Silvera (Cheung, "Reviewing Asian American Literary Studies" 13), *Rice: Explorations into Gay Asian Culture and Politics* (1998) by S. Cho, *Best Gay Asian Erotica* (2004) by Andy Quan.

15. In 1995 authors of Proposition 187 were unsuccessfully trying to force drastic measures like for example the exclusion of illegal immigrants' children from primary and secondary education. They also failed to introduce legislation that would reduce the number of immigrants in states with a large concentration of non-white population. In 1996 states gained control over welfare and health care. Previously that responsibility rested with the federal government. Federal benefits and health care for immigrants were terminated (Gotanda 130).

16. See Note 6 to Chapter Three and page 166 of Chapter Four.

17. Jesse Jackson's Rainbow Coalition was dominated by African Americans and even African Americans did not enjoy a truly all-embracing representation within the coalition. The voices of "black progressives" were muffled by Jesse Jackson, who relegated African American social democrats to the margins of the coalition (Marable, "Memory and Militancy" 154). The Rainbow Coalition was founded on November 3, 1983 during Jackson's first bid for the U.S. presidency. In his speech Jackson said "blacks, women, Hispan-

ics, workers, Indians, Chinese, Europeans — we must come together and form a rainbow coalition" (Rainbow Coalition — Britannica Student Encyclopædia 1). The Rainbow Coalition merged with PUSH Operation (founded in 1971) into Rainbow Push Coalition, which has a limited leverage.

18. A Social Security "reform" promoted by President Bush would channel money from Social Security into private investment funds. A repeatedly asked question is where the resources (three trillion dollars) necessary to finance the "reform" would come from. The move would inevitably lead to the dramatic reduction of Social Security benefits.

19. An additional assumption is that if you pay higher taxes, your children are entitled to better education. Suspicious as it is in itself, it becomes even more suspicious if we take into account sweeping tax cuts for the wealthiest. The budget proposed by Mr. Bush for the year 2005 introduced further cuts in federal spending on education. It significantly limited the number of various education programs. Other federal cuts included among others spending on medical care, food stamps for the poor, literacy and anti-drug programs, environment and subsidies for farmers. The poor bore the brunt of the record deficit created by the tax cuts for the wealthiest sections of American society.

20. This is not to say that the Ku Klux Klan has disappeared completely. Yet it is significantly weakened and it has split into a number of racist organizations. In 2003 there were about 5500 to 6000 members of the Klan. In the old days Klansmen identified themselves as an "invisible empire" ("US Map of Hate Groups" 1). Today the label "empire" would definitely be a misnomer, but "invisibility" would be more fitting than in the past. Even if their faces were hidden under white sheets, their presence was still visible and tangible to the persecuted. One of the split Klan organizations calls itself America's Invisible Empire Knights of the KKK (active in Alabama). There are also a number of other hate groups in the United States, including various skinhead and neo nazi organizations like: Knights of Freedom, National Alliance, Nazi Party USA, New Order, Volksfront, Fascist Action Group Boca Raton, Florida, Central New York White Pride, Aryan Racial Loyalist Party, Aryan Nations/Church of Jesus Christ Christian. To see a list of hate groups by state, visit the website: http://www.borg.com/~jdgdread/racism.htm.

Bibliography

Aanerud, Rebecca. "Fictions of Whiteness: Speaking the Names of Whiteness in U.S. Literature." *Displacing Whiteness.* Ed. Ruth Frankenberg. Durham: Duke, 1997. 35–59.

Abelman, Nancy and John Lie. *Blue Dreams. Korean Americans and the Los Angeles Riots.* Cambridge: Harvard University Press, 1995.

African American History. 6 Dec. 2003 <afr_am_history.htm>.

Alba, Richard. "The Background to Contemporary Immigration." *Remaking the American Mainstream.* Cambridge: Harvard University Press, 2003.

Aldama, Frederick Luis. "Re-Visioning African American Autobiography." *Modern Fiction Studies* 46.4 (2000): 1004–1006.

Alund, Aleksandra, and Carl-Ulrik Schierup. *Paradoxes of Multiculturalism.* Aldershot: Gover, 1991.

Andrews, William L. *African American Autobiography.* Englewood Cliffs: Prentice Hall, 1993.

_____, Frances Smith Foster, and Trudier Harris, eds. *The Oxford Companion to African American Literature.* New York: Oxford, 1997.

Ang, Ien. *On Not Speaking Chinese. Living Between Asia and the West.* New York: Routledge, 2001.

Appadurai, Arjun. "The Heart of Whiteness." *Callaloo* 16.4 (1993): 796–807.

Asante, Molefi Kete. "The Ideological Significance of Afrocentricity in Intercultural Communication." *Journal of Black Studies* 14.1 (1983): 3–19.

_____. "Systematic Nationalism. A Legitimate Strategy for National Selfhood." *Journal of Black Studies* 9.1 (1978): 115–128.

_____, and Peter Anderson. "Transracial Communication and the Changing Image of Black Americans." *Journal of Black Studies* 4.1 (1973): 69–80.

Asian American Theatre Revue — Directory of Asian American Theatre. 24 Jan. 2005 <http://www.Aatrevue.com/Directory.html>.

Baker, Houston. "From 'The Florescence of Nationalism in the 1960s and 1970s.'" *The Journey Back: Issues in Black Literature and Criticism.* Chicago: University of Chicago Press, 1980. 106–113.

_____. "Scene ... Not Heard." *Reading Rodney King. Reading Urban Uprising.* New York: Routledge, 1993. 38–50.

Baldwin, James. "The Language of the Streets." *Literature and the Urban Experience.* Eds. Michael C. Jaye and Ann Chakmers Watts. New Brunswick, N.J.: Rutgers University Press, 1981. 133–137.

Baraka, Amiri. "Black Nationalism and Socialist Revolution." *Black World* July 1975: 30–42.

Bekerie, Ayele. "The Four Corners of a

Circle. Afrocentricity as a Model of Synthesis." *Journal of Black Studies* 25.1 (1994): 131–149.

Benston, Kimberly W. *Performing Blackness. Enactments of African American Modernism.* London: Routledge, 2000.

Bernstein, Robert. "US Census Press Releases. Hispanic and Asian Americans Increasing Faster than Overall Population." 26 Oct. 2004 <http://www.census.gov/Press-Release/www/releases/archives/race/001839.html>.

Bhabha, Homi K. "Cultural Diversity and Cultural Differences." *The Postcolonial Reader.* Eds. Bill Ashcroft, Gareth Griffith. New York: Routledge, 1995. 206–209.

_____. "Of Mimicry and Man. The Ambivalence of Colonial Difference." *The Location of Culture.* London: Routledge, 1994. 85–92.

_____. "The Other Question: Stereotype, Discrimination and the Discourse of Colonialism." *The Location of Culture.* New York: Routledge, 1994. 66–84.

Bloch, Alice. "Sight Imagery in *Invisible Man.*" *A Casebook on Ellison's* Invisible Man. Ed. Joseph Trimmer. New York: Crowell, 1972. 264–268.

Bondi, Liz. "Locating Identity Politics." *Place and the Politics of Identity.* Ed. Keith and Pile. New York: Routledge, 1993. 84–102.

Boris, Ellen. "'Arm and Arm': Racialized Bodies and Colored Lines." *Journal of American Studies* 35.1 (2001): 1–20.

Bracey, John H. "Capitalism. Buy Black." *Black Nationalism in America.* New York: Bobbs Merrill, 1970. 486–491.

Brooks, Linda Marie. *Alternative Identities: The Self in Literature, History, Theory.* New York: Garland Press, 1994.

Browne, Stephen. "Du Bois, Double-Consciousness, and the Modern City." *Rhetoric and Community: Studies in Unity and Fragmentation.* Ed. Michael Hogan. Columbia: South Carolina University Press, 1998. 75–92.

Brye-Laporte, Roy Simon. "Black Immigrants." *Journal of Black Studies* 3.1 (1972): 31–55.

Busby, Mark. *Ralph Ellison.* Boston: Twayne, 1991.

Butler, Judith. *Gender Trouble. Feminism and the Subversion of Identity.* New York: Routledge, 1990.

_____, Ernesto Laclau, and Slavoj Žižek. *Contingency, Hegemony, Universalism. Contemporary Dialogues on the Left.* New York: Verso, 2000.

Butterfield, Stephen. *Black Autobiography in America.* Amherst: University of Massachusetts Press, 1974.

Carmichael, Stokely. "Pan-Africanism — Land and Power." *Modern Black Nationalism. From Marcus Garvey to Louis Farrakhan.* William Van Deburg, ed. New York: New York University Press, 1997.

Cassirer, Naomi. "Race Composition and Earnings: Effects by Race, Region and Gender." *Social Science Research* 25 (375–399). 7 Jan 2005 <http://www.pressroom.com/~afrimale/cassirer.htm>.

Caws, Mary Ann. "Literal or Liberal: Translating Perception." *Critical Inquiry* 13.1 (1986): 49–63.

Chan, Sucheng. *Asian Americans: An Interpretive History.* Boston: Twayne, 1990.

Chang, Edward T. "Jewish and Korean Merchants in African American Neighborhoods: A Comparative Perspective." *Amerasia Journal* 19.2 (1993): 5–21.

_____. "New Urban Crisis: Korean-African American Relations." *Koreans in the Hood. Conflict with African Americans.* Baltimore: The Johns Hopkins University Press, 1999. 39–59.

Chang, Hsiao-hung, "Gender Crossing in Maxine Hong Kingston's *Tripmaster Monkey.*" *MELUS* 21.1 (1997): 15–34.

Chesnutt, Charles Waddell. *The Marrow of Tradition.* Glasgow, Caledonian, 1998.

———. "The Passing of Grandison." *Call and Response: The Riverside Anthology of African American Literary Tradition.* Ed. Patricia Hill. Boston: Houghton Mifflin, 1998.

Cheung, King-Kok. "Of Men and Men. Reconstructing Chinese American Masculinity." *Other Sisterhoods. Literary Theory and United States Women of Color.* Ed. Sandra Kumamoto. Chicago: University of Illinois Press, 1998. 173–199.

———. "Reviewing Asian American Literary Studies." *Interethnic Companion.* Ed. King-Kok Cheung. New York: Cambridge University Press, 1997. 1–37.

———. "The Woman Warrior versus the Chinaman Pacific: Must a Chinese American Critic Choose between Feminism and Heroism?" *Conflicts in Feminism.* Ed. Marianne Hirsch and Evelyn Fox Keller. New York: Routledge, 1990. 234–251.

Chin, Frank. Afterword. *MELUS* 3.2 (1976): 13–17.

———. "Come All Ye Asian American Writers of the Real and the Fake." *The Big Aiiieeeee.* New York: Meridian, 1991.

———. "Confessions of a Number One Son." *Ramparts* 11.9 (1973): 41–48.

———. Introduction to Yardbird Reader. *Yardbird* 3 (1974): IV-X.

———. "The Iron Moonhunter" from *The Iron Moonhunter.* Source unrecorded.

———. "Letter to Y' Bird." *Y' Bird* 1.1 (1977): 42–45.

———. "Railroad Standard Time" an excerpt from *Gunga Din Hihgway.* Minneapolis: Coffee House Press, 1995.

———. "This Is Not an Autobiography." *Genre* XVIII (1985): 109–130.

———, Jeffrey Paul Chan, Lawson Fusao Inada and Shawn Hsu Wong, eds. *Aiiieeeee! An Anthology of Asian American Writers.* Washington, D.C.: Howard University Press, 1974.

———, ———, ——— and ———, eds. *The Big Aiiieeeee. An Anthology of Chinese American and Japanese American Literature.* New York: Meridian, 1991.

Chiu, Monica. "Being Human in the World." *Journal of American Studies* 34.2 (2000): 187, 206.

Choi, InChul, and Shin Kim. "Portrait of a Community Program: The African American and Korean American Community Mediation Project." *Koreans in the Hood.* Ed. Kwang Chung Kim. Baltimore: The Johns Hopkins University Press, 1999. 178–202.

Chow, Karen Har-Yen. "Imagining Panethnic Community and Performing Identity in Maxine Hong Kingston's *Tripmaster Monkey: His Fake Book.*" *Contemporary Asian American Communities.* Eds. Linda Trinh Vo and Rick Bonus. Philadelphia: Temple, 2002. 177–190.

Chu, Patricia. *Assimilating Asians. Gendered Strategies of Authorship in Asian America.* Durham: Duke University Press, 2000.

Clark, Kenneth. *Dark Ghetto.* New York: Harper and Row, 1965.

Cole, Johnetta. "The Black Bourgeoisie." *Black and White Perspectives on American Race Relations.* Ed. Rose Rothman. Wilson, N.Y.: Oxford, 1973. 25–43.

Cooperman, Robert. "Across the Boundaries of Cultural Identity: An Interview with David Henry Hwang." *Staging Difference.* Ed. Marc Maufort. New York: Peter Lang, 1995. 365–373.

———. "New Theatrical Statements: Asian-Western Mergers in the Early Plays of David Henry Hwang." *Staging Difference.* Ed. Marc Maufort. New York: Peter Lang, 1995. 201–213.

Daniels, Roger. "The Asian American Experience: The View from the 1990s." *Multiculturalism and the Canon of American Culture.* Ed. Hans Bak. Amsterdam: Vrije University Press, 1993. 131–145.

Bibliography

Darden, Joe T. "Black Residential Segregation since Shelley v. Kraemer Decision." *Journal of Black Studies.* 25.6 (1995): 680–691.

Davis, Mike. *City of Quartz: Excavating the Future of Los Angeles.* New York: Vintage, 1989.

Davis, Thulani. *1959.* New York: Harper, 1992.

Davis, Yula. *Gender and Nation.* London: Sage, 1997.

Degler, Carl. *Neither Black nor White.* Madison: Wisconsin University Press, 1986.

Denton, Nancy, and Douglass Massey. *American Apartheid.* Cambridge: Harvard University Press, 1992.

_____, and _____. "Residential Segregation of Blacks, Hispanics and Asians by Socioeconomic Status and Generation." *Social Science Quarterly* 69.4 (1988): 797–817.

"Diallo Chronology." Court TV Online–U.S. 24 Jan. 2005 <http://www.courttv.com/archive/national/diallo/chronology.html>.

"Diallo — Medical Examiner." Court TV Online — U.S. 24 Jan. 2005 <http://courttv.com/national/diallo/chronology>.

Dirlik, Arif. "Asians on the Rim: Transnational Capital and Local Community in the Making of Contemporary Asian America." *Amerasia Journal* 22.3 (1996): 1–24.

Divakaruni, Chitra Banerjee.. "Yuba City School." *The Open Boat Poems in Asian America.* Ed. Garrett Hongo. New York: Anchor-Doubleday, 1993. 79–80.

Douglass, Frederick. *Narrative of the Life of Frederick Douglass: An American Slave.* In *Call and Response: The Riverside Anthology of African American Literary Tradition.* Ed. Patricia Hill. Boston: Houghton Mifflin, 1998.

_____. "Our Composite Nationality: An Address Delivered in Boston, Massachusetts on 7 December 1869," *The Frederick Douglass Papers,* Vol.4 New Heaven: Yale University Press, 1991.

Dowd, James J. "Aporias of the Self." *Alternative Identities.* Ed. L. M. Brooks. New York: Garland Press, 1994. 245–266.

Du Bois, W.E.B. *Black Reconstruction.* New York: Russell & Russell, 1963.

_____. *Dusk of Dawn.* In *Writings.* Ed. Nathan Huggins. New York: Library of America, 1986.

_____. *The Souls of Black Folk.* New York: Penguin, 1989.

Du Plessis, "HOO, HOO, HOO": Some Episodes in the Construction of Modern Whiteness." *American Literature* 67.4 (1995): 667–700.

Duster, Troy. "The 'Morphing' Properties of Whiteness." *Making and Unmaking Whiteness.* Eds. Brigit Brander Rasmussen et al. Durham: Duke University Press, 2001. 113–137.

Eakin, Paul John. "Malcolm X and the Limits of Autobiography." *African American Autobiography.* Ed. William L. Andrews. Englewood Cliffs: Prentice Hall, 1993. 151–161.

Edelstein, Marilyn. "Resisting Postmodernism; or, 'A Postmodernism of Resistance.'" *Other Sisterhoods.* Ed. Sandra Kumamoto Stanley. Chicago: University of Illinois Press, 1999. 86–117.

Ellison, Ralph. *Flying Home and Other Stories.* New York: Random House, 1996.

_____. Introduction. *Invisible Man.* By Ralph Ellison. New York: Vintage, 1972: V-XIX.

_____. *Invisible Man* [1952]. New York: Vintage, 1972.

_____. *Shadow and Act.* New York: Signet, 1966.

Eng, David L. *Racial Castration. Managing Masculinity in Asian America.* Durham: Duke University Press, 2001.

Engles, Tim. "'Visions of me in the whitest raw light': Assimilation and Doxic Whiteness in Chang-rae Lee's Native Speaker." *Hitting Critical Mass:*

Bibliography

A Journal of Asian Cultural Criticism 4.2 (1997): 1–16.

Erikson, Erik. *Identity Youth and Crisis*. New York: Norton, 1968.

Espiritu, Yen Le. *Asian American Panethnicity. Bridging Institutions and Identities*. Philadelphia: Temple University Press, 1992.

Farred, Grant. "Endgame Identity? Mapping the New Left Roots of Identity Politics." *New Literary History* 31 (2000): 626–648.

Feng, Peter X. "Asian Americans and the Modern Imaginary." *American Quarterly* 52.4 (2000): 756–764.

———. *Identities in Motion. Asian American Film and Video*. Durham: Duke University Press, 2002.

Ferens, Dominika. *Edith and Winnifred Eaton: Chinatown Missions and Japanese Romances*. Urbana: University of Illinois Press, 2002.

Fine, David. *Los Angeles in Fiction*. Albuquerque: University of New Mexico Press, 1984.

Fishkin, Fisher Shelley. "Interrogating 'Whiteness,' Complicating 'Blackness': Remapping American Culture." *American Quarterly* 47.3 (1995): 428–466.

Flacks, Richard. "The Liberated Generation: An Exploration of the Roots of Student Protest." *Black Power and Student Rebellion*. Eds. James Mc Evoy and Abraham Miller: University of California, Davis, 1969. 355–378.

Flowers, Sandra Hollin, *African American Nationalist Literature of the 1960s. Pens of Fire*. New York: Garland, 1996.

Fong, Colleen. "From Margin to Centre"(?): Teaching Introduction to Asian American Studies as a General Education Requirement." *JGE: The Journal of General Education* 44.2 (1995): 108–129.

Foucault, Michel. "Body/Power." *Power/Knowledge. Selected Interviews and Other Writings*. Ed. Colin Gordon. Brighton: Harvester, 1980. 55–62.

———. "The Eye of Power." *Power/Knowledge. Selected Interviews and Other Writings*. Ed. Colin Gordon. Brighton: Harvester, 1980. 146–165.

Frankenberg, Ruth. "Introduction: Local Whiteness, Localizing Whiteness." *Displacing Whiteness: Essays in Social Criticism*. Durham: Duke University Press, 1997. 1–31.

———. "Whiteness and Americanness: Examining Constructions of Race, Culture, and Nation in White Women's Life Narratives." *Race*. Eds. Steven Gregory and Roger Sanjek. New Brunswick: Rutgers University Press, 1994. 62–77.

Friedman, Susan Stanford. "Beyond White and Other: Relationality and Narratives of Race in Feminist Discouse." *Signs: Journal of Women in Culture and Society* 21.11 (1995): 1–49.

Furth, Isabella. "Bee-e-een! Nation, Transformation and the Hyphen of Ethnicity in Kingston's *Tripmaster Monkey*." *Modern Fiction Studies* 40.1 (1994): 34–49.

Fuss, Dana. "Interior Colonies: Frantz Fanon and the Politics of Identification." *diacritics* 24.2 (1994).

Gale, Dennis. *Understanding Urban Unrest. From Reverend King to Rodney King*. London: Sage, 1996.

Galster, George, and Edward W. Hill, eds. *The Metropolis in Black and White. Place, Power and Polarization*. New Brunswick, N.J.: Centre for Urban Research, 1992.

Gates, Henry Louis. "Good-Bye Columbus? Notes on the Culture of Criticism." *Multiculturalism: A Critical Reader*. Ed. David Theo Goldberg. Oxford: Blackwell, 1995. 203–217.

———, ed. *"Race" Writing and Difference*. Chicago: University of Chicago Press, 1986.

———. *The Signifying Monkey: A Theory of Afro-American Literary Criticism*. New York: Oxford University Press, 1989.

Bibliography

———. "Two Nations ... Both Black." *Reading Rodney King. Reading Urban Uprising*. Ed. Robert-Gooding Williams. New York: Routledge, 1993.

Gayle, Addison, ed. *The Black Novel in America*. Gardena City, N.Y.: 1975.

Georgoudaki, Ekaterini. "Nikki Giovanni: The Poet as Explorer of Outer and Inner Space." *Women, Creators of Culture*. Ed. Ekaterini Georgoudaki and Donna Pastourmatzi. Hellenic Association of American Studies, Thessaloniki, 1997. 170–183.

Gibson, Donald. Introduction. *The Souls of Black Folk*. By W.E.B. Du Bois. New York: Penguin, 1989.

Giovanni, Nikki. *Black Feeling. Black Talk/ Black Judgment*. New York: William Morrow, 1979.

Glicksberg, Charles. "The Symbolism of Vision." *Twentieth Century Interpretations of Invisible Man. A Collection of Critical Essays*. Ed. John M. Reilly. England Cliffs, New Jersey: Prentice Hall, 1970. 49–55.

Gooding-Williams, Robert, ed. *Reading Rodney King. Reading Urban Uprising*. New York: Routledge, 1993.

Gordon, Avery, and Christopher Newfield. "White Philosophy." *Critical Inquiry* 20.4 (1994): 737–757.

Gotanda, Neil. "Exclusion and Inclusion. Immigration and American Orientalism." *Across the Pacific: Asian Americans and Globalization*. Ed. Evelyn Hu De Hart. Philadelphia: Temple University Press, 1999: 129–147.

Gottesman, Ronald. "The Art of Fiction: An Interview with Ralph Ellison." *The Merrill Studies in Invisible Man*. Ed. Ronald Gottesman. Columbus: Merrill, 1971. 43–45.

Greenlee, Sam. *Blues for an African Princess*. Chicago: Third World Press, 1971.

———. "An Interview with Sam Greenlee." *Black World* 20.9 (1971): 42–47.

———. *The Spook Who Sat by the Door* [1969]. Chicago: Lushena, 2002.

Grossberg, Lawrence. *Dancing In Spite of Myself*. Durham: Duke University Press, 1997.

Hahn, Harlan. "Black Separatists. Attitudes and Objectives in a Riot-torn Ghetto." *Journal of Black Studies* 1.1 (1970): 35–53.

Hall, Stuart. "Cultural Identity and Diaspora." *Colonial Discourse and Postcolonial Theory*. Ed. Patrick Williams and Laura Chrisman. New York: Columbia University Press, 1994. 392–403.

Hamamoto, Darrell. *Monitored Peril. Asian Americans and the Politics of TV Representation*. Minneapolis: University of Minnesota Press, 1994.

Harper, Philip Brian. "Nationalism and Social Division in Black Arts Poetry of the 1960s." *Identities*. Eds. K. A. Appiah and H. L. Gates. University of Chicago Pres, 1995. 220–241.

Harris, Cheryl. "Whiteness as Property." *The Harvard Law Review* 106.8 (1993): 1709–1791.

Harris, Daryl B. "The Logic of Black Urban Rebellions." *Journal of Black Studies* 28.3 (1998): 368–385.

Harris, Rosalind, and Julie N. Zimmerman. "Children and Poverty in the Rural South." 1 Jan. 2005 <http://srdc.msstate.edu/publications/srdpolicy/harris_Zimmerman.pdf>.

Hartigan, John. "Locating White Detroit." *Displacing Whiteness*. Ed. Ruth Frankenberg. Durham: Duke University Press, 1997. 180–185.

Healy, J.J. "Literature, Removal and the Theme of Invisibility in America: A Complex Fate Revisited." *Dalhousie Review* 61.1 (1981): 127–142.

Hellwig, David J. "Afro-American Reactions to the Japanese and the Anti-Japanese Movement, 1906–1924." *Phylon* 38.1 (1977): 93–104.

———. "Black Reactions to Chinese Immigration and the Anti-Chinese Movement: 1850–1910." *Amerasia* 6.2 (1979): 25–44.

Hersey, John. "'A Completion of Personality': A Talk with Ralph Ellison." *Speaking For You*. Ed. Kimberly W. Benston. Washington: Howard University Press, 1987. 286–307.

Hill, Patricia. *Call and Response: The Riverside Anthology of African American Literary Tradition*. Boston: Houghton Mifflin, 1998.

Himes, Chester. *Lonely Crusade* [1947]. New York: Thunder's Mouth Press, 1994.

Hing, Bill Ong. *Making and Remaking Asian America Through Immigration*. Stanford: Stanford University Press, 1993.

Hirsch, Arnold. *Making the Second Ghetto: Race and Housing in Chicago 1940–1960*. Cambridge University Press, 1983.

Holmes, Robert A. "The Afro-American in the Urban Age." *Journal of Black Studies* 4.4 (1974): 441–456.

Holt, Thomas. "The Political Uses of Alienation: W.E.B. Du Bois on Politics, Race and Culture, 1903–1940." *American Quarterly* 42.2 (1990): 301–323.

Holte, James Craig. "The Representative Voice: Autobiography and the Ethnic Experience." *MELUS* 9.2 (1982): 25–46.

Hom, Marlon K. "A Case of Mutual Exclusion: Portrayals by Immigrant and American-born Chinese of Each Other." *Amerasia Journal* 11.2 (1984): 29–45.

Hong, Grace. "'Something Forgotten Which Should Have Been Remembered': Private Property and Cross-Racial Solidarity in the Work of Hisaye Yamamoto." *American Literature* 71.2 (1999): 291–310.

Hongo, Garrett, ed. *The Open Boat: Poems from Asian America*. New York: Anchor-Doubleday, 1993.

hooks, bell. "Cultural Identity and Diaspora." *Colonial Discourse and Postcolonial Theory*. Ed. Patrick Williams and Laura Chrisman. New York: Columbia University Press, 1994. 421–427.

———. "Representing Whiteness in the Black Imagination." *Displacing Whiteness*. Ed. Ruth Frankenberg. Durham: Duke University Press, 1997. 165–179.

Horowitz, Ellin. "The Rebirth of the Artist." *Twentieth Century Interpretations of Invisible Man. A Collection of Critical Essays*. Ed. John M. Reilly. New Jersey: Prentice Hall, 1970. 80–88.

Huang, Joan. "Oral Fixations: An Exploration of *Native Speaker*." *Hitting Critical Mass* 6.1 (1999). 79–88.

Huggan, Graham. "(Post)Colonialism, Anthropology, and the Magic of Mimesis." *Cultural Critique* Winter 38 (1998): 91–106.

Huggins, Nathan, Chronology. *Du Bois. Writings*. Ed. Nathan Huggins. New York: Library of America, 1986.

Hurh, Won Moo, and Kwang Chung Kim. "The 'Success' Image of Asian Americans: Its Validity, and Its Practical and Theoretical Implications." *Ethnic and Racial Studies* 12.4 (1989): 512–537.

Hwang, Henry David. *M. Butterfly*. New York: Plume, 1988.

Ichigashi, Yamato. "Emigration from Japan and Thence Their Immigration Into the State of California." Diss. Harvard University, 1913. 274

James, William. *The Principles of Psychology*. New York: Henry Holt, 1905.

Jaynes, Gerald David. *Branches Without Roots. Genesis of the Black Working Class in the American South, 1862–1882*. New York: Oxford University Press, 1986.

Jasnowitz, Morris. "Patterns of Collective Violence." *Violence in America*. Hugh Davis Graham: New York, 1969. 412–445.

Jennings, Regina. "Poetry and the Black Party Metaphors of Militancy." *Journal of Black Studies*. 29.1 (1998): 106–129.

Johnson, James Weldon. *The Autobiography of an Ex-Colored Man* [1912]. New York: Dover, 1995.

Karrer, Wolfgang. "Integration or Sepa-

Bibliography

ratism: The Social History of the Afro-American Dilemma After World War II." *The Afro-American Novel Since 1960.* Eds. Peter Bruck and Wolfgang Karrer. Amsterdam: Grüner Publishing, 1982. 29–52.

Kearny, Reginald. *African American Views of the Japanese. Solidarity or Sedition?* Albany: State University of New York, 1998.

Keating, Analouise. "(De)Centering the Margins? Identity Politics and Tactical (Re)Naming." *Other Sisterhoods.* Ed. Sandra Kumamoto. Chicago: University of Illinois Press, 1998. 23–43.

———. "Interrogating 'Whiteness,' (De)Constructing 'Race.'" *College English* 57.8 (1995): 901–918.

Keith, Michael, and Steve Pile. Introduction Part 1 and Part 2. *Place and the Politics of Identity.* Ed. Keith and Pile. New York: Routledge, 1993. 1–41.

——— and ———. Conclusion: Towards New Radical Geographies. *Place and the Politics of Identity.* Ed. Keith and Pile. New York: Routledge, 1993. 220–227.

——— and ———, eds. *Place and the Politics of Identity.* New York: Routledge, 1993.

Kemp, Kathleen. "Race, Ethnicity, Class and Urban Spatial Conflict: Chicago as a Crucial Test Case." *Urban Studies* 23 (1986): 197–208.

Kennedy, John F. "Letter on Revision of the Immigration Laws." *Presidential Papers Historical Series.* 18 Feb. 2005 <http://www.ilw.com/lawyers/articles/2004, 0301-kennedy.shtm>.

Kim, Elaine H. "Room for a View from a Marginal Sight: Texts, Contexts, and Asian American Studies." *Hitting Critical Mass* 1.2 (1994): 1–14.

Kim, Kwang Chung. *Koreans in the Hood. Conflict with African Americans.* Baltimore: The Johns Hopkins University Press, 1999.

———, and Shin Kim. "The Multiracial Nature of Los Angeles Unrest in 1992." *Koreans in the Hood.* Ed. Kwang Chung Kim. Baltimore: Johns Hopkins University Press, 1999. 17–38.

———, and Won Moo Hurh. "Korean Americans and the 'Success' Image: A Critique." *Amerasia* 10.2 (1983): 3–21.

King, Rebecca Chiyoko. "Racialization, Recognition and Rights: Lumping and Splitting Asian Americans in the 2000 Census." *Journal of Asian American Studies* 3.2 (2000): 191–217.

Kingston, Maxine Hong. *China Men* [1980]. New York: Ballantine, 1986.

———. *Conversations with Maxine Hong Kingston.* Ed. Paul Skenazy and Tera Martin. Jackson: University Press of Mississippi, 1998.

———. "Cultural Misreadings by American Reviewers." *Asian and Western Writers in Dialogue.* Ed. Guy Amirthanayagam. Hong Kong: Macmillan, 1982: 55–65.

———. *The Fifth Book of Peace.* New York: Vintage, 2004.

———. "The Novel's Next Step." *Mother Jones* 14.10 (1989): 37–41.

———. *Tripmaster Monkey: His Fake Book.* New York: Vintage, 1989.

———. *The Woman Warrior* [1976]. New York: Vintage, 1977.

Kirby, Kathleen. "Thinking through the Boundary: The Politics of Location, Subjects and Space." *boundary 2* 20:2 (1993): 173–189.

Knopf, Terry Ann. "Sniping… A New Pattern of Violence?" *Ghetto Revolts.* Ed. Peter H. Rossi. New York, Dutton. 1973. 153–175.

Kogawa, Joy. *Obasan* [1981]. New York: Doubleday, 1994.

Kostelanetz, Richard. *Politics in the African American Novel.* New York: Greenwood, 1991.

Kwong, Peter. *The New Chinatown.* New York: Hill and Wang, 1987.

Lauter, Paul, ed. *The Heath Anthology of American Literature.* Lexington, Mass.: Heath, 1994.

Lazarus, Emma. "The New Colossus." 1 Jan. 2005 <http://www.nps.gov/stli/newcolossusindex.html>.

Lee, Chang-rae. *Native Speaker* [1995]. New York: Riverhead, 1996.

Lee, Don L. *Groundwork: New Selected Poems of Don L. Lee/Haki R. Madhubuti from 1966–1996*. Chicago, Third World Press, 1996.

Lee, Heon Cheol. "Conflict between Korean Merchants and Black Customers: A Structural Analysis." *Koreans in the Hood. Conflict with African Americans*. Baltimore: The Johns Hopkins University Press, 1999. 113–130.

———. "The Dynamics of Black-Korean Conflict: A Korean American Perspective." *Koreans in the Hood. Conflict with African Americans*. Baltimore: The Johns Hopkins University Press, 1999. 91–112.

Lee, James Kyung-Jin. *Urban Triage*. Minneapolis: University of Minnesota Press, 2003.

Lee, Josephine. *Performing Asian America*. Philadelphia: Temple University Press, 1997.

Lee, Marjorie. "On Contradiction: The Second Generation." *Origins and Destinations: 41 Essays on Chinese America*. A joint project of Chinese Historical Society of Southern California and UCLA Asian American Studies Centre in Los Angeles, California, 1994: 103–110.

Lee, Rachel. "Claiming Land, Claiming Voice, Claiming Canon: Institutionalized Challenges in Kingston's *China Men* and *The Woman Warrior*. Re Viewing Asian America. Locating Diversity. Ed. Wendy L. Ng, Gary Okihiro. Washington: Washington State University, 1995. 147–159.

Lee, Robert G. *Orientals. Asian Americans in Popular Culture*. Philadelphia: Temple University Press, 1999.

Leong, Andrew. "How Public-Policy Reforms Shape, and Reveal the Shape of Asian America." *Contemporary Asian American Communities*. Eds. Linda Trinh Vo and Rick Bouns. Philadelphia: Temple University Press, 2002. 229–241.

Leong, Russell. Foreword. *On a Bed of Rice. An Asian American Erotic Feast*. Ed. Geraldine Kudaka. New York: Doubleday, 1995. XI–XXX.

———. "Lived Theory (notes on the run)." *Amerasia* 21.1–2 (1995): V-X.

———, and Edward T. Chang. *Los Angeles Struggles Toward Multiethnic Community*. Seattle: University of Washington Press, 1994.

Leslie, Antonette. *The Rhetoric of Diversity and the Traditions of American Literary Study. Critical Multiculturalism in English*. London: Bergin, 1998.

Lesser, Jeff H. "Always 'Outsiders': Asians, Naturalization and the Supreme Court." *Amerasia* 12.1 (1985–86): 83–100.

Levine, Lawrence W. *Black Culture and Black Consciousness. Afro-American Folk Thought from Slavery to Freedom*. New York: Oxford University Press, 1977.

Li, David Leiwei Li. "The Formation of Frank Chin and the Formation of Chinese American Literature." *Reflections on Shattered Windows*. Eds. Shirley Hune and Gary Okihiro. Washington: Washington State University Press, 1988. 211–223.

———. "The Production of Chinese American Tradition: Displacing American Orientalist Discourse." *Reading the Literatures of Asian America*. Ed. Shirley Geok-lin Lim and Amy Ling. Philadelphia: Temple University Press, 1992. 319–331.

Lim, Shirley Geok-lin. "The Ambivalent American: Asian American Literature on the Cusp." *Reading the Literatures of Asian America*. Eds. Shirley Geok-lin Lilm and Amy Ling. Philadelphia: Temple University Press, 1992. 13–32.

———. "Immigration and Diaspora." *An*

Bibliography

Interethnic Companion. Ed. King-Kok Cheung. New York: Harvard University Press, 1997. 289–312.

Lin, Patricia. "Clashing Constructs of Reality: Reading Maxine Hong Kingston's *Tripmaster Monkey: His Fake Book* as an Indigenous Ethnography." *Reading the Literatures of Asian America.* Eds. Shirley Geok-lin Lim and Amy Ling. Philadelphia: Temple University Press, 1992.

Ling, Amy. *Between Worlds. Women Writers of Chinese Ancestry.* New York: Pergamon, 1990.

―――. "Contemporary Asian American Issues. Demographics, Economics and Politics." *Asian Americans. Comparative and Global Perspectives.* Washington: Pullman, 1991: 191–197.

―――. "Whose America Is It?" *Weber Studies* 12.1 (1995): 27–35.

Ling, Jinqi. *Narrating Nationalisms. Ideology and Form in Asian American Literature.* New York: Oxford University Press, 1998.

Linton, Patricia. "What Stories the Wind Would Tell": Representation and Appropriation in Maxine Hong Kingston's *China Men.*" *MELUS* 19.4 (1994): 37–48.

Lipsitz, George. *The Possessive Investment in Whiteness. How White People Profit From Identity Politics.* Philadelphia: Temple University Press, 1998.

Loewen, James W. "Interracial Families." *The Mississippi Chinese: Between Black and White.* Cambridge, Mass.: Harvard University Press, 1971. 135–151.

Lorde, Audre. *Sister Outsider: Essays and Speeches.* Freedom, Calif.: Crossing Press, 1984.

Lott, Eric. "After Identity, Politics: The Return of Universalism." *New Literary History* 31 (2000): 665–680.

Louie, Andrea. "Chineseness across the Borders: A Multisited Investigation of Chinese Diaspora Identities." *Cultural Compass. Ethnographic Explorations of Asian America.* Ed. Martin F. Manalansan. Philadelphia: Temple University Press, 2000.

Lowe, Lisa. *Immigrant Acts.* Durham: Duke University Press, 1996.

Lyons, Eleanor. "Ellison's Narrator as Emersonian Scholar." *Approaches to Teaching Ellison's* Invisible Man. Ed. Susan Rosneck Parr and Pancho Savery. New York: MLA, 1991. 75–78.

Ma, Sheng-mei. *Immigrant Subjectivities in Asian America and Asian Diaspora Literatures.* Albany: State University of New York Press, 1998.

Maffi, Mario. "Some Remarks on Ethnic Writing in New York City." *Multiculturalism and the Canon of American Culture.* Ed. Hans Bak. Amsterdam: Vrije University Press, 1993. 160–171.

Mangiafico, Luciano. "A Short History of Korean Immigration to the United States." *Contemporary American Immigrants Patterns of Filipino, Korean and Chinese Settlement in the United Sates.* New York: Praeger, 1988. 77–104.

Maini, Irma. "Writing the Asian American Artist: Maxine Hong Kingston's *Tripmaster Monkey: His Fake Book.*" *MELUS* 25.3–4 (2000): 243–264.

Marable, Manning. "African American Empowerment in the Face of Racism: The Political Aftermath of the Battle of Los Angeles." *Beyond Black and White.* New York: Verso, 1996. 177–184.

―――. "Beyond Racial Identity Politics: Toward a Liberation Theory for Multicultural Democracy." *Privileging Positions: The Sites of Asian American Studies.* Eds. Marilyn Alquizda, et. al. Pullman: Washington State University Press, 1995. 315–334.

―――. "History and Black Consciousness: The Political Culture of Black America." *Beyond Black and White.* New York: Verso, 1996. 216–229.

―――. "Memory and Militancy in Transition." *Beyond Black and White.* New York: Verso, 1996. 142–156.

_____, and Leith Mullings. "The Divided Mind of Black America: Race, Ideology and Politics in the Post-Civil-Rights Era." *Beyond Black and White*. New York: Verso, 1996. 203–215.

Martin, Jay. *Downcast Eyes. The Denigration of Vision in the Twentieth Century Thought*. Berkeley: University of California, 1994.

Martin, John Stephen. "Vision and Visibility: The Phenomenology of Power and the American Literary Consciousness of Self." *Canadian Review of American Studies* 18.2 (1987): 181–196.

Massey, Doreen. "Politics and Space/Time." *Place and the Politics of Identity*. Ed. Keith and Pile. New York: Routledge, 1993. 141–162.

McCarthey, John T. *Black Power Ideologies*. Philadelphia: Temple University Press, 1992.

McLaren, Peter. "White Terror and Oppositional Agency: Towards a Critical Multiculturalism." *Multiculturalism. A Critical Reader*. Oxford: Blackwell, 1995. 46–73.

McQuarie, Donald, and Marc Spaulding. "The Concept of Power in Marxist Theory: A Critique and Reformulation." *Critical Sociology* 16.1 (1989): 3–26.

Meier, August, and Elliott Rudwick. "Black Violence in the 20th century: A Study in Rhetoric and Retaliation." *Violence in America*. Hugh Davis Graham: New York, 1969. 399–413.

Meyer, Adam. "Sam Greenlee." *Contemporary American Novelists*. Ed. Emanuel S. Nelson. Westport, Con.: University of Connecticut Press, 1999. 185–191.

Michaelson, Scott. Introduction. *The Limits of Multiculturalism*. Minneapolis: University of Minnesota Press, 1999: IX-XIII.

Miller, R. Baxter. "The Performance of African American Autobiography." *Style* 27.2 (1993): 285–299.

_____. "The Rewritten Self in African American Autobiography." *Alternative Identities. The Self in Literature, History, Theory*. Ed. Linda Marie Brooks. New York: Garland, 1995. 87–104.

Miller, Stuart Creighton. "Chinese Exclusion in Historical and National Perspective." *The American Image of the Chinese, 1785–1882*. Los Angeles: University of California Press, 1969. 191–245.

Mills, Charles. *Blackness Visible*. New York: Cornell University Press, 1998.

Min, Pyong Gap, and Andrew Kolodny. "The Middleman Minority Characteristics of Korean Immigrants in the United States." *Koreans in the Hood. Conflict with African Americans*. Ed. Kwang Chung Kim. Baltimore: Johns Hopkins University Press, 1999. 131–157.

Mitchell-Kernan, Claudia. "Signifying." *Mother Wit from the Laughing Barrel*. Ed. Alan Dundes. Englewood Cliffs, N.J.: Prentice Hall, 1973. 310–328.

Moore, Jack B. "The Art of Black Power: Novelistic or Documentary." *Revue Francaise D'Etudes Americaines* 12.31 (1987): 79–90.

_____. "Black Power Revisited: In Search of Richard Wright." *Mississippi Quarterly* 41.2 (1988): 161–186.

Morrison, Toni. *Beloved*. New York: Knopf, 1987.

_____. *Playing in the Dark. Whiteness and Literary Imagination*. Cambridge: Harvard University Press, 1992.

Moses, Wilson. "The Poetics of Ethiopianism: W. E. B. Du Bois and Literary Black Nationalism." *American Literature* 47.3 (1975): 411–426.

Mosley, Walter. *Devil in a Blue Dress*. New York: Pocket Books, 1997.

Moy, James. "Asian American Visibility: Touring Fierce Racial Geographies." *Staging Difference*. Ed. Marc Maufort. New York: Peter Lang, 1995. 16–28.

_____. *Marginal Sights. Staging the Chinese America*. Iowa City: University of Iowa Press, 1993.

Mullen, Harryette. "Optic White: Blackness and the Production of Whiteness." *diacritics* 24.2 (1994): 25–36.

Mullen, Robert W. *Blacks and Vietnam*. Northern Kentucky University: University Press of America, 1981.

Mura, David. *Where the Body Meets Memory: An Odyssey of Race, Sexuality and Identity*. New York: Doubleday, 1995.

Murphy-Shigematsu, Stephen. "Addressing Issues of Biracial/Bicultural Asian Americans." *Reflections on Shattered Windows*. Washington: Washington State University Press, 1988. 111–116.

Nakanishi, Don T. "Asian American Politics: An Agenda for Research." *Amerasia* 12.2 (1985–1986): 1–27.

Nee de Bary, Brett and Victor. *Longtime Californian. A Documentary Study of an American Chinatown*. New York: Pantheon, 1973.

Nelson, Emanuel S. *Contemporary African American Novelists*. Westport, Con.: Greenwood Press, 1999.

Ng, Fae Myenne. *Bone*. New York: Harper, 1994.

Ng, Wendy L., Soo-Young Chin, James Moy and Gary Okihiro. Introduction. ReViewing Asian America: Locating Diversity. *Reviewing Asian America*. Eds. Wendy L. Ng, Soo-Young Chin, James S. Moy and Gary Okihiro. Washington: Washington State University Press, 1995. 1–14.

Nguyen, Viet Thanh. "Model Minorities and Bad Subjects." *Race and Resistance. Literature and Politics in Asian America*. Oxford: Oxford University Press, 2002. 143–154.

_____. "The Remasculinization of Chinese America: Race, Violence, and the Novel." *American Literary History* 12.1 (2000): 130–157.

Niiya, Brian. "Asian American Autobiographical Tradition." *The Asian American Pacific Heritage*. New York: Garland, 1999. 427–434.

Nishime, LeiLani. "Engendering Genre: Gender and Nationalism in *China Men* and *The Woman Warrior*." *MELUS* 20.1 (1995): 67–82.

Nunez, Sigrid. *A Feather on the Breath of God*. New York: Harper Collins, 1995.

Ogawa, Dennis Masaaki. "Small Group Communication Stereotypes of Black Americans." *Journal of Black Studies* 1.3 (1971): 273–280.

Okihiro, Gary Y. "African American and Asian American Studies: A Comparative Analysis and Commentary." *Asian American Comparative and Global Perspectives*. Ed. ShirleyHune. Washington: Pullman, 1991. 16–28.

_____. *Margins and Mainstreams: Asians in American History and Culture*. Seattle: University of Washington Press, 1994.

_____, ed. *Reflections on Shattered Windows*. Washington: Washington State University Press, 1988.

Olney, James. "The Value of Autobiography for Comparative Studies: African vs. Western Autobiography." *African American Autobiography*. Englewood Cliffs: Prentice Hall, 1993. 212–223.

Omatsu, Glenn. "The 'Four Prisons' and the Movement of Liberation: Asian American Activism in the 1960s and the 1990s." *The State of Asian America: Activism and Resistance in the 1990s*. Boston: Southland, 1994. 16–67.

O'Meally. "The Rules of Magic: Hemingway as Ellison's 'Ancestor.'" *The Southern Review* 21.3 (1985): 751–769.

Omi, Michael. "(E)racism: Emerging Practices of Antiracist Organizations." *Making and Unmaking Whiteness*. Eds. Brigit Brander Rasmussen et al. Durham: Duke University Press, 2001.

_____. "It Just Ain't the Sixties No More: The Contemporary Dilemmas of Asian American Studies." *Reflections on Shattered Windows.* Eds. Gary Okihiro and Shirley Hune. Washington: Washington State University Press, 1988: 117–125.

_____, and Howard Winant. "The Los

Bibliography

Angeles 'Race Riot' and Contemporary U.S. Politics." *Reading Rodney King. Reading Urban Uprising.* New York: Routledge, 1993. 96–114.

———, and ———. *Racial Formation in the United States (from the 1960s to the 1980s).* New York: Routledge, 1986.

Ong, Paul M., and David E. Lee. "Changing of the Guard? The Emerging Immigrant Majority in Asian American Politics." *Asian Americans and Politics. Perspectives, Experiences, Prospects.* Ed. Gordon H. Chay. Stanford: Stanford University Press, 2001. 153–172.

Onishi, Norimitsu. "Affirmative Action: Choosing Sides." *New York Times* March 31 1996: 26–29, 32–34.

Osajima, Keith. "Asian Americans as the Model Minority: An Analysis of the Popular Press Image in the 1960s and 1980s." *Reflections on Shattered Windows.* Eds. Shirley Hune and Gary Okihiro. Washington: Washington State University Press, 1988. 165–174.

Osterndorf, Berndt. "The Costs of Multiculturalism." Working Paper No. 50 *Abteilung für Kultur* (1992): 1–30.

Palumbo-Liu, David. "Assumed Identities." *New Literary History* 31.1 (2000): 765–780.

———. Introduction. *The Ethnic Canon.* Minneapolis: University of Minnesota Press, 1995: 1–19.

———. "Los Angeles, Asians and Perverse Ventriloquisms: On the Functions of Asian America in the Recent American Imaginary." *Public Culture* 6 (1994): 365–381.

———. "Theory and the Subject of Asian American Studies." *Amerasia Journal* 21.1&2 (1995): 55–65.

Park, Kyeyoung. "Use and Abuse of Race and Culture: Black-Korean Tension in America." *Koreans in the Hood. Conflict with African Americans.* Baltimore: The Johns Hopkins University Press, 1999. 60–74.

Peavy, Charles D. "Four Black Revolutionary Novels, 1899–1970." *Journal of Black Studies* 1.2 (1970): 219–223.

"Persons Below Poverty Level." 11 Nov. 2004 <http://www.infoplease.com/ipa/A01044525.html>.

Piper, Adrian. "Passing for White, Passing for Black." *Critical Whiteness Studies. Looking Behind the Mirror.* Eds. Richard Delgado, Jean Stefancic. Philadelphia: Temple University Press, 1997. 425–431.

"Poetry by Anonymous Chinese Immigrants." *The Literature of California.* Eds. Jack Hicks, James D. Houston, Maxine Hong Kingston and Al Young. Los Angeles: University of California Press, 2000.

Pomerantz, Linda. "The Background of Korean Immigration." *Labor Immigration Under Capitalism.* Eds. Lucie Cheng and E. Bonacich. Berkeley: University of California Press, 1984. 277–303.

Posnock, Ross. "Before and After Identity Politics." *Raritan* 15.1 (1995): 95–115.

"Poverty Spreads" Census Bureau, 26 Aug. 2004. 10 Jan. 2005 <http://money.cnn.com/2004/08/26/news/economy/poverty_survey/?cnn=yes>

Prashad, Vijay. *Afro-Asian Connections and the Myth of Cultural Purity.* Boston: Beacon, 2001.

Radhakrishnan, R. "Cultural Theory and the Politics of Location." *Views Beyond the Border Country.* Eds. Leslie Ranan and Dennis Dworkin. New York: Routledge, 1993. 275–353.

———. "Negotiating Subject Positions in an Uneven World." *Feminism and Institutions.* Ed. Linda Kaufman. Oxford: Basil Blackwell, 1989. 277–290.

"Rainbow Coalition." Britannica Student Encyclopedia. 24 Jan. 2005 <http://www.britannica.com/ebi/article?tocId=9313130>.

Razaf, Andy. "(What Did I do to Be So) Black and Blue." *Cultural Contexts for*

Bibliography

Ralph Ellison's Invisible Man. Ed. Eric Sundquist. Boston: St. Martin's Press, 1995. 115–118.

Reed, Ishmael. "Integration or Cultural Exchange?" *Yardbird Reader* V (1976): 3.

———. "Interview with Ralph Ellison." *Y' Bird* 1.1 (1977): 126–159.

Reilly, John M. "Discovering an Art of the Self in History: A Principle of Afro-American Life." *Approaches to Teaching Ellison's* Invisible Man. Ed. Susan Rosneck Parr and Pancho Savery. New York: MLA, 1991. 37–42.

Rich, Adrienne. "Notes Toward a Politics of Location." *Blood, Bread and Poetry.* New York: Norton, 1986. 210–231.

Rilke, Rainer Maria. Excerpts of *The Notebooks of Malte Laurids Brigge.* Tripmaster Monkey. Maxine Hong Kingston. *Tripmaster Monkey: His Fake Book.* New York: Vintage, 1989.

Roberts, John W. *From Trickster to Badman. The Black Folk Hero in Slavery and Freedom.* Philadelphia: University of Pennsylvania, 1989.

Roediger, David. *The Wages of Whiteness: Race and the Making of the American Working Class.* London: Verso, 1991.

Rondon, Stewart. "Ralph Ellison's *Invisible Man*: Six Tentative Approaches." *The Merrill Studies in* Invisible Man. Ed. Ronald Gottesman. Columbus: Merrill, 1971. 100–119.

Rose, Peter I. "Asian Americans. From Pariahs to Paragons." *Multiculturalism and Intergroup Relations.* Ed. James S. Friders. New York: Greenwood, 1989. 107–122.

Ross, Marlon B. "Commentary: Pleasuring Identity, or the Delicious Politics of Belonging." *New Literary History* 31 (2000): 827–850.

Roy, Parama. "Oriental Exhibits: Englishmen and Natives in Burton's *Personal Narrative of a Pilgrimage to Al-Madinah and Meccah. boundary 2* 22.1 (1995): 185–202.

Said, Edward. *Orientalism.* London: Penguin, 1978.

Samarth, Manini. "Affirmations: Speaking the Self into Being." *Parnassus: Poetry-in-Review* 17.1 (1992): 88–101.

"San Francisco Chronicle Obituary." 19 Mar. 2006 <http://www.sfgate.com/cgi-bin/article.cgi?f=/c/a/2006/03/19/BAGNDHQOO31.DTL>

San Juan, E. "Beyond Identity Politics: The Predicament of the Asian American Writer in Late Capitalism." *American Literary History* 3.3 (1991).

Sanchez, Sonia. "the final solution." *Home Coming.* Detroit: Broadside Press, 1969.

Savery, Pancho. "'Not Like an Arrow, but a Boomerang.' Ellison's Existential Blues." *Approaches to Teaching Ralph Ellison's* Invisible Man. Eds. Susan Rosneck Parr and Pancho Savery. New York: MLA, 1991. 65–74.

Schaffer, William J. "Ralph Ellison and the Birth of the Anti-Hero." *A Collection of Critical Essays.* Ed. John Hersey. New Jersey: Prentice-Hall, 1974. 115–126.

Schaub, Thomas. "Ellison's Masks and the Novel of Reality." *New Essays on* Invisible Man. Ed. Robert O'Meally. Cambridge: Cambridge University Press, 1988. 123–156.

Schraufnagel, Noel, ed. *The Black American Novel.* Deland, Florida: Everett, 1973.

Schultz, Elizabeth. "To Be Black and Blue: The Blues Genre in Black American Autobiogphy." *The American Autobiography.* Ed. Albert E. Stone. Englewood Cliffs, N.J.: Prentice Hall, 1981. 109–132.

Schwentker, Wolfganag. "'The Yellow Peril' Reconsidered. Western Perceptions of Asia in the Age of Imperialism." *Cultural Negotiations.* Ed. Cedric Brown. Düsseldorf: Tübigen and Basel, 1998. 4–49.

Shankman, Arnold. *Ambivalent Friends. Afro-Americans View the Immigrant.* London: Greenwood Press, 1982.

Shapiro, Elliott H. "Authentic Watermelon: Maxine Hong Kingston's American Novel." *MELUS* 26.1 (2001): 6–28.

Shimakawa, Karen. *National Abjection. The Asian American Body Onstage.* Durham: Duke University Press, 2002.

Shin, Linda. "Koreans in America, 1903–1945." *Amerasia Journal* 1.3 (1971): 84–91.

Shirley, Hune. "The International History of Asian American Studies: Remembering 1968." *Asian Americans. Comparative and Global Perspectives.* Washington: Pullman, 1991. 39–43.

Shugart, Helene A. "Counterhegemonic Acts: Appropriation as a Feminist Rhetorical Strategy." *Quarterly Journal of Speech* 83 (1997): 210–229.

"Silk Cycle." *Time* 9 March 1942: 62.

Simon, Myron. "Two Angry Ethnic Writers." *MELUS* 3.2 (1976): 20–24.

Sin Far, Sui. "Chinese Workmen in America." *Mrs Spring Fragrance and Other Writings.* Eds. Amy Ling and Annette White Parks. Urbana: University of Illinois Press, 1995.

_____. "Leaves from the Mental Portfolio of an Eurasian." *The Heath Anthology of American Literature.* Ed. Paul Lauter. Lexington, Mass: Heath, 1994. 884–895.

Sirkanth, Rajini. "Gender and the Image of Home in the Asian Diaspora." *Hitting Critical Mass* 2.1 (1994): 1–20.

Skenazy, Paul, and Tera Martin, eds. *Conversations with Maxine Hong Kingston.* Jackson: University Press of Mississippi, 1998.

Smith, C. Edward. "Red Chinese Influence on the Politics of the Black Panther Party." *Black World* 20.9 (1971): 75–79.

Smith, Neil, and Cindi Katz. "Grounding Metaphor: Towards a Spatialized Politics." *Place and the Politics of Identity.* Ed. Keith and Pile. New York: Routledge, 1993: 67–84.

Soja, Edward. *Postmodern Geographies.* New York: Verso, 2003.

Soja, Edward, and Barbara Hooper. "The Spaces that Difference Makes: Some Notes on the Geographical Margins of the New Cultural Politics." *Place and the Politics of Identity.* Ed. Keith and Pile. New York: Routledge, 1993. 183–206.

Sollors, Werner. *Amiri Baraka/Leroi Jones: The Quest for a "Populist Modernism."* New York: Columbia University Press, 1978.

_____. *Neither Black Nor White Yet Both.* Cambridge: Harvard University Press, 1997.

Song, Min Hyoung. "A Diasporic Future? *Native Speaker* and Historical Trauma." *LIT* 12 (2001): 79–98.

Spillers, Hortense. "Mama's Baby, Papa's Maybe" [1987]. *Feminisms.* Eds. Robyn Warhol and Diane Price Herndl. New Brunswick: Rutgers University Press, 1997. 384–405.

Spivak, Gayatri Chakravorty. "Can the Subaltern Speak?" *The Postcolonial Reader.* Eds. Bill Ashcroft, Gareth Griffith. New York: Routledge, 1995. 24–28.

_____. "The Problem of Cultural Self-representation." *The Postcolonial Critic: Interviews, Strategies, Dialogues.* Ed. Sarah Harasym. New York: Routledge, 1990. 50–58.

_____. "Questions of Multiculturalism." *The Postcolonial Critic: Interviews, Strategies, Dialogues.* Ed. Sarah Harasym. New York: Routledge, 1990. 59–66.

Spoehr, Luther W. "Sambo and the Heathen Chinee: Californians' Racial Stereotypes in the Late 1870s." *Pacific Historical Review* 42 (1973): 185–204.

Spurlin, William J. "Theorizing Signifying and the Role of the Reader: Possible Directions for African American Literary Criticism." *College English* 52.7 (1990): 732–741.

Sten, Christopher. "Losing It 'Even As He Finds It': The Invisible Man's Search

For Identity." *Approaches to Teaching Ellison's Invisible Man*. Eds. Susan Rosneck Parr and Pancho Savery. New York: MLA, 1991. 80–95.

Stepto, Robert. *From Behind the Veil. A Study of Afro-American Narrative*. Chicago: University of Illinois Press, 1991.

Stewart, Charles J. "The Evolution of a Revolution: Stokely Carmichael and the Rhetoric of Black Power." *Quarterly Journal of Speech* 83.4 (1997): 429–446.

"Success Story, Japanese American Style." *New York Times Magazine* 9 Jan. 1966: 20–22.

"Success Story: Outwhiting the Whites." *Newsweek* 21 June 1971: 26–27.

"Success Story of One Minority Group." *U.S. News and World Report* 26 Dec. 1966: 6–9.

Sumida, Stephen. "Centres Without Margins: Responses to Centrism in Asian American Literature." *American Literature* 66.4 (1994): 803–815.

Sun, William H., and Faye C. Fei. "Masks or Faces Revisited. A Study of Four Theatrical Works Concerning Cultural Identity." *The Drama Review* 38.4 (1994): 120–132.

Sundquist, Eric. J. *Cultural Contexts for Ralph Ellison's* Invisible Man. Boston: St. Martin's Press, 1995.

Suzuki, Bob H. "Education and Socialization of Asian Americans: A Revisionist Analysis of the 'Model Minority' Thesis." *Amerasia* 4.2 (1977): 23–51.

Tabb, William K. "Black Capitalists." *The Political Economy of the Black Ghetto*. New York: Norton, 1970. 40–49.

Takagi, Dana. "Maiden Voyage: Excursion into Sexuality and Identity Politics in Asian America." *Amerasia Journal* 20.1 (1994): 1–17.

———. "Post-Civil Rights Politics and Asian American Identity: Admissions and Higher Education." *Race*. New Brunswick, NJ: Rutgers University Press, 1994. 229–242.

Takaki, Ronald. *Strangers from a Different Shore*. Boston: Little, Brown, 1989.

Takeshi, Jere. "Japanese American Responses to Race Relations: The Formation of Nisei Perspectives." *Amerasia* 9.1 (1982): 29–57.

Tanner, James T. F. "Walt Whitman's Presence in Maxine Hong Kingston's *Tripmaster Monkey: His Fake Book*." *MELUS* 20.4 (1995): 61–74.

Tanner, Tony. "The Music of Invisibility." *Ralph Ellison. A Collection of Critical Essays*. Ed. John Hersey. New Jersey: Prentice-Hall, 1974. 80–94.

Tate, Claudia. "Notes on the Invisible Women in Ralph Ellison's *Invisible Man*." *Speaking For You: The Vision of Ralph Ellison*. Ed. Kimberly Benston. Washington: Howard University Press, 1987. 163–172.

Taylor, Charles. *Multiculturalism and the Politics of Recognition*. Princeton: Princeton, University Press, 1992.

———. *Sources of the Self*. Cambridge: Cambridge University Press, 1996.

Taylor, Gordon. "'Adding On,' Not 'Giving Up': Ceremonies of Self in Frank Chin's *Donald Duk*. *Asian American Literature in the International Context. Readings on Fiction, Poetry and Performance*. Ed. Rocío G. Davis and Sämi Ludwig. London: Transaction, 2002. 59–69.

Thomas, Brook. "*China Men*, United States v. Wong Kim Ark and the Question of Citizenship." *American Quarterly* 50.4 (1998): 689–715.

Thomas, Joyce Carol. "Paint me like I am." *Yardbird Reader* 4 (1974): V.

Thornton, Michael C., and Robert J. Taylor. "Intergroup Attitudes: Black American Perceptions of Asian Americans." *Ethnic and Racial Studies* 11.4 (1988): 474–488.

Torres, Sasha. *Black, White and in Colour. Television and Black Civil Rights*. Oxfordshire: Princeton University Press, 2003.

Trombley, Lura E. Skandera, ed. *Critical Essays on Maxine Hong Kingston*. New York: G.K. Hall and Company, 1998.

Trudeau, Lawrence J. "Chang-rae Lee" *Asian American Literature*. Ed. Lawrence Trudeau. Detroit: Gale, 1999: 241–249.

Truth, Sojourner. "An Address to the First Annual Meeting of the American Equal Rights Association, 9 May 1867." *Call and Response: The Riverside Anthology of African American Literary Tradition*. Ed. Patricia Hill. Boston: Houghton Mifflin, 1998.

Umoja, Akinyele. "The Ballot and the Bullet. A Comparative Analysis of Armed Resistance in the Civil Rights Movement." *Journal of Black Studies* 29.4 (1999): 558–578.

"U.S. Census Press Releases. Report Released by Census Director at Black Mayors' Annual Conference in Houston." 26 Nov. 2004 <http://www.census.gov/Press-Release/www/releases/Archives/race/000928.html>.

"U.S. Map of Hate Groups." 24 Jan. 2005 <http://www.tolerance.org/maps/hate/state.jsp?T=12&m=2>.

Van Deburg, William. *New Day in Babylon. The Black Power Movement and American Culture, 1965–1975*. Chicago: University of Chicago Press, 1992.

____, ed. *Modern Black Nationalism. From Marcus Garvey to Louis Farrakhan*. New York: New York University Press, 1997.

Vanderwerken, David L. "Focusing on the Prologue and the Epilogue." *Approaches to Teaching Ellison's* Invisible Man. Ed. Susan Rosneck Parr and Pancho Savery. New York: MLA, 1991. 119–123.

Vogler, Thomas. "*Invisible Man:* Somebody's Protest Novel." *Ralph Ellison. A Collection of Critical Essays*. Ed. John Hersey. New Jersey: Prentice-Hall, 1974. 127–150.

Walker, Alice. *Meridian*. New York: Pocket Books, 1986.

Wallace, Michelle. *Invisibility Blues*. New York: Verso, 1990.

Waller, Nicole. "Past and Repast: Food as Historiography in Fae Myenne Ng's *Bone* and Frank Chin's *Donald Duk*." *Amerikastudien/American Studies* 40.3 (1996): 485–502.

Wang, Jennie. "*Tripmaster Monkey*: Kingston's Postmodern Representation of a New 'China Man.'" *MELUS* 20.1 (1995): 101–114.

Watanabe, Paul Y. "Building on the Indigenous Base: The Fund-Raising Controversy and the Future of Asian American Political Participation." *Asian Americans and Politics. Perspectives, Experiences, Prospects*. Ed. Gordon H. Chang. Stanford: Stanford University Press, 2001.

West, Cornel. "The Paradox of the Afro-American Rebellion." *Social Text* 3.3 (1984): 44–58.

White, Walter. "Defending Home and Hearth: Walter White Recalls the 1906 Atlanta Race Riot." 2 Oct. 2004 <http://historymatters.gmu.edu/d/104>.

Wiegman, Robyn. "Whiteness Studies and the Paradox of Particularity." *boundary 2* 26:3, (1999): 115–150.

____, and Judith Roof, eds. *Who Can Speak? Authority and Critical Identity*. Chicago, University of Illinois Press, 1995.

Williams, Noelle. "Parody and Pacifist Transformations in Maxine Hong Kingston's *Tripmaster Monkey: His Fake Book* (1995): 83–100.

Williams, Patricia. *The Alchemy of Race*. Harvard: Harvard University Press, 1991.

Winant, Howard. "White Racial Projects." *Making and Unmaking Whiteness*. Eds. Brigit Brander Rasmussen, et al. Durham: Duke University Press, 2001. 97–115.

Winters, Clyde Ahmad. "Afrocentrism. A Valid Frame of Reference." *Journal of Black Studies* 25.1 (1994): 170–190.

Bibliography

Wong, Bernard. "Chinese Americans." *Multiculturalism in the United States: A Comparative Guide to Acculturation and Ethnicity*. Eds. John D. Buenker and Lorman A. Ratiner: New York: Greenwood Press, 1992. 193–214.

Wong, Sau-ling. "Denationalization Reconsidered: Asian American Cultural Criticism at a Theoretical Crossroads." *Amerasia Journal* 21.1–2 (1995): 1–27.

_____. "Immigrant Autobiography: Some Questions of Definition and Approach." *American Autobiography. Retrospect and Prospect*. London: University of Wisconsin Press, 1991. 142–170.

Wong, Yen Lu. "Chinese American Theatre." *The Drama Review* 20.2 (1976): 13–18.

Wright, Richard. Introduction. *Black Metropolis*. By St. Clair Drake and Horace R. Cayton. New York: Harcourt, Brace, 1945. XVII–XXXIV.

Yamada, Mitsuye. "Invisibility is an Unnatural Disaster." *Gender Reader*. Eds. Evelyn Ashton Jones, Gary A. Olson, Mary G. Perry. London: Longman, 2000.

Yamamoto, Hisaye. "The Fire in Fontana." *Rereading America: Cultural Contexts for Critical Thinking and Writing*. Boston: Bedford, 1992. 366–373.

Yamamoto, Traise. "Different Silence(s): The Poetics and Politics of Location." *Re Viewing Asian America*. Eds. Wendy L. Ng and Gary Okihiro. 137–145.

Yun, Chung-Hei. "Beyond 'Clay Walls': Korean American Literature." *Reading the Literatures of Asian America*. Ed. Shirley Geok-lin Lim and Amy Ling. Philadelphia: Temple University Press, 1992. 79–95.

Zhang, Ya-Jie. "A Chinese Woman's Response to Maxine Hong Kingston's *The Woman Warrior. A Casebook*." New York: Oxford University Press, 1999. 17–21.

Zubrinsky, Charles. "Process of Racial Residential Segregation." *Urban Inequality. Evidence from Four Cities*. Eds. Alice O'Connor, Chris Tilly and Lawrence Bobo. New York: Russell Sage Foundation, 2001.

Index

Abelman, Nancy 130, 188–189
Accommodation 47, 76, 103
Adorno, Theodor 80, 181
Affirmative action 128, 132; in education 163–164, 191
Africa 58–59, 62, 121, 184
African Americans 76–78, 181; family 65–66; leaders 76–77, 85, 169; participation in Vietnam war 63–64; violence against 32, 99; women 65–67, 162
African Nationalist Pioneer Movement in Harlem 163
Afrocentric movement 163, 179
Agency 101, 104, 154
Aiiieeeee 21, 98, 112–113, 119–120, 164, 185, 190
Albinos 50
Algeria 62
Alien land law 138
Alien rhetoric 22, 36–37, 77, 93, 95–96, 99, 101, 114, 122, 126, 131, 164, 167, 182
All-African People's Revolutionary Party 58
Alter identity 149
Althusser, Louis Pierre 70
American Colonization Society 184
Anglo-Americans 125
Anglo-Saxons 22, 35, 134, 169
Anti-imperialism 62
Anti-Semitism 163, 180
Appropriation 159
Armstrong, Louis 38, 41, 52
Asante, Molefi Kete 163, 179
Ashcroft, John 189
Asia 62, 64, 87
Asian Americans: activism of the 1960s 5; cultural nationalists 5, 7, 11–13, 91, 100, 107, 111–122, 140, 165, 186; genealogy 100–101; hyphen 101–102, 185; studies 113, 115–116, 163–166, 191–192; theater 10, 91–92, 104–111, 165, 192; violence against 94, 99, 184; women 119–120, 122, 166
Assimilation 91, 103, 132, 136, 146, 153
Au, Yat-Pang 191
Audibility 17, 72
Authenticity 11, 91, 107–108, 164
Autobiography 10–11, 38–42, 52, 102, 124, 141–142, 144, 149–151, 188, 190
Autobiography 176

Back to Africa Movement 184
Bagehot, Walter 176
Bakke, Allan 191
Baldwin, James: *Notes of a Native Son* 97
Bambara, Toni Cade 190–191
Baraka, Amiri 57, 59, 66, 182
Be-Bop Man/Be-Bop Woman 67
Beloved 173
Bernstein, Robert 189
Bhabha, Homi 14, 79, 96, 149, 154, 181, 186
Bible 19, 175
Big Aiiieeeee 108, 118, 151, 190
Binarism 2, 4, 94–95, 102, 122, 131
Binga, Jesse 176
Biracial descent 176
Black belt 33, 47, 78, 191
Black civil rights: activists 62; leaders 63–64
Black cultural nationalism 58–59
Black entrepreneurship 68
Black Jamaicans 19
Black labor 30, 32, 175
Black lower class 82–83, 86, 162
Black Metropolis 17–18, 179–180, 184
Black middle class 7, 14, 33–34, 55, 68, 75–78, 83–84, 86, 154, 162, 179, 181
Black militant nationalism 10, 55, 59, 61–62
Black nationalists 5, 10, 13, 33, 56–69, 89–90, 100, 112, 121–122, 162–163

213

Index

Black outmigration to the suburbs 75, 77
Black Panthers, 58–59, 61, 63, 68
Black Power 179
Black Power 61, 78, 89, 100, 130, 163, 179
Black pride 57–58, 69, 163, 179
Black Reconstruction 30, 146
Black working class 68
Bloch, Alice 47
Blues for an African Princess 21, 66–67, 77, 180
Boas, Franz 27, 176
Bob Jones University 160
Bondi, Liz 4, 112
Bradley, William 131
Brotherhood Crusade 163
Brown, James 58, 178
Brown, Rap 179
Browne, Stephen H. 173
Burton, Richard 15
Bush, George Herbert Walker 161, 168
Bush, George W. 131, 161–162, 168, 182, 189, 193
Butler, Judith 121, 142, 145, 182
Butterfield, Stan 42

Cambodia 63
Camouflage 79
Canon 113
Caribbean Americans 140
Carmichael, Stokely 58, 67–68, 121, 179
Carson, Sonny 139, 163
Cassirer, Naomi 162
Centrism 64, 186
Chan, Jeffrey Paul 112
Chan, Sucheng 93–94, 99, 138, 184
Chang, Edward T. 129, 132, 138, 188–189
Chang, Hsiao-hung 188
Chao, Elaine 189
Chauvinism 65, 119–120, 188
Cherry, Robert 188
Chesnutt, Charles Waddell 44, 46, 174, 184
Cheung, King-Kok 2, 118, 190
Chicago 32, 176
Chicago School of Sociology 176
Chickencoop Chinaman 104–105, 109, 120
Chief Sam movement 184
Chimurenga, Coltrane 139
Chin, Frank 5, 22, 92, 98, 107, 112, 114, 116, 119, 186; *Aiiieeeee* 21, 98, 112–113, 119–120, 164, 185, 190; *Big Aiiieeeee* 108, 118, 151, 190; *Chickencoop Chinaman* 104–105, 109, 120; *Donald Duk* 175; *Year of the Dragon* 120
Chin, Marilyn 187
China Men 21, 173, 184–185
Chinatown 117, 133, 184, 187
Chinese American labor 21, 93–94;
Promontory Summit 21; on the transcontinental railway 21, 113
Chinese Americans 7, 20, 91, 93, 98–99, 101, 104–106, 108, 182, 188
Chinese myths 107–108, 119
Chinese Revolution 61–62
Chu, Louis: *Eat a Bowl of Tea* 119–120
Chu, Patricia 108, 186
Cipher 44
Civil disobedience 51
Civil rights 65, 95, 187
Clark, Kenneth 69–70, 72–73, 181
Class 12, 30, 68, 140
Clay, Amowale 139
Cleaver, Eldridge 59, 61, 180
Clinton, Bill 161
Cold War 62, 103
Colonialism 63–64
Color blindness 30, 81, 128
Color line 171
Colorlessness 50
Communication gap 17–18
Compensatory wages of whiteness 30, 146, 175
Congress of African People 59
CORE 59, 179
Counter-discourse 113
Criminalization of blackness 103, 162
Crummel, Alexander 184
Cultural deprivation rhetoric 75, 83
Culture definitions 134–135

Davis, Angela 66
Davis, Mike 180–181
Davis, Thulani: *1959* 64
Dawson, William 76
Dean, Howard 79
December 12 Movement 139, 163
Degler, Carl 30
De Gobineau, Arthur 27, 176
Delaney, Martin 184
Democrats 168
Denton, Nancy and Douglass Massey 32, 70–71, 76, 78, 129, 161, 176–177, 180
Diachronism 4, 158
Diallo, Amadou 191
Diaspora 116, 143, 165
Dinkin, David 191
Dirlik, Arif 116
Displacement 92
Divakaruni, Chitra 170
Diversity 166–167, 169
Dole, Elizabeth 190
Donald Duk 175
Double-consciousness 9, 17, 27, 101, 173, 175, 184

214

Index

Douglass, Frederick 157, 185
Dowd, James 110, 117
Du Bois, W.E.B. 18, 20; *Black Reconstruction* 30, 146; *Dusk of Dawn* 16–17, 27, 35, 73, 84, 158, 170, 174; *The Souls of Black Folk* 9, 17–20, 173, 175, 177
Dusk of Dawn 16–17, 27, 35, 73, 84, 158, 170, 174

Eat a Bowl of Tea 119–120
Egypt 19
Eliot, T.S. 42
Ellison, Ralph 15, 173–174, 177; *Flying Home and Other Stories* 177; *Invisible Man* 3–9, 11–12, 15, 25–54, 61, 82, 86, 88, 91, 97, 104, 108, 111, 140, 146, 150–151, 158, 160–161, 170–171, 174–177
Eng, David 116, 185
Engles, Tim 152
Equiano, Olaudah 190
Erikson, Erik 134
Espiritu, Yen Le 95, 100–101, 111, 115
Essentialism 101, 103, 112, 115, 171
Ethiopia 19
Ethnocentricity 64
Ethnographic gaze 18–19, 25, 77, 102, 104
Ethos of masculinity 107, 114, 119
Eugenics 176
European immigration 72
Evictions 33
Exceptionalism 167
Exclusion Acts 20, 22, 93, 99, 184
Exploitation 7, 153–155

Fair Housing Act 72, 161
Farrhakan, Louis 163
Faulkner, William 42
Federal Housing Administration 71
Ferens, Dominika 174, 176, 179, 186
Fifth Book of Peace 122, 190
Filipinos 100
Flowers, Sandra Hollin 63, 66
Flying Home and Other Stories 177
f.o.b. (Fresh Off the Boat) 114, 115, 144
Folk tradition 32, 45, 50
Foster, Ernest 139
Foucault, Michel 28, 69, 158, 174
Fox, Vicente 182
Frankenberg, Ruth 8, 148
Franklin, Aretha 58, 178
Friedman, Susan Stanford 4, 142, 173
Frontier 106
Furth, Isabella 105

Gale, Dennis 180
Galton, Francis 27

Garvey, Marcus 184
Gates, Daryl 180
Gates, Henry Louis 40, 44, 77–78
Geourgoudaki, Ekaterini 178
German Americans 148
Ggeh 136, 141–143, 188
Ghana 184
Ghetto/inner city 7, 55–56, 58, 61, 68–79, 82–84, 86, 91, 128, 139–140, 161–162, 168–169, 176, 179–181; drugs 75, 180–181
Gibson, Donald B. 173
Giovanni, Nikki 57–58, 65, 76, 177–178, 180
Giulianni, Rudy 191
Gold Mountain 21, 93, 99, 146
Gonzales, Alberto 189
Gooding-Williams, Robert 189
Gore, Albert 131, 188
Gotanda, Neil 20, 62, 93, 187, 192
Gotanda, Philip 92
Graham, William 176
Greek Americans 148
Greenlee, Sam 5, 15, 55, 66, 90, 177–178; *Be-Bop Man/Be-Bop Woman* 67; *Blues for an African Princess* 21, 66–67, 77, 180; *The Spook Who Sat by the Door* 3, 5, 7, 9–14, 55–89, 111, 121, 134, 139, 141, 152, 154, 158, 161–163, 170–171, 177–182
Gurley, Leo 45

Hacker, Andrew 190
Haiti 130
Haley, Alex: *Roots* 109
Hall, Stuart 4
Ham (biblical) 19, 175
Hansberry, Lorraine: *Raisin in the Sun* 109
Hare, Nathan 63
Harlem 51
Harlins, Latasha 6, 137
Harris, Cheryl 27, 30, 73, 176, 190
Harris, Joel Chandler 44
Harris, Marvin 176
Harte, Bret 186
Hate groups 193
Hemingway, Ernest 42
Hernandez, Heike Raphael 2
Heroic epic tradition 107, 110, 118
Hersey, John 42, 177
Himes, Chester: *Autobiography* 176; *If He Hollers Let Him Go* 174, 181
Hing, Bill Ong 187
Hiroshima 64
Hirsh, Arnold: *Making the Second Ghetto* 71
Hispanics 125, 128, 141, 166, 190; voters 2, 95, 131, 182
History 1, 48, 57–58, 101, 105, 184
Holden, Nat 138

215

Index

Holliday, Billie 89, 108, 181
Holmes, Robert A. 72
Holt, Thomas C. 173
Hom, Marlon K. 187
Homosexuals 12, 103, 122, 166, 192
Hong, Grace 189–190
Hongo, Garret 192
Horowitz, Ellin 46, 50
Hose, Sam 174
Huggan, Graham 80, 181, 186
Huggins, Nathan 174
Hughes, Langston 41
Humphrey, Hubert 180
Hune, Shirley 166
Hwang, David Henry 192
Hypodescent 176

Ichigashi, Yamato 22
Identity 13, 34–35, 39, 43, 49, 88, 92, 110, 112, 117, 149, 179
Identity politics 11; conventional 11–13, 65, 90, 112, 122–123, 127, 139, 141–142, 160; transformational 1, 11–13, 112, 140–143, 155, 167, 171
If He Hollers Let Him Go 174, 181
Imitation 14, 80, 86, 106, 181, 186
Immigrants 5, 7, 10–12, 22, 32, 64–65, 94, 98–100, 113–115, 122–123, 125–126, 130, 134, 136, 140, 143–146, 149–150, 152, 154, 165–167, 176, 187, 189
Immigration law 65, 91, 93, 95, 114, 116, 129, 131, 167, 182, 184, 187
Imperialism 64
Inada, Lawson Fusao 112, 186
Inaudibility 16, 86
Income gap 162
Innis, Roy 59, 179
Institutional injustice 19, 83, 180
Integration 5, 11, 32, 36, 60, 62, 76, 78, 83, 111
Interaction between Korean Americans and African Americans 5, 127–141, 163, 189–190
Interdisciplinarity 1, 3
Internalized racism 35
Internment of Japanese Americans 174
Interracial relations 2, 5, 10, 13, 19, 26, 52, 59, 61, 63, 86–88, 90, 92, 94–95, 98, 100, 102–103, 109, 121–122, 126–142, 155, 167, 173–174, 179, 182, 189–190, 192–193
Interracial studies 2
Intertextuality 106, 186
Invisibility: as blinding force 10, 36, 141; cultural invisibility of Chinese Americans 98; figurative 6–7, 47, 50, 147; genealogy of the term 4, 15–22; as inspiration 3,
8–9, 25, 37, 104–105, 150; internal 1, 3, 6, 7, 10, 13, 22–23, 28, 33–34, 41, 46, 55, 64–67, 75–79, 90, 117, 126, 153, 158, 165, 181, 187; literal 6, 7, 45, 47, 49–50, 55–57, 61–62, 67–68, 79–89, 146–147; post civil rights gains of the 1960s 21, 59; potential of 8–10, 14, 37, 45, 48–52, 89, 104–105, 110; as source of illumination 10, 25, 37, 39, 152; as source of protection 7, 40, 45, 49, 61, 63, 89
Invisible Man 3–9, 11–12, 15, 25–54, 61, 82, 86, 88, 91, 97, 104, 108, 111, 140, 146, 150–151, 158, 160–161, 170–171, 174–177
Irish Americans 12, 174
Iwamatsu, Mako 192

Jackson, George 180
Jackson, Jesse 191
Jamaica 19
James, William 15
Japanese Americans 93–94, 101, 134, 138, 144, 174, 188–189
Japanese and Korean Exclusion League, 21
Japanese Canadians 175
Japheth 19, 176
Jay, Martin 182
Jaynes, Gerald 175
Jazz 41
Jefferson, Thomas 184
Jewish Americans 127–128, 188
Jews 12, 59, 65,
Johnson, James Weldon 184, 185; *The Autobiography of an Ex-Colored Man* 181
Johnson, Lyndon Baines 65, 180, 187

Kallen, Horace Meyer 27, 176
Karenga, Maulana 57, 66, 178
Katz, Cindi 4, 70, 112, 126
Kearney, Reginald 2, 174, 179
Keating, Analouise Keating 4, 11, 142, 159
Kennedy, John Fitzgerald 187
Kerner Commission 71
Kerry, John 168
Kim, Elaine H. 166
Kim, Kwang Chung 129, 189
Kim, Shin 129
King, Martin Luther 58, 63, 179
King, Steven 182
Kingston, Maxine Hong 5, 15, 90, 96, 107–108, 151, 185; *China Men* 21, 173, 184–185; *Fifth Book of Peace* 122, 190; *Tripmaster Monkey* 3, 5, 7, 9–14, 22, 90–122, 126, 140, 143–144, 158, 163–165, 169–171, 182, 185, 187–188; *The Woman Warrior* 10, 108–109, 118–119, 151, 187
Kipling, Rudyard 95, 105, 169

216

Index

Kirby Kathleen 4
Kogawa, Joy: *Obasan* 22, 175
Kolodny, Andrew 127, 188
Korean Americans 11, 22, 126–141, 148, 154, 188–189
Ku Klux Klan 193
Kuan Yin 187–188
Kwong, Peter 184
Kye 129, 188

Lacan, Jacques 79
Latin America 58
Latinos 2
Lazarus, Emma 167
Lee, C.Y. 114
Lee, Calvin 188
Lee, Chang-rae 15; *Native Speaker* 3, 5, 7, 9–15, 22, 76, 123–155, 158, 166–171, 178
Lee, Don L. 66
Lee, Heon Cheol 132, 139–140, 190
Lee, James Kyung-Jin 2, 72, 190
Lee, Robert 74, 87, 103, 180, 182, 188
Lee, Virginia 22
Leong, Russell 87, 189–190
Levine, Lawrence 45
Liberia 184
Lim, Shirley Geok-lin 116, 166
Lincoln, Abraham 184
Ling, Amy 103
Lipsitz, George 27, 85, 176
Location 1, 3, 69–70, 79, 112, 116, 126–128, 173
Lorde, Audre 118, 159
Lowe, Lisa 20, 93, 116
Lowe, Pardee 188

Magnuson Act 93, 187
Mainstream 111, 123, 128, 145, 159
Making the Second Ghetto 71
Malcolm X 58–59, 66, 179
Malinowski, Bronisław 144
Mao Tse-tung 62
Marable, Manning 2, 68, 76, 140, 179, 192
Margin-center 70, 90
Masculinity 112
Mass media 73–75, 130, 137–139, 146–147, 161, 164, 170
Massey, Doreen 70
McCarran Walter Act 93, 187
McCarthey, John T. 64, 179, 184
McCarthy, Karen 166
McLaren, Peter 124–125, 142
Melville, Herman 47
Middle Passage 146
Middleman 86, 127, 142; minority 127–128, 139, 188

Mimesis 80
Mimicry 14–15, 46, 55–56, 67, 79–89, 91, 105–107, 110, 112–114, 125, 149, 152–155, 181, 186
Min, Pyong Gap 127, 129, 188
Mineta, Norman Y. 189
Miscegenation 78, 103, 176, 186
Mississippi 176
Model minority rhetoric 13–14, 22, 73–75, 103, 132–137, 146, 150, 164, 185, 189
Monogenesis 27
Monrovia 184
Morrison, Toni: *Beloved* 173; *Song of Solomon* 36
Mosley, Walter 57, 138
Moynihan, Daniel Patrick 65, 73, 134, 180
Muhammed, Elijah 179
Multiculturalism 6, 158; conservative 125, 159, 169–170; critical 1, 11, 124, 155; liberal 74, 124–125, 159
Mura, David: *Where the Body Meets Memory* 144

Nagasaki 64
Naming/signification 34–35, 100–101, 124
Nation of Islam 163
National Association for the Advancement of Colored People 174
National Negro Committee 174
Nationalism 115; cultural 5, 90; militant 5, 55, 90
Nationality Act 93
Native Americans 2, 35, 95, 173, 176
Native Speaker 3, 5, 7, 9–15, 22, 76, 123–155, 158, 166–171, 178
Nativity 112, 115, 121
Naturalization 93–94, 187
Nee de Bary, Brett and Victor 133
New Historicism 1
New York 31–32, 129, 176
Niagara Movement 174
1959 64
Nixon, Richard 71
Non-normativity 165
Northern United States and racial issues 31–32, 42, 49, 176
Notes of a Native Son 97
Nunez, Sigrid 157

Obasan 22, 175
Okihiro, Gary 2, 94, 188
Oklahoma 184
Okubo, Mine 189
Omatsu, Glenn 192
Omi, Michael 128, 168, 176
Onishi, Norimitsu 163, 191

Index

Oral tradition 45
Organization of African Unity 58, 66
Orientalism 21, 87, 95–96, 100, 108–109
Osajima, Keith 132, 185
Othering practices 4, 8, 21, 77, 113–114, 164
O-Young, Lee 152

Pacifism 13, 118
Palumbo-Liu, David 81, 113, 137
Pan-Africanists 58–59, 121, 179
Pan-Asian organizations 100–101, 115
Panethnicity 101, 111, 140
Park, Kyeyoung 128, 188–189
Park, Robert E. 27, 176
Particularism 142, 157, 167
Passing 42, 49
Paternalism 31, 45–46
Patriarchy 114, 119, 134
Payton, Philip 176
Pentagon 63, 174
Performativity 13–15, 43–54, 79–80, 90–92, 113, 116–117, 122, 182
Philippines 62
Piper, Adrian 176
Police in the conflict between African Americans and Korean Americans 139
Polish Americans 148
Polygenesis 27
Positionality 4, 22, 44, 70, 79, 141–142, 148, 184
Poverty among African Americans 161
Power dynamics 3, 7–8, 11, 15, 31, 37, 40, 46–47, 57, 68–69, 82, 98, 119, 124–125, 130, 148, 151–152, 154–155, 158, 171, 174, 177
Prejudice 17, 19, 26, 29, 91
Privilege 8, 10, 17, 19, 31, 60, 77, 85, 98, 140, 159, 171, 176
Prometheus 15
Promontory Summit 174
Property relations 27, 45, 66, 72, 137–139, 168–169, 176, 190
Proposition 187 192
Pseudoscience 27, 175
Public housing projects 71, 76
Puerto Ricans 130, 148

Quest, Richard 189
Quotas 163–164

Racial profiling 162, 176, 191
Racist organizations 193
Rags to riches rhetoric 136–137
Rainbow Coalition 192–193
Raisin in the Sun 109
Reagan, Ronald 72, 128, 161, 168

Reappropriation 100, 185
Recentering 90, 111–122
Redlining in real estate 32, 72, 161
Reed, Ishmael 177
Relationality 4, 123, 141–142, 173
Representation 41, 80, 92, 104, 158–159, 181
Republicans 71, 161–162, 168, 182
Rilke, Rainer Maria 104, 111
Riots (ghetto rebellions) 69, 71–72, 75, 77, 94, 138–139, 162, 180, 184
Rodney King rebellion 6, 8, 73, 137, 139, 168, 189
Roediger, David 175
Roots 109
Ross, Diana 191
Roy, Parama 15, 149
Rubin, Robert 135
Rugged individualism 74
Russian revolutionaries 62

Said, Edward 87–88, 96
Saito, Leland T. 190
Sanchez, Sonia 57, 63, 76, 177
Sarandon, Susan 191
Schaub, Thomas 177
Second-sight 9–10, 26, 57, 79, 122, 152, 173, 175
Segregation 16, 20, 27, 32, 45, 55, 70, 130, 160–161, 176–177, 179–181; restrictive covenants 33; trespassing 45
Self 15, 28, 39, 41, 46, 48, 57, 82, 88, 97, 117, 149–150, 152
Self-consciousness 28, 34, 39, 41–42, 122, 175
Separatism 5, 11, 59–60, 62, 78
September 11 169
Sexuality 87
Sharecroppers 29, 34, 47, 57
Sharpton, Al 79, 191
Shem 19, 176
Shimakawa, Karen 92, 109, 192
Shugart, Helene A. 185
Signifying 14, 44, 46
Silence 9, 22, 149–150
Sin Far, Sui (Eaton, Edith) 18–20, 106, 174, 186
Slavery 46, 66, 94–95, 100, 173, 182; revolts 58, 178
Slippage 14, 80–82, 86, 88, 186
Smith, Edward C. 62
Smith, Neil 4, 70, 112, 126
SNCC 58, 178–179
Social Darwinism 27, 176
Sollors, Werner 174, 176
Song of Solomon 36
The Souls of Black Folk 9, 17–20, 173, 175, 177

218

Index

South Central Los Angeles 139, 189
South East Asia 187
Southern United States and racial issues 27, 31–32, 42, 49, 130, 160, 176
Space 69–70, 173–174
Spectatorship 138
Spencer, Herbert 176
Spillers, Hortense 65–66
Spirituals 59, 177
Spivak, Gayatri 55, 184
The Spook Who Sat by the Door 3, 5, 7, 9–14, 55–89, 111, 121, 134, 139, 141, 152, 154, 158, 161–163, 170–171, 177–182
Sten, Christopher 41
Stereotyping 6, 8, 13–14, 22, 25–26, 40, 47, 56, 67, 79, 81, 87, 91–92, 95–97, 101, 103 107, 109–110, 112–114, 120, 122, 127, 130, 146, 151–152, 154, 162–166, 186, 188
Sting 182
Structures of oppression 7, 17, 61, 64, 90, 97, 139, 147–148, 155, 170
Sumida, Stephen 113
Supreme Court 33
Syncretism 106

Takagi, Dana 191
Takaki, Ronald 99, 138
Tan, Amy 151
Tanner, Tony 39, 47–49
Taussig, Michael 80, 181
Taylor, Charles 39–40
Taylor, Robert 76, 181
Theater 91–92, 104–111, 182
Tokenization 55, 60, 111, 189
Torres, Sasha 139
Tricksterism 6, 14–15, 25, 43–54, 79
Tripmaster Monkey 3, 5, 7, 9–14, 22, 90–122, 126, 140, 143–144, 158, 163–165, 169–171, 182, 185, 187–188
Truth, Sojourner 58, 178
Turner, Bishop M. 184
Turner, Nat 58
Twain, Mark 186

Underclass 162, 181
Underground 48, 52–53, 56–57,
Underground railway 59, 89
Unions 29–30
Universalism 114, 142, 159
Uno, Roberta 166
Urban restructuring 71

Van Deburg, William L. 58–59, 163, 178–179
Van Horn, James 180
Veil 10, 17, 42, 175

Vesey, Denmark 58, 178
Viet Cong 62, 151, 180
Vietnam war 100, 180
Vietnamese 115
Vietnamese Americans 148
Violence against African Americans 32, 99
Violence against Asian Americans 94, 99, 184
Visibility 3, 10–11, 15, 17, 22, 25–26, 28, 36, 40, 42, 50, 52, 55–56, 70, 72, 84, 88–92, 97, 99, 104, 108, 111–112, 117, 121–123, 132, 139–140, 144–145, 148, 150–151, 153, 155, 157–158, 163, 165–166, 170–171, 181
Vision 6, 9–11, 15, 20, 27, 31, 36–38, 40, 43, 57, 83, 138, 148, 152, 175, 182
Vogler, Thomas 35, 39, 52

Wallace, Michelle 190
Washington, Booker T. 41–42, 47
Watanna, Onoto (Eaton, Winnifred) 106, 186
Wells, H.G. 49–50
West, Cornel 68, 75
Where the Body Meets Memory 144
White, Walter 184
Whiteness 2, 19, 21, 26–28, 33, 35, 44–45, 51, 54, 58, 60, 64, 85, 97–98, 102, 106, 112–113, 121, 123, 125, 128, 137, 140, 153–154, 159, 164, 168–169, 184, 190; conservative whites 60, 74, 85; internal stratification within whiteness 8, 10, 12, 148, 171; liberal whites 8, 60, 74, 83, 85; National Guard 61; whiteness aggravating the tensions between and inside minorities 7, 34, 77, 126–128, 132–133, 139; white apparatus of power 3, 7, 60–61, 70, 73, 75, 78, 138, 154–155, 157, 159, 170–171, 180; white blindness 9, 17, 20, 22, 25–27, 29, 31, 36–37, 45–46, 56, 81, 83, 88, 90, 95–97, 175; white flight to the suburbs 70–71; white invisibility 8, 126, 139, 147–148, 193; white man's burden 28, 98; white middle class 83; white police 31, 61, 75, 176, 180; white sociologists 65, 73–74, 83, 134; white working class 21–22, 29–30, 146, 175
Whitman, Walt 185
Williams, Patricia 191
Winant, Howard 85, 128, 168, 176
The Woman Warrior 10, 108–109, 118–119, 151, 187
Wong, Cynthia Sau-ling 116, 190
Wong, Diane Yen-Mei 166
Wong, Eugene 188
Wong, Jade Snow 106, 119, 135, 186

Index

Wong, Shawn Hsu 112
World War II 144
Wright Richard 42; *Black Power* 179; introduction to Drake and Cayton's *Black Metropolis* 17–18, 179–180, 184

Yamamoto, Hisaye 138
Yamauchi, Wakako 92
Year of the Dragon 120

Yellow Peril 13, 100, 135, 146
Yellow Power 61, 100
Yellow Seed 100
Yoruba cultures 44
Yun, Leong Gor 188
Yutang, Lin 114

Zenner, Walter 188
Žižek, Slavoj 159

www.ingramcontent.com/pod-product-compliance
Lightning Source LLC
Chambersburg PA
CBHW032053300426
44116CB00007B/714